WORKING WITHIN TWO KINDS OF CAPITALISM

CONTEMPORARY STUDIES IN CORPORATE LAW

Edited by John Parkinson,
Professor of Law, University of Bristol

Contemporary Studies in Corporate Law exists to act as a focus for fresh approaches to thinking about the law and its role, scope, and effectiveness in the context of corporate activity. The series both espouses a broader meaning for 'corporate law' than is found in the textbooks and also encourages the use of methodologies and analytical styles which are not necessarily 'legal'. As such it aims to publish books of high intellectual quality and theoretical rigour and to promote the further development of scholarly research and writing on the whole range of subjects comprising corporate law, including corporate governance, corporate finance, insolvency, financial services law, securities, and multinational enterprises.

Titles in this Series

Working Within Two Kinds of Capitalism: Corporate Governance and Employee Stakeholding: US and EC Perspectives
Irene Lynch Fannon

Contracting with Companies
Andrew Griffiths
(due summer 2003)

The Jurisprudence of the Takeover Panel
Tunde Ogowewo
(due autumn 2003)

Working Within Two Kinds of Capitalism

Corporate Governance and Employee Stakeholding: US and EC Perspectives

IRENE LYNCH FANNON
BCL (NUI), BCL (Oxon.), SJD (UVa.),
Solicitor

·HART·
PUBLISHING
OXFORD – PORTLAND OREGON
2003

Published in North America (US and Canada) by
Hart Publishing
c/o International Specialized Book Services
5804 NE Hassalo Street
Portland, Oregon
97213–3644
USA

Hart Publishing is a specialist legal publisher based in Oxford, England.
To order further copies of this book or to request a list of other publications please write to:

Hart Publishing, Salters Boatyard, Folly Bridge,
Abingdon Rd, Oxford, OX1 4LB
Telephone: +44 (0)1865 245533 Fax: +44 (0) 1865 794882
email: mail@hartpub.co.uk
WEBSITE: http//:www.hartpub.co.uk

British Library Cataloguing in Publication Data
Data Available
ISBN 1–84113–286–1 (hardback)

Typeset by Hope Services, Abingdon
Printed and bound in Great Britain by
Biddles Ltd, www.biddles.co.uk

Preface

Working Within Two Kinds of Capitalism is aptly titled. It contrasts, from the perspective of employee welfare, the American model of corporate governance, in which the maximisation of returns to shareholders in a lightly regulated environment is the dominant goal, with a European model, where the company 'is tempered by state regulation in the name of macro-economic policy and by state supported social policies regarding the welfare of employees and others'.[1] One of the features that distinguishes this work from much of the existing literature on comparative corporate governance is its emphasis on policies towards the company adopted at the level of the European institutions, rather than on the corporate law and practice of individual states. It also transcends the conventional boundaries between company law and employment law scholarship to look at measures designed to improve the position of employees within the enterprise in the round. This facilitates an assessment of the relative merits of 'employment law' and 'company law' approaches, namely strategies aimed at strengthening the rights of employees against the company on the one hand, and on the other, interventions intended to broaden the goals of the company itself to include the promotion of employee welfare, for example, by altering directors' duties or mandating employee participation in the company's decision-making structures.

While engaging with the theory of the firm and financial economics literatures that have been so influential in Anglo-American company law scholarship, *Working Within Two Kinds of Capitalism* also draws on a broader range of disciplines, emphasizing in particular the role of politics in shaping governance arrangements and examining the capacity of public-policy choices to reorder corporate priorities and alter power relationships within the company. In adopting this approach it makes a useful contribution to the growing body of writing that argues that the institutions and objectives of corporate governance cannot be explained simply by reference to stylised economic interactions, but must instead be examined in the light of the social and political contexts and different forms of market system within which they have developed. This writing, for example, the *Varieties of Capitalism* literature,[2] draws attention to the comparative economic advantages of different forms of capitalism and the institutional complementarities on which they depend. It also suggests that attempts to transplant desired features of one system into another are likely to be problematic. In what may be a related phenomenon, *Working Within Two Kinds of Capitalism*

[1] Below, at 5.

[2] See Peter A Hall and David Soskice (eds), *Varieties of Capitalism: The Institutional Foundations of Comparative Advantage* (OUP, Oxford, 2001). See also Mark J Roe, *Political Determinants of Corporate Governance: Political Context, Corporate Impact* (OUP, Oxford, 2003).

highlights the differing preoccupations of those advocating pro-employee governance reform within the distinct systems, with an emphasis in the United States on fiduciary duty amendments and employee shareholding, and less on employee participation in decision-making favoured in (continental) Europe.

In common with many who eschew a purely economic interpretation of the company, Irene Lynch Fannon views the corporation not simply as 'private'—the product of contracting between the economic participants—but also as a form of public body, the decisions of whose controllers have a profound impact on the lives of their employees and society more generally. She takes this approach further, however, moving beyond an analysis of how governance structures might be reformed in the light of it, to give the concept of the company as a public or social enterprise substantive content, by reference to EU social policy. The function of the company is not just to maximise abstract social welfare, but rather 'improving overall living and working conditions is a social aspiration for which all major institutions, including corporations, [should] take responsibility.'[3] EU social policy is drawn on in an illuminating way to suggest the detail of how this aspiration might be realised.

Working Within Two Kinds of Capitalism is an excellent beginning to the Contemporary Studies in Corporate Law series. It deserves a wide readership among scholars and policy makers interested in corporate governance, employment law and related disciplines, and social policy more generally.

John Parkinson

[3] Below, at 9.

Acknowledgements

This work developed from an interest which I have in the interface between company law and labour and employment law. I have spent many years teaching both subjects and have now developed a strong interest in company law theory, in particular as it relates to stakeholders other than shareholders. My career at University College Cork has brought me to this point and I would like to acknowledge the support which the University has given me in practical terms to achieve this publication. The granting of sabbatical leave is very important to academics, particularly those of us who are involved in teaching in a committed way.

I would like to acknowledge the support and interest of a number of individuals with different backgrounds who have supported the publication of this book. Most importantly I would like to thank Professor Michael P Dooley, William S Potter Professor of Law at the University of Virginia who engaged with me on the issues touched on here, when I started this research at the University of Virginia. I have a number of colleagues at University College, Cork and in the broader academic community who have been supportive in a collegiate way as I continued with this work over the ensuing years, they know who they are. I am grateful for their interest and encouragement. I would like to thank David Walsh, my research assistant, for trojan efforts made in tracking documents and sources, and more importantly for his interest. Hart Publishing must be acknowledged for their wonderful efficiency and in particular Richard Hart for his encouragement and support. It has been a pleasure to work with such a dynamic team.

On a personal note none of this would have been possible without the dedication and kindness of Sarah Davidson. Finally, and of course not least, my thanks are publicly due to Tom Fannon for his advice, his insights gained from practical experience in this field, his encouragement and support.

Contents

Introduction

'The decisive power in modern industrial society is exercised not by capital but by organisation, not by the capitalist but by the industrial bureaucrat'.[1] JK Galbraith (1978)

'An infectious greed seemed to grip much of our business community . . . It is not that humans have become any more greedy than in generations past. It is that the avenues to express greed had grown so enormously.' Alan Greenspan US Federal Reserve Chairman, *New York Times*, July 2nd, 2002

INTRODUCTION

THE ECONOMIC POWER of large corporations has become a significant force in all western economies. The power of these corporations is in turn controlled by management whose relationship with the corporation is not that of primary owner (although stock ownership is common) but a relationship of employment. Yet many decisions they make have drastic effects on other employees of those firms or corporations, who of course work and live a good many rungs down the corporate and social ladder. This book focuses on the factors, political and legal, which influence the motivations of those controlling corporate wealth and power in their relationship to employees and the justifications utilised by them for decisions they make.

CORPORATE GOVERNANCE

The corporate governance debate rises in cycles. In the current round of debate which could be described as stretching over the last 25 years, approximately coin ciding with the start of the take-over era in the United States, a number of dominant themes have emerged. These can be characterised as follows: Firstly, building on the work of Berle and Means,[2] commentators have described how the division between owners (shareholders) and controllers has become the established reality in large publicly held firms. The consequent rise in managerial

[1] JK Galbraith, *The New Industrial State* 3rd edn (Mentor, New York, 1978) p xiv.

[2] Adolph Berle and Gardner Means, *The Modern Corporation and Private Property* (Commerce Clearing House Inc, New York, 1932).

power and prerogative raises issues of accountability. Secondly, a debate has emerged as to whether the lack of management accountability to shareholders ought to be remedied.[3] (Initially shareholders as owners of the corporation were the primary focus of the revived corporate governance debate.) Those in favour of legislation giving shareholders more voice assume, or, in the course of their arguments, try to establish that the development of the separation of ownership and control is an historical aberration. Those against giving shareholders more voice argue that whether or not this is an historical aberration, (some argue that it is not),[4] modern corporate theory cannot and should not make management any more accountable to shareholders. Moreover, the argument is continued by some, shareholders do not want more voice and prefer the passive role.[5] Others argue that in any event sufficient monitoring devices exist to protect shareholders' interests.[6]

[3] In the United Kingdom the most recent cycle of the corporate governance debate has taken the Cadbury report, published in 1992, Report of the Committee on the Financial Aspects of Corporate Governance (London, December, 1992), and the subsequent Greenbury, Turnbull and Hampel Reports as its central reference points and has thus focused almost exclusively on accountability to shareholders, as compared with the current US debate which has also considered, over a longer period, issues regarding other stakeholders. See further: *Contemporary Issues in Corporate Governance,* DD Prentice and PRJ Holland (eds) (Oxford University Press, Oxford, 1993). The Greenbury Report issued guidelines for UK publicly quoted companies aimed at improving boardroom practice by reforming internal controls to prevent further corporate scandals which had a huge impact on members of the public, such as the collapse of the Maxwell empire and of the banking group, BCCI. A second goal was to control the activities and caliber of both executive and non-executive directors of larger companies in the UK. Accountability to stakeholders has not been such a hotly debated issue although very considered contributions have been made to the debate. See for example W Hutton, *The State We're In* (Vintage, London, 1995) and *Journal of Law and Society*, Special Issue on Enterprise and Community: New Directions and Corporate Governance. Vol 24, March 1997. JE Parkinson, *Corporate Power and Responsibility* (Clarendon Press, Oxford, 1993).

[4] The notion that the modern corporation represents an accidental or historical perversion of the original intended structure is described by Walter Werner 'Corporation Law in Search of its Future' (1981) 81 *Columbia Law Review* 1611 as the 'erosion doctrine'. Werner disagrees with this doctrine and argues that it was not necessarily envisaged that property and control should remain under a unified possession. Although interesting, the historical debate detracts from the present situation which in my opinion presents far more pressing concerns. It is interesting that the US publicly held corporation and companies quoted on the London Stock Exchange seem to share these characteristics ie a wide dispersal of share ownership, whereas European corporations and Japanese corporations do not demonstrate this huge separation of ownership and control. E Wyermeesch, 'The Corporate Governance Discussion in some European States' in D Prentice and PRJ Holland (eds) *Contemporary Issues in Corporate Governance ibid* n 3. See further Ch 8.

[5] Eugene Fama, 'Agency Problems and the Theory of the Firm' (1988) 88 *Journal of Political Economy* 288 'Our description of modern economy, insofar as it deals with the quasi-public corporation, must be in terms of the two forms of property, active and passive, which for the most part lie in different hands . . . In and of itself, the corporate device does not necessarily bring about this change.' Berle and Means: above n 2 p 4.

[6] See ch 3.

OTHER STAKEHOLDERS

Finally, the corporate governance debate has been extended to a debate as to whether other constituencies or 'stakeholders' ought to be given more participatory rights. Stakeholders usually considered in this part of the debate include investors other than shareholders such as bondholders, employees and communities affected by corporate activity. Variations of this argument include an argument that management accountability to these stakeholders should be increased in addition to accountability to shareholders. Others argue that accountability to these stakeholders should be increased whilst leaving the shareholders' position as it is. Issues surrounding other stakeholders seemed to have been the primary focus of the debate in the US during the last decade,[7] amongst academic writers at least.

The term corporate governance clearly is multi -faceted and indeed the debate has raised more issues than have been resolved. However at the core is a fundamental question about corporate power and wealth and how this should be controlled. Events in the US during the Summer of 2002 have brought some of these basic questions into sharper focus, in particular in relation to the position of the shareholder. This book, however, seeks to consider the nature of the relationship between the corporation, management[8] and directors on the one hand and employees on the other within a large publicly held corporation.

[7] In the last decade debate amongst corporate law scholars in the US seems overall to have focused on obligations owed to non-shareholder constituencies and in particular the function of other stakeholder statutes in this context. 'Corporate Malaise-Stakeholder Statutes: Cause or Cure?' *The Stetson Law Review Symposium* 1991 xxi (1). The Law School of the University of Toronto held a symposium in Summer 1993 again focusing on the stakeholder concept, particularly in the context of what are described here as pathological situations ie where the corporation/plant is closing or facing takeover. (1993) 43 *Toronto Law Journal*. The Stetson Symposium focused on non-shareholder constituency statutes, particularly in the context of the rash of high leveraged buy-outs occurring in the US in the 1980s. Even though at the time of this symposium, this chapter of American corporate history had all but closed, it left, in its aftermath, according to O'Connor in an Introductory article to this symposium, a vulnerability on the part of US corporations to competitive pressure to restructure. O'Connor describes the malaise referred to in the title of the symposium as a concern among commentators (presumably business analysts and economists, although none are actually referred to) that 'various crisis-oriented responses may adversely affect American competitiveness in the long-run'. Marleen A O'Connor, 'Corporate Malaise-Stakeholder Statutes: Cause or Cure?' *ibid* p 3. This theme has been returned to a number of times by the scholars writing in both the Stetson Law Review and the Toronto Law Journal. See LE Mitchell (ed) *Progressive Corporate Law* (Westview Press, Boulder Co, 1996).

[8] References to management here indicate managerial employees who are not directors, executive or otherwise, of boards. The latter will be referred to as directors. Interestingly, although employees, and therefore having the same legal relationship to the corporation as all other employees it is clear that management do not consider themselves as having quite the same relationship to the corporation as their fellow workers. This is because of the very basic fact, that managerial employees, by virtue of their positions exercise a considerable deal of power over other employees of the corporation. Furthermore managerial employees consider themselves to have a shared identity with the corporation, as distinct from other workers, and this identification is a matter of some pride. In the Anglo-American model this shared identity is underpinned by managerial stock

TWO KINDS OF CAPITALISM

In considering the issues raised here, a comparison is made between the Anglo-American corporate model (which has been described as the 'US Megacorp model'[9]) and its nearest equivalent in the EU. A number of US academic writers in this field refer to the German experience but it is argued here that this is insufficient. The concept of the EU corporation is by far the more apt comparator. This is particularly relevant at the dawn of a new age for Europe with the initiation in December 1999 of European Monetary Union and the introduction of the Euro in January 2002. It is clear that present corporate governance structures in Europe and the US[10] are very different, both in a broad sense in terms of ownership and accountability structures generally, and in a particular way in relation to the role of employees. This work proposes that there are two different types of capitalism at large:[11] American capitalism operating through the US Megacorp model which is underpinned with legal and economic theory supportive of profit maximisation as a goal pursued in a relatively unregulated environment. In this model the corporation is viewed as essentially a private actor. Then there is the European model of capitalism where the corporation is

ownership, a social phenomenon that has become problematic in European countries. The phenomenon has been elegantly described by JK Galbraith, *The New Industrial Estate*, n 1 above.

'The question automatically asked when two men meet on a plane or in Florida is, "Who are you with?" Until this is known, the individual is a cipher. He cannot be placed in the scheme of things; no-one knows how much attention, let alone respect he deserved, or whether he is worthy of any notice at all. If, however, he is with a large well-known corporation—a good outfit—he immediately counts. The organization man has been a subject of much sorrow. But all who weep should recall that he surrenders to organization because organization can do more for him than he can do for himself . . . it is still normally a matter of pride that the corporation absorbs nearly all his waking energy. All else including family, politics, sex and even alcohol is secondary'.

'The corporation, the job has dominated my whole life. Everything else has been secondary, and I know I have paid a price for it. I have had some fun and some successes but I have paid a price—there is no question about that but I would probably pay the price again. I lost two wives to my job and I have reached a conclusion that there's no way to be happily married and successful in business at the same time. I believe that to-day.'

[9] Margaret M Blair, *Ownership and Control* (Brookings Institute, Washington DC, 1995). See also Margaret M Blair, *Wealth Creation and Wealth Sharing* (Brookings Institute, Washington DC, 1996).

[10] Although some of the writers in this area, particularly in the US also refer to features of Japanese corporate governance structures, this work will not examine the Japanese corporation.

[11] The idea that there are two different types of capitalism at large has been mooted by Michael E Porter, *The Competitive Advantage of Nations* (Macmillan, London, 1990). Porter identifies a US-British model, an Anglo-Saxon model, where the emphasis is on short-term profitability and a mobile workforce and refers to other countries, including Germany and Japan, but also Sweden and Korea, as examples of a different type of capitalism. This model of capitalism is characterised as emphasising long-term stability, both economically and in the workforce and placing a greater emphasis on investment in training and skills development. In a more recent text a French writer, Emmanuel Todd, *The Economic Illusion: Essay on the Stagnation of Developed Societies* (1998) has developed this theme in the context of the attainment of Monetary Union and the sustained period of economic success in the United States. He criticises both; the former as unattainable, the latter as lacking foundation. However it is argued here that the different types of capitalism are essentially American and European in character, in particular in relation to employees.

tempered by state regulation in the name of macro-economic policy and by state supported social policies regarding the welfare of employees and others. Here the corporation is viewed as a public actor. Questions are raised as to the importance of these differences in the context of globalisation, particularly as governance structures affect employees. Furthermore questions will be asked as to whether corporate governance structures really matter, both in terms of employee welfare and in terms of efficiency and productivity.

> The phrase corporate governance is often applied narrowly to questions about structure and functioning of boards of directors or the rights and prerogatives of shareholders in boardroom decision making . . . [but] a broader view of corporate governance, [is] one that refers to the whole set of legal, cultural, and institutional arrangements that determine what publicly traded corporations can do, who controls them, how that control is exercised, and how the risks and returns from the activities they undertake are allocated.[12]

[12] Blair, above n 9 p 3.

1

The Corporation and Its Employees

INTRODUCTION TO THE CORPORATE GOVERNANCE DEBATE

TWO ISSUES HAVE been the focus of much of the debate on corporate governance in recent years, both in the US and the UK. Firstly, possible solutions to ineffective or even fraudulent management have been proposed. Secondly, lack of management accountability in any meaningful way to shareholders continues to be a difficult issue and even more so in relation to auditing scandals in the United States in the summer of 2002. These issues have been the primary focus of projects that have addressed the need for legislative reform in this area.[1] In response, present theories of the corporation tend towards justification for continuing the status quo in management structures and the management shareholder relationship.[2] But the status quo represents an accountability vacuum which has been, and is, theoretically troublesome in its own right.[3]

It is clear that in modern companies employees, as stakeholders, are more vulnerable than any other constituency to management adoption of specific (possibly fashionable) management theories. Such theories are pursued in the

[1] See the *Ali Principles of Corporate Governance: Analysis and Recommendations* American Law Institute Principles of Corporate Governance (1994) and drafts. See Michael P Dooley, *Fundamentals of Corporation Law*, Ch III. (Foundation Press, New York, 1995). See further: Melvin A Eisenberg, 'Legal Models of Management Structure in the Modern Corporation: Officers, Directors and Accountants' (1975) 63 *California Law Review* 375. John C Coffee, 'Beyond the Shuteyed Sentry: Toward a Theoretical View of Corporate Misconduct and an Effective Legal Response' (1977) 63 *Virginia Law Review*. Victor Brudney, 'The Independent Director-Heavenly City or Potemkin Village' (1982) 95 *Harvard Law Review* 597. Lewis D Solomon, 'Restructuring the Corporate Board of Directors: Fond Hope-Faint Promise?' (1978) 76 *Michigan Law Review* 581.

[2] The predominant theory, particularly in the US, is that developed by the law and economics school: RH Coase, 'The Nature of the Firm' (1937) 4 *Economica* (NS) 386 and Armen Alchian and Harold Demsetz, 'Production, Information, Costs and Economic Organisation' (1972) 62 *American Economic Review* 777–783. See Mark Kelman, 'Consumption Theory, Production Theory and Ideology in the Coase Theorem' (1979) 52 *Southern California Law Review* 669 for a criticism of this theory. Alternative theories will be described and considered in ch 6. See also Eugene Fama, 'Agency Problems and the Theory of the Firm' (1988) 88 *Journal of Political Economy* 288 (1988) and Eugene Fama, 'Efficient Capital Market Markets' (1991) 46 *Journal of Finance* 1575 where the capital markets theory, describing management accountability to the market, is developed.

[3] See Ronald M Green, 'Shareholders as Stakeholders: Changing Metaphors of Corporate Governance' (1993) 50 *Washington and Lee Law Review* 1415 who argues that the power exercised by corporate managers today lacks even the moral persuasiveness of ownership and consequently allows action without responsibility. See further ch 6.

name of profit maximisation. Examples include the rash of corporate take-overs and reconstructions which occurred in the US in the late 1980s,[4] and the current emphasis in both Europe and the US on extensive 'downsizing' as a means of cost reduction, which is likely to increase in the short-term given the slow-down in both economic regions. Both these management strategies have recently been reconsidered and replaced by newer emerging theories, yet management accountability to the thousands of workers whose lives have been irrevocably altered as a result is almost nil.[5]

A second area of difficulty for the modern worker arises from inadequate protection from current management views of what is required from *individual* workers. The expansion of working hours and the decline of leisure and family time may well be a source of pride for some workers but, they nevertheless have a significant impact on the quality of the lives of many, and in particular of families.[6] In Europe, some but not all of these problems are addressed through the provision of mandated rights, but not so in the US. Fears of losing a competitive

[4] The problems presented by disregarding the employee constituency during the rash of hostile takeovers and leveraged buy-outs in the 1980s led to the enactment of the other stakeholder constituency statutes by many states.

[5] Hamel and Prahalad, *Competing for the Future* (Harvard Business School Press, Cambridge, MA, 1994). See below Joseph W Singer, 'Jobs and Justice: Rethinking the stakeholder debate' (1993) 43 *Toronto Law Journal* 475. His starting point in this article is the announcement by GM in February 1992 that it planned to lay off permanently 74,000 workers over several years. Joseph W Singer, 'The Reliance Interest in Property' (1987–1988) 40 *Stan. L. Rev.* p 713. 88,000 steelworkers lost their jobs between January 1979 and January 1984 due to plant closures. 25% of those workers left the workforce entirely. 40% of workers were still looking for work in January 1984. Reductions in wages for those who did eventually find jobs seemed to reach a median of 40% below the wages earned by those workers in the steel industry. Furthermore a disproportionate number of those suffering these harsh effects were older, less well educated, female workers or workers from racial minorities.

[6] Juliet B Schor, *The Overworked American: The Unexpected Decline of Leisure* (Basic Books, New York, 1993). Ellen Goodman of the Boston Globe has described dissatisfaction with long working hours, which gave rise to industrial action at the GM plant in Flint, Michigan in October 1994. (Syndicated to The Washington Post of Saturday 8 October 1994.)

'When the auto workers struck at the GM plant in Flint, Mich., last week, the tired middle-aged men and women carrying picket signs talked of 66 hour workweeks, of mandatory overtime, of missed little league games and birthday parties, of lives that weren't lived. The overtime had once been gravy. Now they were drowning in gravy. What good is more money, they said in a dozen different voices, if you don't have time.'

Reviewed in (1993) 46 *Industry and Labour Relations Law Review* 419–20. For further analysis from Juliet Schor see Juliet B Schor, *The Overspent American: Upscaling, Downshifting and the New Consumer* (Basic Books, New York, 2001).

Arlie Hoschschild, and Anne Machung, *The Second Shift: Working Parents and the Revolution at Home* (Avon Books, New York, 1989).

See the following reviews: Debbie Ward, Review of the Second Shift (1991) 16 *Journal of Health Politics, Policy and Law* 823–830; Susan Boyd, Review of the Second Shift (1990) 4 *Canadian Journal of Women and the Law* 325–330.

This work involves a sociological study of the lives of a number of modern American couples with children and their attempts to reconcile the demands of their careers and jobs with home and family demands. The couples were largely middle class and would probably describe themselves as having careers rather than jobs and for our purposes this might indicate a time commitment to their working lives outside the home that might not be actually demanded of them by their employers.

advantage are often at the root of arguments against this kind of regulation of the labour market in the US and increasingly, against the extension of further rights in EU15. Yet even now it is clear that many European countries with highly regulated corporate responses to employee welfare are also highly competitive in markets where the US is also a competitor.[7]

Overall, there seems to be a lack of management accountability to employees in view of their vulnerability to the profit imperative. More importantly, there is a lack of 'moral persuasiveness' justifying management prerogative as it exists today. The same lack of moral persuasiveness attaches to the profit imperative. Consideration of specific issues will allow us to identify alternative solutions or theories.

There are consequently two issues: the legitimacy of the management function within the present corporate structure; and the need to alter the corporate structure in recognition of the fact that the corporation has a public role, through its actions, in shaping the lives of workers and consequently society.[8]

THE CORPORATION AND ITS EMPLOYEES

At present corporate governance theory in the US as expressed in academic legal literature is clearly focused on shareholder wealth maximisation as the dominant corporate function. In contrast, when officials within the European Union attempt to describe business and economic policy for the coming decade and beyond, it is clear from policy documents, that improving overall living and working conditions is a social aspiration for which all major institutions, including corporations, take responsibility. In this context the 'social responsibility' model of governance seems more dominant in Europe.[9]

There is a correlation between corporate law theory and understandings of the corporate function on the one hand and the treatment of workers in terms of benefits and conditions of work on the other. This phrase is intended to mean all non-wage benefits and rights such as mandated rights to paid leave, including parental leave, sick leave and other leave rights but will also include rights

[7] This issue is returned to in ch 10.

[8] 'I have already chronicled the many barriers to becoming a more leisured society. Corporations remain the most significant obstacle. Most will be vociferous opponents to my ideas. At last count, the Conference Board reports that fewer than fifty firms nation wide have comprehensive programs for work and family issues'. Schor, above n 6 p 163. Among them Schor mentions Hewlett Packard, Black and Decker and Levi-Strauss. Schor also considers the arguments against reducing working hours put forward by CEOs of many US corporations which specifically address the problems which shorter working hours would present in terms of competition with countries such as Japan and Korea. Schor points out that Germany and Sweden, both competitive economies, have much shorter working hours than the US and Japan, but she also points out that competitiveness is really about productivity and that wage levels and standards of living are also factors to be considered. p 153. With these criteria in mind the European worker fares better than the US worker does. See comparisons made by Schor, above n 6 p 82.

[9] See COM(2001)366 on Corporate Responsibility.

to information regarding corporate policy, consultation and participation rights. Compared with his European counterpart, the US worker is much more vulnerable to management decisions to save costs by limiting 'ordinary benefits' such as leave, and to other more radical decisions to downsize, restructure and relocate. The European worker, on the other hand, is protected by a considerable degree of legislation and is thus accorded a certain status in relation to corporate decision making and activity. This in turn translates into legislative protection for the employee in situations where the effects of corporate activity may have harsh results. In describing the relative positions of corporate employees in the US and the European Union, it is hoped to illustrate that there are real life issues at stake in relation to the exercise of managerial and corporate power. In other words that the outcome of the corporate governance and other stakeholders debate is politically and socially significant. Furthermore, in light of the continued globalisation of corporate activity such comparisons are essential to our understanding of the problems facing multinational corporations.

At this point an interesting contrast can be introduced in the context of considering environmental law controls. Interference in management prerogative and corporate freedom to benefit workers is frowned upon and resisted from a number of theoretical perspectives, which in legal terms can be characterised as resistance to statist intervention. However, whilst workers have to fend for themselves, actions of corporations which affect the environment are regulated. Whilst there are theoretical reasons also emanating from the law and economics school, for objecting to such regulation, this theoretical position does not seem to be a popular one on either side of the Atlantic. A similar situation pertains in relation to the regulation of corporate activities to protect consumers. In contrast theoretical resistance to intervention in corporate affairs to protect workers has resonated profoundly in the legislative arena, thus leaving the American worker with very little by way of legislative protection and within EU15 increasing resistance to the expansion of Social Policy initiatives.

REAL LIVES: TOO MUCH WORK AND NO WORK

We're officially into summer as of June 21. Did you notice?

I didn't.

Used to be it was impossible to ignore the first day of summer.

My paterfamilias invariably asked what the first day of summer is called.

'Summer solstice!' came a chorus around the dining room table.

'Derivation?' Dad would ask.

'Latin!' we would answer. ' "Sol" for sun, "sistere" for stand still.'

If we forgot, there was a Webster's Unabridged Dictionary on a walnut stand behind his chair (and an abridged to the right of his knife and spoons).

This recitation officially marked the beginning of summer.

Didn't notice the vernal equinox (Latin. 'Aequus' for equal, 'nox' for night) this March 20, either.

Like millions of us, I'm time-compressed.

. . . Then there are the current management propensities to add 'work-smarter opportunities' (time-management classes), or to hawk employees as corporate products (waving from convertibles in local parades) or to urge workers to 'volunteer' their spare time as a corporate team in a community project.

Tweaking time-management skills for people whose PDAs and Day-Timers are efficiently jammed from 6:15 a.m. (the time I chose to start writing to you) to 9:40 p.m. (the time I came home) isn't going to do it. We know it. Managers know it, though they say otherwise.

. . .

Are we going to get to the autumnal equinox and wonder where summer went?

We've got until Sept. 23 to decide.[10]

. . . The average American worker is spending a startling 12.5 weeks more a year on the job than the average German worker and 6.5 weeks more than the average British laborer.

A recent survey shows that 37 percent of Americans work more than 50 hours a week. We work six weeks more a year than we did 20 years ago and eight weeks more a year than the average European.

Although the average hours worked has risen in America during the last two decades, in Europe they have fallen. France has passed legislation limiting the workweek to 35 hours. Almost 80 percent of male workers in America work more than 40 hours in a typical week, compared with only 11 percent of Dutch men.

Americans also have the least amount of vacation time in the industrialized world, averaging two weeks a year as compared with our European counterparts, who average six. The difference is even more significant because in Europe, paid vacation is a guaranteed right, mandated by federal statutes. Union agreements have added time to the federally mandated time.

The recent International Labor Organization report surprisingly showed the United States third behind France and Belgium in productivity per hour. France provided $33.71 of value per hour, compared with $32.98 in Belgium and $32.84 in the United States. Though the report ranked the United States No. 1 in productivity per worker, that was due only to the high number of hours that Americans work.[11]

In her book Juliet Schor[12] documents the increase in work hours of the American worker and a contemporaneous reduction in rates of pay from the 1970s on with wage levels now at the level of the mid- sixties.

[10] Betty Booker, Summer Of Work; Will We Play, Too? The Richmond Times-Dispatch, 24 June 2002 Monday City Edition.

[11] Lee Scheier, 'Call it a day, America; Some think it's time we quit working so hard and start playing a little more'. Chicago Tribune, 5 May 2002.

Annual Average Country Hours at Work; US 1,979; Japan 1,842; Canada 1,767; Britain 1,719; Germany 1,480; Source: International Labor Organization; The European Foundation for Living and Work state that for the year 1998 the figures were US: 1,991; Japan: 1,947; Britian: 1,925; Germany: 1,517; and France: 1,672.

See Directive 93/104/EC which provides for a maximum working week of 48 hours (on average over a reference period not exceeding four months), a minimum daily rest period of 11 hours and a daily hours limit of eight hours for night workers.

[12] Juliet Schor, *The Overworked American: The Unexpected Decline of Leisure* (Basic Books, New York, 1993).

> This erosion [of rates of pay] . . . has a profound effect on hours: in order to maintain their current standard of living, these employees must now put in longer hours. Like the piece-rate workers who were forced to produce more as the rates fell, a large number of American families are now in a similar bind.[13]

This has continued to be a growing problem in the US into the 21st century with figures published by the International Labour Organisation in July 2002 showing that American workers now work longer hours than all other workers in developed economies, including Japan. The authors of *Competing for the Future*[14] describe how downsizing has become a corporate addiction in the US:

> Although perhaps inescapable and in many cases commendable, restructuring has destroyed lives, homes and communities. To what end? For efficiency and productivity. Although arguing with these objectives is impossible, their single minded-and sometimes simple-minded pursuit has often done as much harm as good.
>
> In every workplace that has been downsized and sped up, in every office where workers are doing three jobs for the price of two, in every office where the CEO brags that 'productivity' is up, the workload is going up and up.

Concern with the detrimental effects of plant closures and downsizing on communities and workers has been the focus of some of the current US debate on corporate governance which has focused on questions of accountability to employees as a constituency. This has also been of concern in the formulation of European Social Policy. In the US, this concern translated initially into the implementing of 'other constituency statutes' in certain States and this was followed inevitably by an assessment of such statutes by corporate lawyers. Within the European Union, various measures have been taken to increase consultation and dialogue and to afford some financial protection to workers. However, even in non-pathological situations, ie situations that do not involve plant closures or downsizing, the quality of working lives is deteriorating. These difficulties are

[13] Juliet Schor, *The Overworked American: The Unexpected Decline of Leisure* (Basic Books, New York, 1993) p 82. In the same passage Schor also notes that eight out of 10 Americans consider that it is no longer possible for them to 'make it' on a single income but also points out that 'our understanding of what we "need" turns out to be quite complicated.' Schor posits that the nature of long working hours in itself creates a demand for more goods, (p 157 'Overcoming Consumerism'). In addition she describes a phenomenon described earlier by JK Galbraith in his work, *The Affluent Society*, that beginning in the 1920s corporations sought to create needs in the consuming public which they wished to supply through the power of advertising. In her words, business began to use advertising 'as a psychological weapon against consumers'. *Ibid* p 119.

[14] Hamel and Prahalad, *Competing for the Future* (Harvard Business School Press (Cambridge, MA, 1994). From the lawyer's perspective arguing with efficiency, as the sole criterion is not 'impossible'. Singer has argued that job creation and job security are 'crucial issues of both justice and liberty'. Economic efficiency ought not to be the end of the story for lawyers and legislators. He says that 'the issue of who controls corporations implicates the values underlying democratic government'. Joseph W Singer, 'Jobs and Justice: Rethinking the Stakeholder Debate' (1993) 43 *Toronto Law Journal* 475. This work is considered in detail in ch 6.

further exacerbated by the addition of family responsibilities.[15] This issue has been described by Hoschschild and Machung in their book *The Second Shift*[16] who conduct a survey of how middle class couples with two jobs cope in their efforts to combine work and family responsibilities. There are a number of striking issues arising from this book; the first is the nature of the demands made on these couples by their work . . . and their acceptance of this. The second is the lack of social support for their endeavours. The lack of legal regulation of employer demands made on them is remarkable. Finally, although a lot of emphasis has been placed on the demands this social problem makes on women, it is also clear that despite the social importance of their endeavour as a family, and the importance generally attached to the creation of a nurturing environment for children, these couples and consequently their children are not protected from the demands of corporations and employers generally.[17]

A very topical example, because this has become so much a part of management strategy to cut labour costs and increase profits, is the growing popularity amongst corporations of employing many part-time and temporary or seasonal workers. The disadvantages of these kinds of work structures are sometimes not apparent in terms of pay (until the rates are compared with those of unionised full-time permanent workers) but are very clear when benefits such as pension rights and healthcare are considered.[18] In Europe this growing phenomenon is

[15] In an article in the *Chicago Tribune*, 13 November 1994 headed the 'Cadillac of Child Care', the child care facility at GM HQ in Flint, Michigan which is operated jointly by GM and the UAW was described in glowing terms. 'Working Mother magazine recently named GM as one of the top 100 companies for working mothers.' However, one of the working mothers featured in this happy scenario worked on the 2nd shift beginning at 3.00 pm. She routinely dropped her 4 year old to the center at 2.15 and her 10 year old was collected by the day care van from school. She picked the children up between 12.00 pm and 2.00 am 'depending on overtime'. As a 'special treat' the mother could visit her sons during her '35 minute lunch hour' because the facility is so near where she works. When one actually realises what this means, one can appreciate the overtones of corporate propaganda in this piece. Essentially, the child at school may see his mother at 8 am as he leaves for school in the morning. The children's sleep is interrupted when they are brought home between 12 pm and 2.00 am. The mother must get an average of 5 hours sleep every night if she is taking care of the younger child during the day. And the 'lunchtime treat' in fact occurs somewhere around 7pm and realistically could last between 10–15 minutes only.

[16] A Hoschschild and a Machung, n 6 above (1989).

[17] This problem has traditionally been resolved by arguments against mothers working outside the home. Similarly, in more recent times this sort of problem is considered as a feminist issue, a mistake the authors tend to make here also. 'The stalled revolution' is a phrase much used by the author and although reading the book one might be forgiven for sometimes presuming that the revolution has a somewhat narrow focus (on the burdens of housekeeping) I would argue that the revolution will be about how we think of work and corporate life and its relationship to the other parts of the life of the individual. European Foundation for Living and Work figures for 2001 state that the statutory minimum leave including public holidays in the US is 10, in Sweden and France this figure is 36 with most European countries averaging about 32 with the UK at 28 and Japan at 25. www.eiro.eurofound.ie. Feminism is a very important milestone on this path, particularly in American history, but a broader conception of the community and society as a whole is the ultimate goal.

[18] The Teamsters strike at UPS in August 1997 focused primarily on the issue of part-time employees of the company. 38,000 of the 46,000 jobs created by UPS from 1993 were part-time. An average hourly rate for a worker employed as a loader, employed typically on a part-time basis was $9. In contrast the company's drivers, usually employed full-time came out with an hourly rate of

described as the emergence of 'atypical work contracts' and is considered a serious enough issue to be the subject of considered legislation at Commission and Council level.[19]

Corporate strategies pursued over the last two decades which have focused on reorganisations, mergers, acquisitions and so on, have had the effect, (which of course was the intended outcome) of driving down wages and benefits.[20] Recent OECD figures have shown that in the US there is a greater wage disparity between the rich and the poorly or low paid than in any other industrialised western country. In the US 25 per cent of the workforce are low-paid where low paid is defined as those earning less than two thirds of the median weekly wage.[21] These are often referred to as the 'working poor.' In Europe the comparative problem is the ongoing high rate of unemployment which has varied between approximately 8 per cent to 11 per cent over the ten year period 1991–2001 in contrast to the much lower figure of between five per cent and six per cent in the US.[22] Within the European Union, however, there is a considerable variation in unemployment figures ranging from 2.1 per cent in Luxembourg to 13.9 per cent in Spain.[23] In 2000 the US figure had dropped to 3.9 per cent, 'the lowest level in a generation.'[24] Whilst these figures are encouraging, it is not clear whether they will be sustainable in the context of slower economic growth. Strategies of relocation, restructuring and downsizing have been adopted without challenge either by policy makers or lawmakers.[25] Whilst

$19.95 (a fact which was made much of by the company during the strike). UPS boasted that it provided generous benefits) (specifically health insurance), to all its employees in comparison with other employers, specifically UPS provided health insurance to all its employees. See 'Part-time Workers at UPS See Cause for Full-Scale Fight' *New York Times*, 12 August 1997.

[19] See further below ch 3.

[20] Charles Craypo, 'The Impact of Changing Corporate Strategies on Communities, Unions and Workers in the United States of America' (1997) 24 Journal of Law and Society 10. Craypo points out that this has consequently diminished the material living standard of the bottom 60% of Americans, left the next 20% slightly better off and enriched the highest 20%, especially the top 1%. These figures are cited by Craypo from Mishel and Bernstein, *The State of Working America 1994–1995* (1996) 35–44.

[21] OECD 1997.

[22] European Commission, European Commission Directorate General for Economics and Finance 2001.

[23] Note that connections have been identified between these problems and the need to address, inter alia, 'structural rigidities' . . . in labour markets and high labour costs. www.usatrade.gov

[24] Economic Report of the President (Government Publications Office, Washington DC, 2000).

[25] See Craypo above n 20 at p 13. A further consequence is that now locations and communities in the US compete with one another for the location of manufacturing and other jobs. Craypo claims that the national average cost to a community for each job is $4,000 in terms of reduced taxes, grants and so on. A startling comment is related by Craypo in relation to the decision of BMW to locate a manufacturing plant in Spartanburg, South Carolina. The average wage of a German auto worker is $23 per hour, the average wage paid by BMW in South Carolina is $10, which reflects prevailing wage rates. Indeed as one BMW board member commented to the local press, BMW were not in South Carolina to pay the high wage levels BMW pay in Germany. Two investigative journalists have observed that to attract the plant which cost $250m–$300m 'South Carolina gave away tax breaks and other taxpayer-funded benefits equal to half the value of the plant'. Craypo refers to D Bartlett and J Steele, *America: Who Really Pays the Taxes?* (1994) 302–06.

such corporate strategies have been pursued aggressively in the 1980s and 1990s, Reich notes that over the same period from 1960–1990 executive pay levels have increased so that the 'typical executive officer of the core American corporation' was about 12 times richer than 'the worker on the line' in 1960 when salaries are adjusted after tax, whereas in 1988 'the chief executive officer of one of America's hundred largest corporations' took home 70 times more than the worker on the line, after tax.[26] Corporate scandals occurring during the summer of 2002 place these figures in an even less inspiring light.

Borrowing a concept from JK Galbraith it is argued in this work that one of the major contributing factors in the growth of the disparity in wealth distribution has been that historically the large corporation has grown from strength to strength and has been influenced very little by the concerns of any 'countervailing power.'[27] Or as another commentator has put it the 'modern business corporation arguably has enjoyed economic and political hegemony in the United States since its inception.'[28] This hypothesis seems to be more true of the United States than of the European Union.[29] The absence of any 'countervailing power' is further reinforced by policies which are justified and politically rooted in corporate governance theories emphasising profit maximisation, and accountability to and through the capital markets, both in terms of earnings per share and managerial competence. Thus the hypothesis is that at this time American capitalism displays marked differences in the context of employee welfare, protection and voice, to European capitalism. The 'countervailing power', representing in our context, labour interests, has not, since the 1950s, been as clearly politically articulated in comparison to European countries. More importantly those representing 'countervailing interests' have not been invited into a social partnership in a manner similar to that which has occurred in modern times in Europe.

[26] R Reich, *The Work of Nations* (Simon and Schuster, London, 1991) 204–05. See further ch 10.

[27] JK Galbraith, *American Capitalism: The Concept of Countervailing Power* (1956).

[28] Craypo, above n *20* traces the historical development of corporate America from the early 1800s. Interestingly Craypo, in considering corporate activity in the 50s and 60s in the US, is of the view that economic prosperity was shared by corporations with the worker or employee. However, in the last two decades this has not been the case, where corporate strategies and policies have been developed which are hostile to worker or employee interests. Craypo points to a number of factors which, in his view, have led to the development of such strategies. Non-competitive products and production processes, technological changes and more importantly, in the context of this work, government deregulation, corporate reorganisation and low-cost labour. The consequent strategy is summarised by Craypo as the decision to use 'the unchallenged power of corporations to grant or withhold capital investment in plant, equipment and product development. Such threats were enhanced by the demonstrated willingness of corporations to relocate operations and by widespread plant closings and downsizings.'

[29] Recent European Industrial Relations Office figures show that in the US 15% of workers are covered by 'direct collective bargaining structures' whereas figures given for European countries vary between 100% in Belgium to 36% in the UK. The survey also notes the prevalence of statutory works councils in many European countries including the major economies.

Table 1 below shows some useful comparisons for 2000:

Table 1: Comparative Relevant Economic Indicators for the EU and US for 2000

	EU	US
GDP Growth	3.3	5.0
Inflation	2.1	3.4
Employment Rate	63.3	74.0
Employment Growth	1.8	1.3
Unemployment Rate	8.2	4.0
Growth in nominal compensation per employee	2.9	4.8
Labour productivity growth	1.6	3.7
Nominal Unit Labour Costs	1.3	1.1

Sources: European Commission, Eurostat, US Bureau of Labor Statistics.

These figures indicate continued US success as judged by these economic indicators. EU performance against these indicators is not as strong but nevertheless gains are indicated. Striking a balance between competitiveness and social protection is a central tenet of EU social policy and the more moderate EU figures might reflect that reality.

Table 2 provides a comparison for earnings growth and working hours:

Table 2: Comparison for Earnings Growth and Working Hours for 2000

	EU	US	Germany	France	UK*
Average nominal earnings increase for 2000	3.7	5.4			
Average real earnings increase for 2000	1.6	2.0			
Annual total hours worked 1998**	N/a	1,991	1,517	1,672	1,925
Average annual leave plus public holidays (2000)	36.4	26.9			
Statutory minimum leave plus public holidays (2000)	32.8	10			

* Individual countries were documented where no EU figure available.

** Based on production workers in manufacturing industry.

Sources: EIRO, BLS (USA), US Department of Labor

2

Firm Theories and Employees as Stakeholders

> Nothing better disguises the reality of life than the assumption that there is a single theory of the firm.[1]

MANAGEMENT AND EMPLOYEES

During the 1990s, the primary focus of the governance debate in the US, amongst academic writers at least, related to other stakeholders. With the events of summer 2002 including corporate accounting scandals and a decrease in stock value, the focus seemed to shift back to the relationship between management and shareholders. Regardless of the focus, at the core of the corporate governance debate is a single issue. It is about corporate wealth. Who should benefit from this wealth and to whom are those who control this wealth accountable? What justifications are presented for management decisions? Are these justifications based in reality? Are they morally acceptable?

FIRM THEORIES AND MANAGEMENT ACCOUNTABILITY

Theories of the firm, which currently underpin the corporate governance debate, are based on neo-classical economic theory.[2] Reference is usually made to the work of Coase[3] who describes, from one perspective, the reasons why an

[1] JK Galbraith and N Salinger, *Almost Everyone's Guide to Economics* (Houghton Mifflin Co, New York, 1978).

[2] For an introduction to these theories see further Michael P Dooley, *Fundamentals of Corporation Law* (Foundation Press, New York, 1995). Brian Cheffins, *Company Law: Theory, Structure and Operation* (Clarendon Press, Oxford, 1997). See also Frank H Easterbrook and Daniel R Fischel, *The Economic Structure of Corporate Law* (Harvard University Press, Cambridge, Mass, 1991).

[3] RH Coase, 'The Nature of the Firm' (1937) 4 Economica (NS) 386. See M Kelman, 'Consumption Theory, Production Theory and Ideology in the Coase Theorem' (1979) 52 *South California Law Review* 669–98 for a criticism of this theory. See also RH Coase, 'The Problem of Social Cost' 3 (1960) *Journal of Law and Economics* 1 where Coase further argues that if all parties are free to contract over the use of resources then all resources will be used efficiently. So, the

organisation or firm develops. In the passage extracted below Coase recognises that a very important part of firm structure is the integration of labour services into that structure:

> When the direction of resources (within the limits of the contract) becomes dependent on the buyer in this way, that relationship which I term a 'firm' may be obtained. A firm is likely therefore to emerge in those cases where a very short-term contract would be unsatisfactory. It is obviously of more importance in the case of services-labour- than it is in the case of the buying of commodities . . .
>
> We may sum up this section of the argument by saying that the operation of a market costs something and by forming an organisation and allowing some authority (an 'entrepreneur') to direct the resources, certain marketing costs are saved. The entrepreneur has to carry out his function at less cost, taking into account the fact that he may get factors of production at a lower price than the market transactions which he supersedes, because it is always possible to revert to the open market if he fails to do this.

This work was developed by Alchian and Demsetz[4] who considered the difficulty of ensuring that members of the firm or team are rewarded for efficient work and induced to work efficiently as part of the team. Put in their terms the problem of 'shirking' is presented. One way to reduce shirking according to Alchian and Demsetz is to introduce a specialist monitor (roughly equivalent to management). Monitoring of management will then present a problem and here the relevant specialist monitor is placed in the structure to resolve the issue, (one could describe the role as the ultimate monitor). The specialist monitor receives the residual rewards of the enterprise. Within the construct of the corporation as it stands this is the shareholder. It is argued that as residual claimant, the shareholder has an interest in monitoring the operations of the firm, and specifically the activities of management.

The endpoint of this analysis is that shareholders as the monitors fill the accountability gap identified by firm theorists. Although Alchian and Demsetz claim that the shareholder as monitor displays a number of significant decision-making or control functions, in reality the shareholder as the ultimate monitor of managerial or corporate activity, in a modern publicly owned corporation, plays only a very limited role as a residual claimant with a right to sell.

argument goes that if property rights, for example to clean air, are properly defined and similarly the industry owner's right to pollute is clearly established, one party will pay the other for the right to pollute or not to pollute whichever right is more valuable to the other. The contract process according to Coase will determine the socially optimal price for polluting. As Blair points out this hypothesis can only hold where 'the information requirements are quite severe'. Margaret M Blair, *Ownership and Control* (Brookings Institute, Washington DC, 1995) at p 225. To transpose to the labour situation this assumes certain things that are clearly untrue and which can be simply summarised as inequality of bargaining power as between labour and employer. Stuart Schwab, 'Coase Defends Coase: why Lawyers Listen and Economists Do Not' (1989) 88 *Michigan Law Review* 1171 at 1195–8.

[4] Armen A Alchian and Harold Demsetz, 'Production, Information, Costs and Economic Organisation' (1972) 62 *American Economic Review* 777–83.

Shareholders without significant stockholding in large publicly quoted companies do not exercise decision-making or control functions. In that sense, the modern corporation does not conform in any real way to the analysis proffered by Alchian and Demsetz.

The claims of neo-classical firm theorists should not be overstated. It should be noted that within economics, neo-classical firm theories represent only one particular theoretical view. It is generally recognised that the theory does not aspire to providing answers in all cases, to all firm problems:

> The economist's notion that there is only one kind of business firm is derived from the neo-classical view of the market, not from the reality of things.[5]

What is curious is that such theories have been accepted so willingly by the majority of corporate law scholars in the US, (as we will see in chapters six and seven) and seem to be gaining in popularity amongst colleagues in the UK, where there are such clear shortcomings in terms of yielding good resolutions from a legal perspective. In considering the marriage of neo-classical firm theories with the majority view in modern corporate law scholarship, a cynic might suggest that these theories have been embraced as a means to an end. The end being the recognition of the de facto control that management and directors have over corporate wealth. These theories attempt to justify the present imbalance of power and control over corporate wealth, by persuading the reader that the status quo is acceptable in view of the fact that the shareholders really do have an important monitoring function. It is argued here that even though corporate law theorists generally accept this as the orthodox view, modern corporate law does not support the idea of the monitoring function in either a principled way or in practice. The most significant point, in this context, is that the division of ownership and control allows managers of the firm or enterprise to attain a position of control. With the support of present doctrines of corporate law on proxy contests, derivative actions and fiduciary obligations maintain this position almost as a self-perpetuating body.[6]

Nevertheless, it is important to recognise the contribution of the theories of Coase and Alchian and Demstz to the governance debate. If one contrasts the 'nexus of contracts' approach with what others have described as the 'legal conceptualisation of a company'[7] (which has as its core the doctrines of separate personality and limited liability), the former has allowed us to reconsider the corporation in terms of the relationships occurring between the constituencies. Thus the nexus of contracts approach has provided subsequent analysis with a

[5] Galbraith and Salinger, above n 1 at p 61.

[6] The capital markets theory discussed below attempts to provide a resolution to the question of who monitors the monitor (management) but it is argued that this is a very poor response and has many shortcomings.

[7] See for example Brian Cheffins, *Company Law: Theory Structure and Operation* (Clarendon Press, Oxford, 1997) 32 ff. Ige Omotayo Bolodeoku, 'Economic Theories of the Corporation and Corporate Governance: A Critique' [2002] Journal of Business Law 411 makes a similar point.

starting point. Indeed the 'other stakeholder statutes' in the US implicitly recognise this point.

CAPITAL MARKETS THEORY: CONNECTIONS BETWEEN OWNERSHIP AND CONTROL

Continuing with an economic analysis of the firm, Fama's[8] description of the firm starts from the premise that our inability to understand the operation of the modern firm has been perpetuated by theories that have assumed that the proper role of the shareholder is that of owner (monitor) of the firm. Fama disputes the necessity of the connection between ownership of the equity capital and ownership of the firm. Whether historically accurate or not, this proposition is acceptable to the modern corporate stockholder, whose main interest is the profit to be made in the market for his shares, and the gains to be made through the payment of dividends. Having debunked the shareholder as the appropriate controller, Fama justifies the role that management have in this regard, as overseer of 'contracts among factors', and at this point he shares common ground with the theories of Alchian and Demsetz and Coase. The fact that this theory tends to debunk the sanctity of share ownership leads us to ask important questions. If shareholders do not own the corporation, then who does? Can a theoretical case be made out for employee ownership claims?

Theories such as Fama's which do not appeal to the shareholder as having a residual monitoring function appeal to other external controls. In Fama's case, managers are monitored in the performance of their functions, firstly, by the operation of the managerial labour market, secondly, by the operation of the capital market which efficiently prices the firm's securities, and thirdly, the manager is monitored by other managers, both those managing below him and those managing above him. However, although this may be an empirically attractive hypothesis, it certainly limits, to a great extent, the accountability of management for decisions having effects which are not taken into account in these fora. Thus capital markets must be limited in terms of what factors of performance they reflect, profitability being clearly the major issue. Furthermore, whether this is short term or long term or some shadowy mixture of both is not clear.[9] The difficulty of accurately measuring performance and ensuring reliable accounting standards are complied with has been highlighted by scandals in ENRON, WorldCom, and closer to home ELAN and to some extent Allied Irish Banks.[10]

[8] Eugene F Fama, Agency Problems and the Theory of the Firm (1988) 88 *Journal of Political Economics* 288.

[9] Eugene F Fama, 'Efficient Capital Market Markets' (1991) 46 Journal of Finance 1575. Jonathan R Macey and P Miller, 'Good Finance, Bad Economics: An Analysis of the Fraud on the Market Theory' (1990) 42 *Stanford Law Review* 4059.

[10] See WorldCom Press Release dated 25 June 2002: WorldCom Announces Intention to Restate 2001 and First Quarter 2002 Financial Statements. 'Two top executives of Elan Corporation resigned to-day after six tumultuous months of questions about accounting practices and a collapse of the company's stock price'. (*New York Times*, 10 July 2002) . 'Major investment banks helped

The managerial labour market will of necessity reflect managerial concerns of the day and be driven in terms of those standards. Thus the manager will be assessed, according to this theory, by his peers above and below him who will all be guided by the same current management theories and with the same vested interests. This sort of assessment will clearly underrate or completely ignore aspects of managerial performance which may be of vital concern to others. Thus, the flaw with Fama's theory is the lack of recognition of the necessity for *an independent outside constituency* to whom management are accountable in any meaningful way. Central to this criticism is the argument that the operation of capital markets is a very incomplete reflection of the entire function of management. In considering the different ownership structures of European companies it will be seen that there is a distinction between this kind of monitoring, sometimes described as 'arm's length finance monitoring' and the more European type of 'relational monitoring'.

However, the strength of Fama's theory is that it reflects reality, insofar as it illustrates that shareholders in large corporations have no monitoring function per se. But here the question can be raised as to what extent the capital markets theory and our acceptance of its potency has shaped current reality. This model of managerial accountability focuses on profit maximisation as a corporate, and thus managerial, goal. This is aspired to in the name of shareholder welfare as indicated by dividend payments and increase in share value. In turn, the way in which profits are measured and accounted for has led to the consideration of labour exclusively as a cost, and we have thus come to the point where shareholder welfare is pitted against employee welfare. The capital markets theory has become the dominant motif and has provided a legitimising theoretical foundation to this approach. This in turn, has led to very harsh results in many cases as far as employee welfare is concerned. In practical terms this often results in huge rises in stock values when announcements are made that employees are being laid off or plants are closing, although the cost of labour may not in fact be the cause of the corporation's difficulties or the solution to its problems. The discussion of the activities of 'Chainsaw Al' in chapter five illustrates this point. Conversely, throughout the summer of 2002 announcements of lay-offs were greeted with further falls in stock prices, based on the perception that lay-offs heralded corporate bankruptcy, illustrating the imperfection of information available to traders on the stock market.

Nevertheless towards the end of the nineties it is clear that, in a limited sense, the dominance of the capital markets theory has taken on a historical flavour of its own. Recent commentators look back at the period of hostile take-overs and

ENRON Corporation for years by lending the fallen energy giant billions of dollars via elaborately disguised commodity trades, a congressional panel said on Monday . . .' (*New York Times*, 22 July 2002). 'Is the P/E Ratio Irrelevant?' (*New York Times*, 21 July 2002).

acquisitions as representing a particular cycle of corporate history.[11] This is why the work of the communitarian corporate governance writers and others presents us with a challenge. It is the challenge to rethink our understanding of the purpose of the corporation.

QUESTIONING THE CONTROL STRUCTURE

The corporate governance debate has reached a point where the only real question is whether we ought to abandon the legal structure of the corporation, which has existed more or less intact since the nineteenth century, so that modern management (an unelected, careerist constituency with clear vested interests of its own) is legally obliged to consider its obligations to labour, suppliers, customers and others?[12] This work focuses only on labour, as a deserving beneficiary.

We have recognised that the shareholder does not have any real control function, leaving a vacuum. In reality this control vacuum is filled by management. The shareholder/owner as controller (the entrepreneur) can immediately be distinguished from the type of management control we are now considering in that he possesses some legitimacy arising from our deep seated and widely held respect for personal and private property, but modern management in this context are different, they are a class of functionaries. Fama attempts to justify their position by describing management as having invested 'a substantial lump of wealth—their human capital—to the firm.'[13] But interestingly this does not distinguish management from the vast majority of corporate employees.[14] Other firm theories, most notably that of Alchian and Demsetz, have been interpreted as justifying the management function as a necessary monitoring function. Their analysis provides us with only one view of human behaviour. Corporate law scholarship seems to ignore this point. For example, the case of the shirking heavy load lifters adopted by Alchian and Demsetz, has been interpreted by corporate law scholars of the law and economics school in a manner which involves a shift from a theoretical description of the firm, and agency problems within the firm, specifically the shareholder-management relationship, to a very real discussion of the labour-management relationship, thus subtly legitimising management control over labour:

[11] See further references to J Pound, 'The Rise of the Political Model of Corporate Goverance and Corporate Control' (1993) 68 *New York University Law Review* 1003 in Ch 9 and the references to Michael C Jensen, 'The Modern Industrial Revolution, Exit and Control Systems' (1993) 48 *Journal of Finance* 831 at 837 (1993) in ch 9. See generally, LE Mitchell (ed), *Progressive Corporate Law* (Westview Press, Boulder Co, 1996).

[12] Oliver E Williamson (1983) 'Corporate Governance' 93 *Yale Law Journal* 1197 where he argues that a mechanism must be created to insure that corporate management 'does right' by these constituencies.

[13] Above n 9.

[14] See further Blair's arguments regarding 'firm specific investments' described in ch 6 below.

> How can members of a team be rewarded and induced to work efficiently? . . . when lifting cargo into the truck, how rapidly does a man move to the next piece to be loaded, how many cigarette breaks does he take, does the item being lifted tilt downward at his side?

They go on to state that

> [O]ne method of reducing shirking is for someone to specialize as a monitor to check the input performance of team members. But who will monitor the monitor? One constraint on the monitor is the aforesaid market competition offered by other monitors, but for reasons already given that is not perfectly effective. Another restraint can be imposed on the monitor; give him title to the net earnings of the team, net of payments to other inputs.

CONCLUSION ON FIRM THEORIES

Many corporate law scholars have based their analysis on the economic models described in this Chapter, which present only one view of the issues. Even within their own terms the approach of the law and economics scholars to legal principles tend to focus on analysis of legal rules from a descriptive perspective. Statements which embody the notion that rule X works because in economic terms it yields result Y, form the core of law and economics analysis, rather than statements of the nature that rule X is the best rule given that result Y is desired. The dominant law and economics analysis of corporation law fails to provide us with good answers to what rules we ought to have if we desire results Y. The law and economics school is at its most impoverished when we ask the question what results or outcomes do we want from the modern corporation. For example, the contractarian approach has resisted the extension of management accountability through fiduciary obligations on the basis that economic analysis of the firm supports existing monitoring devices which operate successfully to control management. Moreover within the contract paradigm, it is argued that further monitoring or accountability can occur through the manipulation of existing structures; for example increased shareholder activism. Both statements are descriptive and provide a reasonably coherent description of the present. But both statements also contain a normative element in the implicit acceptance of the *status quo*: present rules have yielded result Y and that is how it should be. Neither statement will present us with a new way of considering the corporation or with the conceptual tools to advance our understanding of how the corporation should look in the future.

Different Paradigms of Control

What are the appropriate control structures for the modern corporation? Existing legal models offer the possibility of a number of different methods of altering the control structure of corporations so that, in the first instance, management is more accountable to employees, and secondly, employees have more voice in the management of corporations. This may be achieved through reform of both corporate laws and reform of labour law[15] or through models based on the expansion of existing common law doctrines, which have as their effect a radical shift of power in the relationship between management and labour.[16] In considering these models, a distinction must be made between models or arguments which seek to protect the employee from managerial decisions, and models which seek to give control to employees in a more positive way. An example of the first kind of model is found in a move away from a purely contractual understanding of the employment relationship, characterised by freedom of contract, to a more protected relationship whereby employees have gained, inter alia, a degree of legally protected job security. An example of the second kind of model is found in the adoption of worker representatives on to Boards of Directors. Many writers who support arguments for greater employee voice tend to confine themselves in reality to the protection of employees in pathological situations[17] such as plant closure, rather than considering models offering positive control. This approach probably has its roots in the deep-seated perception of management-labour relations as essentially conflictual in character rather than mutual.

This work will consider three models which are derived from a consideration of legislation implemented by the Council and Commission of the European Community in pursuit of its Social Policy. These models are described here as the Proprietorial Interest Model, the Management-Labour Consultative Model, which will include within its rubric a consideration of worker participation on boards of directors, and finally the Trade Union Model, which builds on existing trade union structures and regulation thereof.[18] Other models will also be considered, which are at present found in US corporate culture, but interestingly not to such an extent in Europe. These two models involve a restructuring of the

[15] Note that in the US the term 'labour law' is usually used to describe the regulation of collective organisations and actions and 'employment law' is used to describe individual relationships between employer and employee. This straightforward terminological distinction does not exist in other English speaking common law countries where both terms are used to describe regulation of the entire industrial relations field.

[16] Joseph W Singer, 'The Reliance Interest in Property' (1987–1988) 40 *Stanford Law Review* 713 attempts to reconstruct the power relationship through the use of tort and property doctrines. See p 611 ff.

[17] Alan Hyde, 'Ownership, Contract and Politics in the Protection of Employees Against Risk' (1993) 43 *Toronto Law Journal* 721 at 746; see also Robert Howse and Michael J Treibilcock, *Protecting the Employment Bargain ibid* p 751; see also Katherine Van Wetzel Stone 'Policing Employment Contracts within the Nexus of Contracts Firm: The Adequacy of Stakeholder Contractual Protection' (1993) 43 *Toronto Law Journal* 353 and Ronald Daniels: *Stakeholders and Takeovers: Can Contractarianism Be Compassionate?* 43 *Toronto Law Journal* 315 (1993) who provides a critique of the opposing sides to interference in contract debate in the context of corporate accountability.

[18] This taxonomy is the writer's own, derived from a consideration of the features of each model together with a consideration of the theoretical literature on corporate governance.

power balance within a corporation through the adaptation of corporate law; firstly the extension of existing fiduciary duties either by judicial law making or by statute[19] and secondly the use of share ownership to increase employee voice.

TRANSATLANTIC COMPARISONS

Comparison is made here between US regulation of the labour market at a Federal level and corporate laws by reference to the dominant states of Delaware and New York on the one hand and the legislative initiatives of the European Union in this area, rather than with the particular domestic legislation of any member state of the European Community on the other hand.[20] However, reference will be made to domestic provisions of member states where there are no harmonising provisions in place. In particular this work will focus on the implementation of the European Social Policy because the welfare of workers is dealt with under this rubric, regardless of whether specific provisions in fact regulate corporate or state behaviour.

[19] Usually described as 'other constituency' statutes in the US. See Eric W Orts, 'Beyond Shareholders: Interpreting Corporate Constituency Statutes' (1992) 61 *George Washington Law Review* 26 who describes the text of the original Pennsylvania statute of 1983 which provided a model for other states' statutes in this area. Orts notes that as of 1992, 29 states had passed other constituency statutes including notably New York, but excluding Delaware. An important point regarding these statutes is that the language used is permissive and not mandatory, except in the case of Connecticut. The Pennsylvanian statute states that 'in discharging the duties of their respective positions, the board of directors, committees of the board, individual directors and individual officers may, in considering the best interests of the corporation, consider the effects of any action upon employees, suppliers and customers of the corporation, communities in which offices or other establishments of the corporation are located, and all other pertinent factors.' See further ch 5.

[20] To date US writers have displayed a keen interest in one aspect of German company law, involving mandated worker representation on Boards of Directors, ignoring the fact that this is no longer simply a German phenomenon but a European one, occurring in a number of different countries. For example, although there has been legislation proposed for a number of years mandating worker participation on Boards in all member states, and that there is also proposed legislation for a European company which includes worker participation on Boards, both these draft pieces of legislation have been largely ignored by US commentators. In addition the vast amount of legislation which substantially alters the status and position of those workers within the European corporation is also ignored. See further ch 3.

3

The European Experience: Policy

The objective in the coming period must be to preserve and develop the European social model as we move towards the 21st century, to give to the people of Europe the unique blend of economic well-being, social cohesiveness and high overall quality of life which was achieved in the post-war period.[1]

INTRODUCTION

THE EUROPEAN SOCIAL Policy includes under its rubric Treaty provisions, legislative provisions and policy documents addressing the welfare of employees of all member states. A recurrent and continuing theme underlying the Social Policy is the idea that employee welfare is a fundamental part of a successful economic policy. From a comparative perspective, American academic literature on corporate governance, does not fully appreciate the extent of the influence of the Social Policy, nor of the extent to which the laws of all the member states of the EU are affected by legislative policy formulated in Brussels. It is striking that the only European country, which is focused on, is Germany, and this, so that reference can be made to one small aspect of German company law: the fact that worker representatives are included at Board level.[2] The literature disregards the fact that it is not only Germany which possesses the concept of a

[1] White Paper, below n 5 at p 1a para 13.

[2] See for example the work of Marleen O'Connor referred to in ch 8; Katherine Von Wetzel Stone also considered in ch 8; and Kohler. Similarly in a collection of papers given at a Conference at the Columbia Law School in November 1996 comparative considerations of other countries focused on Germany (and the issue of co-determination) and Japan but not on other European Countries: Symposium, 'Sloan Project on Corporate Governance: Employees and Corporate Governance' (22 November 1996). (Transcript available from Columbia Law School). See further the 5th Draft Directive on Company Law providing for worker representation in all European companies of a certain size. See the original proposal in 1972 OJ (C 7) and amendments thereto in 1983 OJ (C 240) and 1991 OJ (C 7). See further Adriaan Dorresteijn *et al*, *European Corporate Law* (Kluwer, Deventer, The Netherlands, 1994). See in addition proposals for a European Company contained originally in the European Company Statute 1970 OJ (C124) 1 (since amended). The main difficulties experienced with the implementation of these two pieces of legislation have 'to do with the equivalence of employee participation measure.' See The European Information Service 03.16.98. However, agreement has been reached and texts and legislation have been adopted for implementation by 2004. Council Regulation 2157/2001 2001 OJ (L294).

See further ch 4.

two tier board with worker participation, but that also European countries such as France and Italy have adopted this course since World War II. More importantly lack of awareness and knowledge about how legislative policy in this regard is fundamentally affected by membership of the European Union calls for a more complete consideration of the European experience in the context of an increased trend towards globalisation and arguably from the European perspective a more pro-active articulation beyond Europe's borders of the Social Policy.

LEGAL FOUNDATIONS OF THE SOCIAL POLICY

The foundations of the Social Policy are found in the Single European Act of 1986, the Maastricht Treaty 1992 and the Treaty of Amsterdam in 1997. The Treaty on European Union signed at Maastricht, Netherlands in February 1992 was the last major policy document indicating the planned direction of the Social Policy. The special protocol to that Treaty, which was signed by 11 of the then 12 members of the community, outlined the intended goals of the social policy of the community. Article 1 of this Protocol states that

> the Community and member states shall have as their objective the promotion of employment, improved living and working conditions, proper social protection, dialogue between management and labour, the development of human resources with a view to lasting high employment and the combating of exclusion.[3]

The Protocol then goes on to describe the initiatives which the Community and the member states will take in relation to achieving these goals. In 1997 the Treaty of Amsterdam included the Maastricht Social Protocol in the main body of the Treaty and also changed the manner in which social policy measures can be adopted. Under the terms of the Treaty of Nice, Article 137 of the EC Treaty, on social policy concerning the combating of social exclusion and the modernisation of social protection, systems are brought within the qualified majority voting provisions.

In addition to the Treaty provisions and legislation which is passed on the legal authority of these Treaties, the European Commission has, in the last decade published significant policy documents in this area. These are very instructive in expanding on the theory and policies underlying the legislation and in highlighting future trends. The documents also address issues which are debated in the academic literature in the US. At the beginning of the last decade, the publication in 1993 and 1994 of the Green Paper entitled European Social Policy: Options for the Union[4] and a subsequent White Paper entitled European

[3] The term 'exclusion' or social exclusion is used to denote unemployment, poverty and the social isolation, which are its consequences. The United Kingdom derogated from this part of the Treaty of Maastricht, refusing to continue implementing the Social Policy. However, following a landslide victory of the Labour party in 1997 the UK has abandoned this stance.

[4] Commission of the European Communities COM(93) 551 final. [17.11.93] [hereinafter Green paper].

Social Policy: A Way forward for the Union[5] effectively set the stage for the development of the legislative measures described in the next chapter. These papers ought to be considered in conjunction with a further White Paper on *Growth, Competitiveness and Employment*.[6] Since the Lisbon summit in March 2000, continued high unemployment rates and lower productivity compared with that of the US, have been identified as problems and further important communications have emanated from the Commission which effectively establish a policy framework in which these issues can be addressed.[7] In addition the Commission has published an interesting and provocative Green paper on Corporate Social Responsibility.[8]

Without going into too much detail on specific articles or provisions, major themes of the European social policy can be described as they have been outlined in the various Treaty provisions. These include the following:

The improvement of living and working conditions and the approximation of these standards throughout the European community;
The promotion of measures facilitating adaptation to organisational, structural and economic change;
The promotion and protection of management-labour dialogue;
The promotion of lasting high employment;
The combating of social exclusion;
The promotion of equality of men and women at work in relation to equal pay for work of equal value, equality of opportunity in relation to access to employment, promotion and training;
The promotion of health and safety at work;
The protection of the environment and the consumer.

In terms of transatlantic comparisons, four significant features of the EU Social Policy should be mentioned. Firstly, 'harmonisation' of domestic laws has been a very important strategy to ensure that there is a single legislative response to any given issue. In part the aim is to prevent states competing with each other by introducing more generous tax environments, less disclosure obligations for companies and so forth. Emphasis on harmonisation addresses the issues raised by the US debate on 'race to the bottom' problems, in both

[5] Commission of the European Communities COM(94) 333 final/1 and COM(94) 333 final/2. [27.07.1994] [hereinafter White paper].

[6] Supplement 6/93 of the Bulletin of the EC [1993].

[7] Communication from the Commission to the Council, the European Parliament, the Economic and Social Committee and the Committee of the Regions on the Social Policy Agenda COM (2000) 379 28.6.2000.

Communication from the Commission to the Council, the European Parliament, the Economic and Social Committee and the Committee of the Regions on Employment and Social Policies: a framework for investing in quality. Com (2001) 313 20.6.2001.

Communication from the Commission to the Council, the European Parliament, the Economic and Social Committee and the Committee of the Regions on Promoting Core Labour Standards and improving social governance in the context of globalisation. Com (2001) 416 18.7.2001.

[8] COM (2001) 366.

employment and corporate law.[9] Any laws, which impact on the operation of the market, are seen to be within the legislative competence of the institutions of the EU, and in particular, any laws affecting the operation of corporations, and any laws regulating employment relationships would be so regarded. There has been an extensive programme of harmonisation of both employment law and corporate law.[10]

Secondly, the establishment and administration of the European Social Fund (ESF) illustrates vividly the point that we are not simply talking about the odd legislative initiative concerning equal pay or health and safety or whatever; rather we are concerned with a substantive Social Policy that has had and will have profound effects on employment issues in Europe. The Fund was first established in the 1957 Treaty by Articles 123–28 and is now governed by Articles 123–25 of the Maastricht Treaty. The function of the ESF is to:

> improve employment opportunities for workers in the internal market . . . to render the employment of workers easier and to increase geographical and occupational mobility within the Community, and to facilitate their adaptation to industrial changes . . . in particular through vocational training and retraining.

Under Council Regulation 2084/93 the budget for the period 1994–99 was 47.2 billion ECU, equivalent to approximately 90 billion $US.[11] For the period 2000–06 it is 63 billion EUROS equivalent to about the same amount in US dollars under Regulation 1784/99.

In the Commission communication on the Social Policy Agenda of June 2000, the importance of the ESF in conjunction with the structural funds are underlined as 'the main Community financial instruments in underpinning policy.'[12]

Thirdly, the institutions and policy makers of the European Community have a very broad understanding of what comes within the rubric of social policy and in fact do not really concern themselves with distinctions between say, labour pol-

[9] See Michael P Dooley, *Fundamentals of Corporation Law* (Foundation Press, New York, 1995) 867 ff. for a description of this debate. An interesting feature of the 'race to the bottom' problem is the ability of a company in the US to incorporate in one State, say Delaware, and to have its main headquarters and place of business in another State. In the EU this is not permitted by the domestic laws of most of the Member States, with the exception of Ireland, the UK and the Netherlands. The other European Member States operate a strict rule which provides that a company can only be incorporated in that jurisdiction if it is to have its principal place of business in that jurisdiction. This is usually translated as the 'real seat' doctrine. The difference in approach has presented substantial problems in advancing the integration of the European market in the context of company law. This is considered by LS Sealy, *Cases and Materials in Company Law* 6th edn (Butterworths, London, 1996) 80–83.

[10] The relevant harmonising directives here are Council Directive 78/660 1978 OJ (L 222) 11; referred to as the 4th Company Law Directive; Council Directive 83/349, 1983 OJ (L 193), the 7th Company Law Directive; and the 8th Company Law Directive Council Directive 84/253, 1984 OJ (L 126).

[11] 1993 OJ (L193). According to one commentary the Social Fund 'provides support to operations carried out in certain disfavored areas or regions of the European Union.' Assistance for eligible operations under the Social Fund depends on whether or not they take place in 'absolute priority regions.' Coopers and Lybrand, *EC Commentaries* (Coopers and Lybrand, London, 1995).

[12] Above n 7.

icy and corporate policy at all. Thus, any legislative proposal which has an effect on industrial relations, the labour market, management-labour dialogue, welfare payments or living and working conditions would not be distinguished from provisions, say concerning terminations, which would be termed labour law or employment law in a more traditional classification. It is this paradigm of approach which is striking in Community legislation and policy. It enables us to consider issues affecting the worker, and consequently the role of the worker within the firm and society in a wider context. Far from representing an idealistic aspiration, specific legislative measures have given substance to this approach. Even looking at the Treaty provisions we can see that the content varies between provisions more readily classed as 'labour law' or 'employment law'—Article 119 on equal pay as between men and women[13]—and provisions which have a much broader scope, such as Articles 117 and 118 on the improvement of living and working conditions. This broader conception of the employment relationship within the firm allows us to consider, in their entirety, issues such as social security payments, environmental issues affecting workers and measures affecting efficiency of markets, which do not traditionally fit into the labour law/employment law and corporate law paradigm. We can then consider for example, what effect social security payments have on wage levels, which in turn will be one determinant of the cost of job creation. This knowledge will allow us, for example, to more accurately assess the impact of protective legislation on the job creation process, a factor which is often used, particularly by employer groups, to warn against the introduction of further legislative protection for employees.[14]

Fourthly, central to the achievement of the goals of the Social Policy is the perception of the role of the various parties to the employment relationship. The European social policy documents constantly reiterate that responsibility for the

[13] Interestingly from an American perspective the EU Treaty does not address racial discrimination per se, but does attempt to protect workers from discrimination on the basis of nationality. In recent times this policy theme has focused on ensuring equality of access by citizens of all member states to social security in other member states thus facilitating the relocation of migrant workers in other member states. For example, council regulation 2332/89 seeks to ensure the application of social security schemes to employed persons, self-employed persons where applicable and their families moving between member states. Directives passed in 2002 have expanded the equality agenda to include race.

Similarly the Treaty of Nice, introduces some changes to the legal positions of both member states and immigrants into the European Union region.

[14] Although these arguments are made by employer groups in Europe, there are strong arguments made in this vein in the academic literature in the US. See for example, Jonathan R Macey, 'Externalities, Firm Specific Capital Investments, And The Legal Treatment Of Corporate Changes' (1989) *Duke Law Journal* 173 and Jonathan R Macey, 'An Economic Analysis Of The Various Rationales For Making Shareholders The Exclusive Beneficiaries Of Corporate Fiduciary Duties' (1991) 23 *Stetson Law Review* 37, where he argues that all other constituencies have the ability to protect firm specific investments by contract, at least in theory. A second argument put forward by Macey is that if protective statutes are passed, these simply decrease the benefits that workers will get in other spheres. Joseph William Singer 'The Reliance Interest in Property' (1988) 40 *Stanford Law Review* 611 considers these arguments. Describing the 'myth of the free market' he rejects the idea that workers are free to negotiate their own contracts or to choose their terms. See further the section on the Proprietorial Interest Model.

implementation of goals is shared by all constituents, including national and regional authorities, and particularly the 'social partners, ie trade unions and works councils, industries and professional associations and *individual companies*' (my emphasis).[15] In the Communication on the Social Policy Agenda of 2000, again the importance of social dialogue was emphasised as 'one of the most effective ways of modernising contractual relations.'[16] Thus, it is important to understand also that these provisions, aimed at providing a high level of protection for workers throughout all of Europe, impose obligations on companies operating throughout the European Union. This is the case whether these companies are identifiably US, EU or Japanese in origin. Thus employees of US multinationals living and working in the EU gain benefits of EU social policy, which are not available to US employees of the same companies. On the other hand, because of less protection available to workers in the US, European companies are beginning to locate in the US to avail themselves of lower labour standards; sometimes this is referred to as a less rigid labour market.[17] The corporation is central to the furtherance of the European vision in this context and this is further underlined by development of new thinking on corporate responsibility.[18]

COMPETITIVENESS AND SOCIAL PROTECTION

> The premise at the heart of this Green paper is that the next phase in the development of European social policy cannot be based on the idea that social progress must go into retreat in order for economic competitiveness to recover. On the contrary, as has been stated on many occasions by the European Council, the Community is fully committed to ensuring that economic and social progress go hand in hand. *Indeed, much of Europe's influence and power has come precisely from its capacity to combine wealth creation with enhanced benefits and freedoms for its people.*[19]

The policy documents underpinning social policy grapple with difficult questions regarding the correct balance to be struck between efficiency, productivity, labour standards, social responsibility and the role European companies play in this regard and in the context of global competition. The more recent communications from the Commission have identified the need to reconsider social policy aims for the period 2000–2005 and these are discussed below.

To begin with in the Green Paper[20] there is a clear recognition of the tensions involved in ensuring competitiveness and growth amongst the Member States of the EU and at the same time fulfilling the clearly agreed objectives of the EU

[15] europa.eu.int/comm/dg05/esf
[16] Above n 7 p 5.
[17] This issue will be returned to in ch 9.
[18] See below.
[19] Commission of the European Communities COM(93) 551 final [17.11.93] p 7 para 4.
[20] Above n 4.

social policy. It is interesting to note that continual reference is made in the White Paper[21] of 1994, to a further *White Paper on Growth, Competitiveness and Employment*.[22] Thus the White Paper on Social Policy agrees that the Paper on Growth, Competitiveness and Employment raised

> fundamental questions which are central to the future development of social policy, notably that competitiveness is crucial for wealth and job creation and that labour market policies in particular need to be reoriented.

and continues to state that:

> The White Paper and the Green Paper have therefore provided a valuable complementary focus in the debate *about the need to create more jobs and at the same time preserve the basis of social protection which the people of Europe have come to prize*.[23]

Throughout the Green Paper and the White Paper there are repeated commitments to the aspirations of the Social Policy. For example, the Preface to the White Paper clearly states that a fundamental political aspiration is to preserve social progress, but at the same time to examine methods of ensuring continued competitiveness and growth.

It is clear that the Commission is committed to the view that these two important goals, far from being contradictory, are complementary, and closely related in their attainment. Therefore these goals ought to be and will be pursued in tandem.

> Continuing social progress can be built only on economic prosperity and therefore on the competitiveness of the European economy. The key to this is continuing productivity gains, which will enable the Union to reconcile high social standards with the capacity to compete in global markets. Europe needs to move towards an efficient, quality-based economy with a high rate of investment in new technologies. The key resource will be a well-educated and highly motivated and adaptable working population.[24]

The subsequent White Paper goes on to consider the difficult question of mandated labour standards. It states that:

> the issue of labour standards is at the heart of the debate about the relationship between competitiveness, growth and job creation.

At the same time the policy document acknowledges the extensive debate as to the correct balance to be struck and recognises that there are those who argue that 'excessively high labour standards result in costs which blunt the competitive edge of companies in one country or region as compared with others' but also states that 'On the other hand, many believe that productivity is the key to

[21] Above n 5.

[22] Supplement 6/93 of the Bulletin of the EC [1993].

[23] *Ibid* at p 3 paras 9 and 10.

[24] *Ibid* p 4 at para 17; p 11 para 12.

competitiveness and that high labour standards have always been an integral part of the competitive formula.'[25]

EUROPE IN A GLOBAL CONTEXT

At the Lisbon summit continued high unemployment rates and lower productivity rates compared with the US caused a further considered examination of the role of Europe in the global context. In addition, challenges presented by the further enlargement of the Union had also to be addressed. Subsequent communications from the Commission[26] reiterated similar themes described earlier. The Social Policy Agenda document restated 'a new strategic goal' for Europe to become the 'most competitive and dynamic knowledge-based economy capable of sustainable economic growth with more and better jobs and greater social cohesion,' yet the document continually underlines the importance of Europe's 'social model' and reiterates the 'essential linkage between Europe's economic strength and its social model.'[27] These later documents also articulate more clearly the place of Europe within the global context, almost with a new confidence despite somewhat more negative economic indicators than the US. Earlier documents had made some statements in this regard, for example the following passage from the 1994 White Paper:

> The European social model is not impervious to outside influences from other parts of the world, nor can it be ignored that the achievement in Europe of a reasonable balance between wealth creation, freedom and social justice appealed to the peoples of Central and Eastern Europe and contributed to the collapse of Communism. And while European rigidities were the subject of considerable criticism from the United States in the period after the oil shocks, the current US/Europe debate(as for example at the G7 summit on jobs) recognises that much can be learned from the European commitment of a high level of social protection. On the other hand, the Japanese socio-economic model, which has been the subject of debate in Europe is beginning to evolve towards a new balance between security and flexibility.[28]

Later documents are more specific in criticism of other models. The communication on Employment and Social policies[29] notes that the 'European model is distinguished from others by its framework and design, and by the nature, focus and distribution of the policies.' The document goes on to describe the significantly different method of funding of social spending between the EU and US, the former being largely publicly funded, the latter being much more privately funded.[30] It also notes the fact that in Europe 'benefits appear more evenly spread' than in the US where

[25] Supplement 6/93 of the Bulletin of the EC [1993] p 23 paras 10–12.
[26] Above n 7.
[27] Above n 7 COM (2000) 379 p 5.
[28] See below ch 9 and the discussion of the work of Robert Reich therein.
[29] Above n 7 COM (2001) 313.
[30] *Ibid* p 5.

> for example 40% of the population does not have access to primary health care, even though spending per head is actually higher as a proportion of GDP than it is in Europe.

It also notes that distribution of income is much wider in the US than in the EU, although there is evidence of some widening in several EU countries.[31]

CONCLUSION

The description of opposing views on this issue which are alluded to in the above passages, replicate in a microcosm, opposing versions of corporate functions and purpose presented to us by a comparison of the Anglo-American model of corporate accountability and the European model of corporate accountability on the issue of employee welfare. In all the documents ranging from 1993 to more recent documents of 2000 and 2001, the Commission acknowledges that there was and is no overwhelming consensus identifiable from the submissions it had received in relation to this debate. It is interesting that the role of corporations is specifically mentioned in many passages in these documents. In relation to the question of whether the corporation is a public or private actor, there is a clear assumption that the corporation has a public role and responsibility in the macro-economic context.[32]

An interesting feature of the claims made in the White Paper of 1994 is the view that high labour standards are a part of the competitive formula. It is argued in this work that high labour standards are, at the very least, essential to the ability of workers to contribute positively in the context of governance. Any attempt to include worker participation models, along the lines of those present in the corporate laws of many member states of the EU, or in any other format, for example those currently favoured in the US,[33] will never succeed unless workers participating are at the same time guaranteed job security so that they will not be threatened by insecurity of job tenure. Moreover, a further argument is that in the context of the broader governance debate as to corporate purpose and management accountability, high labour standards and good quality of life are ends to be pursued in their own right. Current understandings of the functions of the corporation can be legitimately redefined to include such goals and aims. These ideas are reflected even in the most recent communications from the Commission.[34]

[31] *Ibid* p 6 and Graph 7 p 20. These European countries are interestingly Ireland and the UK, the countries with corporate governance structures most similar to the US which has the widest income distribution figures and also literacy figures.

[32] See further the theoretical debate discussed in this work.

[33] See ch 5.

[34] Above n 7 COM (2001)416 p 10.

'Economic progress and social cohesion, together with a high level of protection and improvement of the quality of the environment, are complementary pillars of sustainable development and are at the heart of the process of European integration. Raising living standards, promoting a high level of employment and social protection, improving living and working conditions and promoting quality of life are goals of the European Union.'

The foregoing description of the EU Social Policy indicates that continued high levels of protection is a stated goal of the EU Commission, but that at the same time the debate on competitiveness and growth, and the impact of the aspirations of the Social Policy is not a closed one. It seems that the same sort of debate is being conducted in a much more loosely defined way within the corporate governance debate conducted in the academy in the US. Although both regional economies are starting from very different positions, the same questions about possible trade-offs are being asked.

Finally, the Green Paper on Corporate Social Responsibility[35] clearly identifies a European understanding of the corporation as having non-legal and social responsibilities in many areas including relationships with consumers, the environment, public authorities and other investors. One of the most important stakeholders identified in the Green Paper are the corporation's 'human capital' and the paper states that 'going beyond basic legal obligations . . . can also have a direct impact on productivity.' At the same time the paper is quick to emphasise that corporate responsibility is not and should not be seen 'as a substitute to regulation or legislation.'[36]

[35] COM (2001) 366.
[36] *Ibid* ch 2.

4

The European Experience: Legislation

'In a market without borders, workers' rights do not stop at the border . . .'—
Horst Guenther, German Deputy Labour Minister

THE MODELS DERIVED from European legislation which accommodate employee stakeholdership are described here, as the Proprietorial Interest Model, the Management-Labour Consultative Model, which will include within its rubric a consideration of worker participation on boards of directors, and finally the Trade Union Model building on existing trade union structures and regulation thereof.[1] The Proprietorial Interest Model involves primarily reform and restructuring of the employer-employee relationship, traditionally based on contract, by implementing labour laws which grant employees a measure of job security and other beneficial rights, such as legal rights to paid vacation and other forms of paid leave. This legislation is thus 'rights based' and *tends* towards protection of employees in pathological situations rather than aspiring to give employees more voice. This kind of legislation is not only important in terms of its own aspirations but is also necessary to allow employees the security to participate in management decisions. Legislation which protects employees from dismissal-at-will recognises the firm specific investment made by many employees and thus accords some proprietorial interests in their jobs to employees.

THE PROPRIETORIAL INTEREST MODEL

One of the fundamental provisions in this set of rights is the protection given to employees from dismissal without cause. In addition, certain grounds for dismissal will be outlawed completely. Thus the employer will have to show reasons for dismissals and typically go through a standard set of warning procedures before dismissal takes place in the first instance. All of the member states within the EU have this type of legislation as part of their employment

[1] This taxonomy is the writers own, derived from a consideration of the features of each model together with a consideration of the theoretical literature on corporate governance.

law.[2] More importantly, in the context of concerns expressed by corporate governance writers, particularly in the US, about accountability of management regarding decisions to close plants, European labour legislation also protects the worker in redundancy situations by mandating certain payments and certain consultative procedures.[3] In contrast, the US employment-at-will doctrine has developed from a very strong commitment to the contractual concepts of equal bargaining power and freedom of contract and has been maintained in many states,[4] due, in part, to strong arguments made in favour of this approach, particularly in the academic arena. In particular it has been argued that state intervention in such matters constrains and distorts the dynamics of private bargaining. Furthermore it has been argued that employees have the ability to protect themselves through bargaining and that there will inevitably be a trade-

[2] See further European Commission DGV CE–06–97–343-EN-K: Termination of Employment relationships: Legal situation in the Member States of the European Union. In Great Britain the Employment Protection Act 1971 and in Ireland The Unfair Dismissals Acts 1977–1993 protect employees with a minimum period of continuous service from dismissal without warning or cause. The burden is on the employer to show that there is a legitimate reason for the dismissal and in doing so the employer is confined to reasons specified in the Act (which may include incompetence, incapability, lack of qualification and specified types of misconduct). More importantly the employer must show that a reasonable warning procedure has been followed except in cases of serious misconduct where summary dismissal is justified. In all states, as with the legislation in the British Isles, the employee must be employed for a minimum period to qualify for protection. The German legislation provides for the shortest period, requiring 6 months; in France and Ireland the qualifying period is 2 years. In all countries the legislation typically provides for compensation for the worker who is arbitrarily dismissed and although all legislation provides for the remedy of reinstatement, this is not usually awarded. See further Samuel Estreicher, 'Unjust Dismissal Laws: Some Cautionary Notes' (1985) 33 *American Journal of Comparative Law* 310; Caroline Fennell and Irene Lynch, *Labour Law in Ireland* (Gill and MacMillan, Dublin, 1993) and Paul Davies and Mark Freedland, *Cases and Materials on Labour Law* (Weidenfeld and Nicholson, London, 1986). See also Erika Szyszczak, *EC Labour Law* (European Law Series, Longman, London, 2000).

[3] Ronald Daniels, 'Stakeholders and Takeovers: Can Contractarianism be Compassionate?' (1993) 43 *Toronto Law Journal* 315 argues that on the data available to him, there is no conclusive support for the conclusion that at least insofar as employees and creditors are concerned '[these] . . . stakeholders suffer certain injury following every change of control transaction.' Although he does concede that in certain instances stakeholders, for example labour, can experience loss. He states for example that employees have 'sometimes lost their jobs' and 'endured wage and pension benefit reductions'. He then canvasses the (p 327) usual arguments regarding private contract approach: he describes the argument that government intervention designed to protect stakeholders will make them worse off as this constrains and distorts the dynamics of private bargaining. He describes this argument as 'highly problematic'. Daniels describes the 'innate antipathy to government intervention' in these theories.

[4] Theodore J St Antoine, 'A Seed Germinates: Unjust Discharge Reform Heads Towards Full Flower' (1988) 67 *Nebraska Law Review* 56 discusses legislation providing just cause protection of this kind which has been introduced in the following legislatures in the US: California, Colorado, Connecticut, Massachusetts, Michigan, Montana, New Jersey, Ohio, Pennsylvania, Virgin Islands, Washington and Wisconsin. Writing in 1994 St Antoine notes that the harshness of the employment-at-will doctrine has been ameliorated in 45 states. Theodore J St Antoine, 'Dedication to Cornelius J Peck: The Making of the Model Employment Termination Act' (1994) 69 *Washington Law Review* 361. William B Gould, 'Job Security in the US: Some Reflections on Unfair Dismissal and Plant Closure legislation from a Comparative Perspective' (1988) 67 *Nebraska Law Review* 28 considers the legislation in a number of different states.

off between such state mandated rights and other benefits.[5] Pragmatically it has been argued that the extent of mandated employee rights in Europe generally, has created a less flexible labour market, and that this lack of flexibility has meant that the European labour market is less able to respond quickly to economic upswings as compared with the US labour market. This may be true and the European experience seems to indicate that the cost of employment, in terms of granting rights and benefits to employees may reduce job creation. However labour market analysts[6] illustrate that there are vast wage differentials amongst industries but also intra industry. A number of explanations are posited for this, including inefficient markets and inefficient dissemination of labour market information. In this context, this kind of analysis is very important because it immediately casts doubt on arguments against protectionist legislation which state that employees will ultimately suffer the cost of protectionist legislation because employers will uniformly and consistently reduce wage levels in response. If there is no pre-existing uniformity and consistency in wage levels there is no reason to suppose that employer responses to one additional external factor will be uniform or consistent.

In addition, it can be argued that the jobs which are created in European countries with legally protected security are 'real jobs' with the full compliment of protections, where the worker is less likely to return to welfare dependency over time. At this point it is simply important to note that arguments such as these, based on concepts such as equal bargaining and market equilibrium,

[5] Katherine Van Wetzel Stone, 'Employees as Stakeholders under State Nonshareholder Constituency Statutes' (1991) 21 *Stetson Law Review* 54 attempts to deal with arguments such as those of Macey's against protectionist legislation. See also Katherine Van Wetzel Stone, 'The Adequacy of Stakeholder Contractual Protection' (1993) 43 *University of Toronto Law Journal* 353. See further Jonathan R Macey, 'Externalities, Firm Specific Capital Investments, and the Legal Treatment of Corporate Changes' (1989) *Duke Law Journal* 173 where the argument is made that all other constituencies have the ability to protect firm specific investments by contract, at least in theory. A second argument put forward by Macey is that if protective statutes are passed these simply decrease the benefits that workers will get in other spheres. However Stone fails to address the basic premise of Macey's objections to initiatives such as mandated worker participation, ie that mandated protection will decrease labour creation. Singer, below n 8 also considers these arguments. Describing the Myth of the Free Market he rejects the idea that workers are free to negotiate their own contracts or to choose their terms. See further Donald H Hermann and Yvonne S Sor, 'Property Rights in One's Job: The Case for Limiting Employment at Will' (1982) 24 *Arizona Law Review* 765, 783.

See further William J Carney, 'Comment: Two Modes Of Discourse In The Stakeholder Debate' (1993) 43 *Toronto Law Journal* 379. Commenting on the work of Daniels, above n 36 and Stone, above, published in the Toronto collection, he describes the latter as advocacy and the former as social science. He considers the gap to be unbridgeable. He criticises Stone, see pp 382 ff on the basis that he objects to her modern restatement of older views of capitalist exploitation of the working classes, which according to him, ignores much of modern transaction costs economics. He also criticises Stone for confining herself to the US labour market without considering effects of globalisation. But he himself ignores Europe and Japan. The entire issue is not only concerned with low wage competition and in fact American manufacturers have suffered more from quality competition. These problems are considered further in Ch 6.

[6] For example Groshen, 'Why Wages Vary Among Employers' (1991) *Industry and Labour Relations Review* 36.

together with arguments against state intervention have been firmly rejected by the EU.

European commentators often cynically describe this type of unfair dismissal legislation or 'just cause legislation' as being merely procedural in nature. The criticism focuses on the argument that the legislation simply obliges the employer to rigidly pursue the reasonable warning systems which are prescribed by the tribunals or courts which administer this legislation, rather than actually guaranteeing job security or preventing the employer from making arbitrary decisions regarding termination. Nevertheless, this sort of legislation serves two very important related functions. Firstly it protects the employee from arbitrary decisions exercised by an individual employer (manager) and in this sense is more socially just[7] in that the legislation specifically addresses the problem of unequal power in the employment relationship. In fact the cynical commentator claiming only a procedural advantage for the employee seems sadly ignorant of what employment relationships can be like without such protection. Secondly, leaving aside instances of abusive employment relationships, these sorts of rights accord the employee positive rights to job security to the extent that no discharge can take place outside the permitted parameters of the legislation. Such legislation thus contributes to the trust element in the employment relationship. This element of trust is vital to encourage both the interest and willingness on the part of employees to express opinions as to how the company should operate, however small their input may be.[8] Trust, as discussed in chapter six has become a very important concept for some corporate governance theorists. It is argued here that this kind of legislation is an essential building block in a model of corporate governance which accords to employees more voice.[9] So for example if we conclude that co-operative management—labour structures such as works councils in the European model, or worker representatives on the Board, contribute to increased productivity, the argument here is that employee participation cannot take place in any meaningful way unless the job security of the employee is somehow protected.[10] It should be clarified that

[7] For examples of arbitrary decisions made by US employers which cannot lead to redress for the employee see *Main v Skaggs Community Hosp*, 812 S W 2d 185 (Mo Ct App 1991); *Rowe v Montgomery Ward & Co* 473 NW 2d 268 (1991). See further J Wilson Parker, 'At Will Employment and the Common Law: A Modest Proposal to De-Marginalize Employment Law' (1995) 81 *Iowa Law Review* 347.

[8] For example, under British and Irish law, employers are expressly prohibited from dismissing employees who are involved in litigation with the employer. In Part IV of his article 'The Reliance Interest in Property' (1988) 40 *Stanford Law Review* 611 at 623 Singer argues that there is a need to develop institutions capable of generating trust among participants in common enterprises. See further the discussion of the theoretical issues below.

[9] See further Singer, *ibid* at 713. Stone, 'Employees as Stakeholders under State Nonshareholder Constituency Statutes' above n 5 argues that this sort of legislation is insufficient to protect workers because workers require *ex ante* influence over decisions. In addition, when exercising this influence, the employee needs to be assured that his or her position is safe regardless of comments he or she makes in the management process.

[10] Blair supports this statement and makes the point that where the prerogative of shareholders is exercised too frequently credibility is lost from the perspective of the employee who in turn *loses*

such legislation does not prevent dismissal for cause, nor does it in any way restrict the rights of the employer to lay employees off for economic reasons.

Finally, leaving issues of trust and voice aside, it is clear that, at the very least, this sort of legislation serves to underpin what is in fact reality for many employers and employees: that employment relationships are long-term and open-ended, reflecting the reality that many employment relationships reflect firm, specific investment of human capital.[11] In the 'US Megacorp model' of the firm, although employees do not have legally mandated job security, and even less so the sort of life -time job guarantee traditionally present in Japanese companies, it has been acknowledged by a number of commentators that in some companies there are:

> Cultural and reputational considerations and in some cases union contracts . . . [which] help to reassure employees that firms will not casually dismiss them or attempt to expropriate all of the rents .[12]

Nevertheless it is highly significant that this sort of security is not mandated and that the law supports a great deal of prerogative on the part of the shareholder in the US Mega Corp model to reorganise the corporation.

Termination of the Employment Contract due to Plant Closures or Other Economically Motivated Restructuring

It is clear that increased decline of traditional industries is anticipated by EU policy makers. The European Community legislators consider that one of the functions of the increased use of management-labour dialogue will be to ease the transition of individual workers and firms from one type of business to another and to ensure that social costs of change are kept to a minimum.

In the context of plant closures and corporate reorganisation, three main directives passed have been in this area. They are:

Firstly, Council Directive 75/129/EEC on the approximation of laws of the Member States relating to collective redundancies.

Secondly, Council Directive 77/187/EEC which is amended by Council Directive 98/50/EC[13] on the approximation of laws relating to the safeguarding of employees' rights on the transfer of undertakings, businesses or parts of businesses mandated further rights for the employee who is affected by corporate restructuring.

incentive or motivation to suggest any innovations which may increase labour efficiency to protect themselves. Margaret M Blair, *Ownership and Control* (Brookings Institute, Washington, DC, 1995) 260–70.

[11] See further discussion of Blair's work in the discussion on theory.

[12] Above n 10 at p 270.

[13] 1977 OJ (L 61) (the original Directive) and 1998 OJ (L 201) for the second Directive. The implementation date for the former was 14.02.1979 and the latter is 17.07.1998.

Thirdly, Council Directive 80/987/EEC on the approximation of laws relating to the protection of employees on the insolvency of the employer.

Council Directive 75/129/EEC relating to collective redundancies and an amending Directive 92/56/EEC have been codified in Council Directive 98/59/EC.[14] This directive has been implemented by domestic legislation in all member states of the EU. This is a 'consultation Directive' and is rather atypical from a traditional labour lawyer's point of view in the sense that it is not viewed as conferring substantive rights on an individual. The efficacy of the legislation depends to a great extent on the employer being a 'good citizen'. This is in contrast to legislation which imposes specific legal obligations. The Directive compels an employer to consult with employees through their representatives in collective redundancy situations with a view to reaching agreement on the possibilities of avoiding such redundancies, having obtained the views of experienced employees. A second stated objective is to reduce the number of employees affected ie to reduce job losses. In addition, other means of mitigating the consequences of the redundancies or lay-offs must be discussed by employers with employee representatives. Even if these discussions are not fruitful, there are nevertheless a number of obligations imposed on the employer to provide specifically described information to employee representatives, including reasons for the redundancies, methods of selection for redundancy or lay-off and methods used by the employer to calculate compensation (severance pay). There is also a provision requiring the notification of the redundancies to a member state public authority, at a level equivalent to the Department of Labor in the US. In this sense the directive is very characteristic of one of the Social Policy's core objectives—that of creating good conditions for adaptation to industrial change. However, there is no obligation on the employer to listen to employee representatives, and typically the legislation as implemented by the member states enforces the obligations it creates by a system of fines, although the directive itself does not contain any provision in relation to sanctions.

In the US, The Worker Adjustment and Retraining Notification Act of 1988 provides for similar notification measures. The Act obliges employers with over 100 full-time employees to notify each union representing the workers affected or, where there is no union, each affected worker of plant closings or 'mass lay-offs'[15] 60 days in advance of the closure or lay-offs occurring. The employer is also obliged to notify the State dislocated worker 'rapid response' units established under the Job Training Act, in addition to the chief elected local government officials. Employers who are in violation of the Act are liable for up to 60 days back-pay and benefits for each affected employee. Unlike the European legislation, these penalties are paid directly to affected workers. However, the Act does not provide for consultation of employees[16] and therefore adds very little

[14] 1998 OJ (L 225).

[15] The term 'mass lay-offs' includes a number of different definitions depending on a variety of numerical thresholds.

[16] Once the employer has given notice, its legal obligations are fulfilled.

to the obligations of management or companies in this context. Nor does it really advance the development of different governance structures within corporations, particularly relating to voice and participation of employees. Unlike the EU provision there is no recognition that the input of the workforce into these sorts of decisions may in fact yield positive benefits to all.

Meanwhile continued efforts are being made to strengthen these particular legislative initiatives at EU level. Impetus for further legislation was provided by the closure by Renault automakers of their plant at Vilvoorde in Belgium with a loss of 3,100 jobs in 1997. The European Parliament passed a resolution[17] deploring this action of the management of Renault, noting that the decision had been made without the consultation and input of the workers. The resolution noted that such input had, in past cases, often saved workers from unnecessary redundancies and also stated that the Parliament 'considers it inadmissible that a transnational company should decide to close a plant, resulting in collective redundancies without prior consultation' and that the Parliament

> strongly condemns the actions of Renault management which demonstrates arrogance and disdain for the most fundamental rules of social consultation which is an essential element of the European social model.

The Parliament called on the Commission to penalise Renault for this action. In response the Commission passed a resolution urging the French government not to provide additional funding to Renault, a state-owned company. Since then Renault has increased corporate support for its European Works Council (EWC) by providing paid time for those on the committee for EWC work and by providing an annual budget of 45,000 Euro to the EWC. Similarly in early 2000 a merger between TotalFina and Elf oil companies was scrutinised under European competition law by the Commission. Whilst the French chemical and energy workers' union FCE-CFDT had meetings with the Competition directorate in relation to the merger, they complained that insufficient information had been given to employees regarding the merger. Concerned about significant job losses or 'downsizing' after the merger the union called for further improvements in EU law regarding information and consultation in situations of corporate restructuring.[18] More recent documents on the social policy agenda reiterate the commitment to developing a:

> positive and proactive approach to change by promoting adequate information for both companies and employees . . . and adapting working conditions and contractual relations to the new economy with a view to fostering a renewed balance between flexibility and security.[19]

The question still remains as to whether it is acceptable for companies to declare individual employees or large numbers of employees redundant purely

[17] 1997 OJ (C 115).

[18] www.icem.org

[19] COM (2000) 379 final p 17.

for economic reasons where the company as a whole is financially healthy, a prohibition sometimes mooted by labour unions in Europe. Some research conducted in the US canvasses situations where employees find lay-offs acceptable and situations where it is not. In a survey conducted by Charness and Levine[20] employees found lay-offs more acceptable when they were due to lower product demand and the introduction of new technologies and when 'CEOs voluntarily shared the pain.'[21]

Secondly, Council Directive 77/187/EEC which is amended by Council Directive 98/50/EC[22] on the approximation of laws relating to the safeguarding of employees' rights on the transfer of undertakings, businesses or parts of businesses mandated further rights for the employee who is affected by corporate restructuring. The essence of this legislation is to protect the interests of employees by guaranteeing the transfer of employment relationships from the transferor to the transferee in a takeover, merger or sale of the business in restructuring. The Directive provides that 'The transferor's rights and obligations arising from a contract of employment existing on the date of transfer are, by reason of such a transfer, transferred to the transferee.' In addition the Directive imposes obligations on both the transferor and the transferee to inform representatives of respective employees affected by a transfer of 'legal, economic and social implications of the transfer for employees'. The Directive excludes restructuring arising from insolvency situations , but allows for the inclusion of such transfers at the discretion of the member state. In essence workers are protected from dismissal solely by reason of the transfer, but there are exceptions which enable the transferor or transferee to dismiss workers for rationalisation purposes, whether these are for economic or technical reasons. Even if termination occurs, the cost of the termination in terms of mandated severance or redundancy pay or compensation for termination must be carried by the transferee. The employee will be able to enforce any rights, which he would have had against the transferor, against the transferee. Despite considerable exemptions in relation to the obligation to continue the employment relationship, but not, it should be stressed, in relation to the monetary obligations, the provisions have been described as having 'revolutionary implications between employers and employees.'[23]

Finally, there is Directive 80/987/EEC on the approximation of laws relating to the protection of employees on the insolvency of the employer which provides for a State-run fund to be established by each Member State, out of which

[20] Gary Charness and David Levine, 'When Are Layoffs Acceptable? Evidence from a Quasi-Experiment' (Economics Working Paper No 368 Universitat Popeu Fabra) http://papers.ssrn.com

[21] However, in many quoted companies stock prices rise when redundancies are declared which often enure to the direct benefit of management. See further the case of Sunbeam in ch 5.

[22] 1977 OJ (L 61) (the original Directive) and 1998 OJ (L 201) for the second Directive. The implementation date for the former was 14.02.1979 and the latter is 17.07.1998.

[23] Barrington J in *Mythen v The EAT, Buttercrust and Ors* [1990] Employment Law Reports, Ireland.

employees claims on corporate bankruptcy will be met. The scheme essentially operates as an insurance fund in cases of acute bankruptcy and is funded by employer contributions.

Mandated Leave Rights

Other rights, which are mandated, compliment the proprietorial interest concept. Employees within the member states of the European Union have mandated vacation rights regardless of status. The Working Time Directive mandates, *inter alia*, at least four weeks annual paid leave for all workers. It provides that no allowance can be paid in lieu of the leave to any worker.[24]

In October 1992 the Council of European Ministers adopted a Directive[25] providing for a minimum of 14 weeks maternity leave and at least 75–80 per cent of the net salary to be paid as a maternity allowance by the social welfare funds of the state or by the employer. This improved existing paid maternity leave provisions which were already in place. In addition, in June 1996 a Directive was passed providing for parental leave rights in addition to maternity leave.[26] This Directive, which was enacted by Member States, at the latest, by June 1998, provides for three months leave, per worker, per child under eight, allowing the worker to take the leave over time, incrementally or otherwise. It also provides for the leave to be paid or unpaid at the discretion of the Member State legislature or employer. These are not bargained for rights but legally protected rights which cannot be ignored by the employer. The rights of American workers compare unfavourably with these standards. Although it can be argued that many US corporations do provide for some paid parental leave, this is often through the use of sick leave by the employee. Most importantly the only federally mandated provisions in this area arises from the Family Leave Act where employees in firms with over 50 employees are entitled to take 12 weeks unpaid leave for family care.

The maternity leave and parental leave provisions have been enacted in Europe as part of an expressly stated and ongoing concern with both the inclusion of women in the workforce and with providing assistance to employees to better balance the demands of work and family. There has also been included in the Working Time Directive, provisions which set a limit on the number of hours which employees can work in a given period of time. Employees are limited to working 48 hours in a seven day period to include overtime hours. Employees must also be given 11 hours rest between periods of work and at least

[24] European Foundation for Living and Work figures for 2001 state that the statutory minimum leave including public holidays in the US is 10, in Sweden and France this figure is 36 with most European countries averaging about 32 with the UK at 28 and Japan at 25. www.eiro.eurofound.ie. See Directive 93/104/EC. 1993 OJ (L 307) p 0018–0024. See ch 1.

[25] See Directive 92/85/EEC OJ (L 348).

[26] See Council Directive 96/34/EC 1996 OJ (L 145) p 0004–0009.

one 24 hour period of rest in seven days. These legislative provisions are explicitly designed to improve the working conditions of all employees. Thus employees are not as vulnerable to demands of employers wishing to impose harsh contractual terms, nor are employees dependent on representation by a trade union. All employees are protected regardless of bargaining power.

Atypical Work

Furthermore, in the context of the growing popularity amongst employers and employees (primarily women with children) of part-time and casual labour the European legislative programme is now seeking to accord this kind of proprietorial interest to part-time and temporary workers described as 'atypical workers'. As part of the Action Programme for the implementation of the Social Charter, the Commission stated its intention to tackle the issue of contracts and employment relationships for workers who do not enjoy full-time, open-ended contracts with their employers. Although part-time and temporary workers are regarded as 'atypical' workers, they constitute a very important proportion of the working population. By the early part of the 1990s there were more than 14 million part-time employees and approximately 10 million temporary employees in the Community. By the end of the 1990s, figures indicate that part-time workers represent about a sixth of all workers in both the EU and the US.[27] Despite their numbers, these types of workers are very often discriminated against because of the nature of their employment contracts and/or because of the different social security coverage provided by the member states. Apart from negative social discrimination, with which the Commission is concerned, it is also clearly concerned that this different treatment adversely distorts competition amongst member states. Hence the submission to the Council of three draft Directives, which aimed to ensure a 'minimum coherence' of treatment amongst member states regarding the very varied forms of work which existed other than full-time open-ended contracts. In all three cases, only workers employed for eight hours or more a week were covered.

The first Directive[28] aimed to grant a minimum set of protective measures to part-time, seasonal and fixed-term contract workers with regard to social security protection, paid leave, bonuses, seniority, promotion and other benefits and advantages which are currently only granted to full-time workers. The second Directive[29] was intended to ensure that part-time and temporary workers enjoy

[27] Based on 1999 Eurostat Labour Force Survey, and BLS labour statistics for the US for January and February 2001 as collated in the EIRO reports. www.eiro.eurofound.ie. This was one of the key issues in the UPS dispute of 1997, see ch 2.

[28] 1990 OJ (C224). The Social Affairs Council revived the proposal during its 22 November 1993 meeting, but was not able to make any progress on it. A Council working group will, however, continue its work. The proposal requires a qualified majority vote from the Council to be adopted.

[29] OJ 1990 (C224).

access to vocational training and social services provided by the firm, under conditions comparable to those enjoyed by workers employed full-time or for an indefinite period. The third Directive sought to encourage improvements in the safety and health provisions at the work place for temporary workers. It was adopted in June 1991 as part of the ongoing drive to ensure high standards of workplace safety throughout Europe.[30] The first two of these Directives were then consolidated into one Directive which attempted to ensure that atypical workers in part time employment, on fixed term contracts and temporary agency work, should receive the same basic remuneration pro rata as full-time workers on open ended contracts; enjoy equal access to social protection schemes; and be counted in relation to the application of employee representation schemes. Finally, the directive also provided that employee representatives should be informed about the use, by an employer, of these forms of employment. This directive was passed in December 1997 and was implemented by all member states by January 2000.[31]

In the US, attempts have been made to adapt common law principles to establish proprietorial rights for workers reflecting the same sorts of concerns which are fundamental to the progress of the European Social Policy, although addressing the problem from a somewhat different legal paradigm.[32] The problem presented by the closure of plants causing mass lay-offs has been described as a divergence of the company's moral and legal obligations.[33] However, the matter is not so easily dispensed with. If there is acceptance of the notion that the corporation has some moral or ethical obligation to its workers in this situation then it is a matter of political will and public policy to ensure that the law gives expression to our sense of what is ethically required.

[30] Council Directive 91/383 1991 OJ (L206).

[31] Council Directive 97/81 1998OJ (L 14) This Directive was amended by Directive 98/23 1998 OJ (L 131) to include the United Kingdom. Interestingly in light of resistance to this legislation on the part of the UK throughout the early 90s, it was decided to pursue initiatives under the legislative authority of the Social Policy Protocol to the Maastricht Treaty 1992 which, at that time did not apply to the UK. The procedure under the protocol provides for the inclusion of 'the social partners' (ie national trade union organisations) at consultation stage and is based on 'qualified majority voting' (ie introduction of initiatives does not require unanimous consent from the representatives of all member states). The European Report reported in February 1997 that the Commission were concerned that there was a significant gender issue regarding the presence of atypical workers in the labour market, noting that 83% of part-time workers were women and over 50% of temporary workers were women. Thus the need to accord such workers similar rights to full-time or permanent workers was also regarded as an employment equality issue. This approach, together with the reconsideration of the UK position on the Social Charter resulted in a positive impact on progress with these directives.

[32] Singer, above n 8. Note in particular an attempted statement of the reliance interest in property which Singer argues accrues to employees to give them a legitimate interest in corporate property. Thus the property cannot be sold or dissipated without their consent. That the community and the corporation may have somewhat divergent interests in the short term is recognised by Singer, but he argues that the externalisation of the costs of closure by the plant or corporation will result in long term effects in the community which are undesirable in a broader way. 'Poverty is the parent of crime and revolution.'

[33] *Ibid.*

The recognition of this ethical or moral obligation on the part of a corporation involved in plant closure or downsizing involves the acceptance of the idea that a corporation, which is publicly held, is a common enterprise. This concept, is the fundamental premise on which the European Social Policy is based. Nevertheless, the various directives described above do not even attempt to limit or constrain a corporation's ability to close or reduce the size of a plant for economic reasons where there is no immediate threat of insolvency. Although all of the legislative measures described above are to be welcomed, there is a long way to go before management are accountable for decisions to terminate jobs, decisions which affect individual workers and which are often justified by reference to a need to reduce costs, without any meaningful scrutiny of such claims.

THE MANAGEMENT—LABOUR CONSULTATIVE MODEL

Worker Participation on Boards of Directors

For comparative purposes it is interesting that in the US,[34] Germany is the European country which has been the sole focus of attention despite the fact that it is only one of a number of European countries with this sort of legislation. Mandated employee representation on Boards or through works councils occurs in several European countries, including France, Netherlands, Belgium and Spain. However, as stated, attempts to restructure Boards to include employee representatives have not been successful at pan-European level. Perhaps it is because worker participation measures in Europe seek to actually change the corporate structure that they have met with difficulties. In particular both the UK and Ireland adopt structures very similar to the US and have resisted change. A further obstacle has been that the member states have structures already operating which are significantly different from each other. The draft Fifth Directive on Company law on the participation of workers on Boards of Directors, and the European Company Statute, which contains proposals on

[34] Marleen A O'Connor, 'The Human Capital Era: Reconceptualising Corporate Law To Facilitate Labor–Management Cooperation' (1993) 78 *Cornell Law Review* 898. See also O'Connor, 'Corporate Malaise-Stakeholder Statutes: Cause or Cure?' (1991) 21 *Stetson Law Review* 3 and O'Connor, 'Restructuring The Corporation's Nexus Of Contracts: Recognizing A Fiduciary Duty To Protect Displaced Workers' (1991) 69 *North Carolina Law Review* 1189. O'Connor in her work concentrates primarily on stakeholder statutes and makes some forays into the worker participation on boards of directors debate. In the Cornell Law Review article she discusses the need for participatory models and proposes a 'neutral referee model' as a preferred option to an employee participatory model such as that of Germany. She also discusses the culture of trust and uses notions such as trust, stemming from the moral nature of the fiduciary relationship, as an explanation for some types of behaviour, or at least as a justificatory principle for some types of behaviour, in contrast to the economic man's motivations based on self -interest. Note, in particular, passages above p 156 and fn 126 regarding Sen and fn 230. See also Amartya Sen, 'Goals Commitments and Identity' (1985) *Journal of Law and Economics and Organisation* 341. O'Connor's work regarding fiduciary relationships is considered below.

similar lines[35] have both met with strong opposition.[36] However, these provisions are only one type of initiative taken by the European Union to increase management–labour dialogue. Works councils have been successfully introduced through legislation. These are considered below.

The regulation implementing the European Company Statute has now been agreed by the Council of Ministers, together with a related Directive on worker involvement in European Companies. The regulation is due to enter into force in 2004.[37] (In contrast there is no Federally operative US company code, with corporations establishing primarily in the States of Delaware, New York and California). Worker participation is again recognised as an important element. The final SE regulation refers to Directive 2001/86/EC which addresses the issue of worker involvement separately. However, the preamble to the Regulation provides in Clause (19) that these rules 'on the involvement of employees in the European Company. . . . are an indissociable complement to this Regulation and must be applied concomitantly.' Originally the draft legislation on the SE included specific models of worker participation similar to the two types of board structure currently operative within European companies, ie to the two-tier system, which distinguishes between the supervisory and administrative boards, and the one-tier system, where non-executive directors sit on the same board as executive directors. Essentially the statute provided that in either system, at least one-third, but not more than half of the members of the administrative or supervisory board of the European Company (SE) will be employee representatives.[38]

[35] See below.

[36] Most notably Ireland and the UK. Clyde Summers, 'Labor Law as the Century Turns: A Changing of the Guard' (1988) 67 *Nebraska Law Review* 7 states that the widespread acceptance of workers on Boards of Directors is highly unlikely in the US. See also Alfred Conard, 'Comparative Law: The Supervision of Corporate Management: A Supervision of Developments in European Community and United States Law' (1984) *Michigan Law Review* 1459. Irene Goll, 'Environment, Corporate Ideology and Employee Involvement Programs' (1991) 30 *Industrial and Labour Relations Review* L 138 contains a survey of 645 US corporations ranked in Business Week 1985, 1986. A response rate of 25% was recorded and the survey revealed that there were many different forms of employee participation utilised among these companies, see p 142. An interesting point raised in this article is what exactly is meant by employee participation. The survey, according to Goll, supports the thesis that corporate ideology is a factor which influences the development of employee participation in addition to environmental factors but does not support the thesis that environmental factors shape corporate ideology which in turn develops employee participation. Goll is of the view, therefore, that employee participation will evolve over time. It is difficult to accept, however, that short of mandatory enforcement, new ways of thinking about these issues will affect the extent of employee participation. It is also clear that in the absence of mandated involvement the extent of employee participation structures was limited.

'In both union and non-union settings, participative programs seem to be designed largely to allow for employee involvement in QWL decisions (ie quality of working life). The traditional issues are handled mainly through collective bargaining in union settings and unilaterally by management in non union settings.'

[37] See Council Regulation 2157/2001 on the Statute for a European Company (SE) and the related Council Directive 2001/86/EC supplementing the Statute for a European Company with regard to the involvement of employees.

[38] See generally Adriaan Dorresteijn *et al*, *European Corporate Law* (Kluwer, Deventer, The Netherlands, 1994) ch 7.

However, the final SE regulation acknowledged the difficulty of reaching agreement on these matters, hence the Directive was passed separately. This Directive essentially sets out a negotiating model for companies proposing to form an SE and sets out a framework within which negotiations with employees regarding their involvement in the new company can take place. The Directive acknowledges the 'great diversity of rules and practice' regarding employee involvement and states that in light of this it is 'inadvisable to set up a single European model of employee involvement applicable to the SE.'[39] It also provides a basic reassurance that rights previously existing for employees regarding involvement should not be abdicated without agreement and relies in part on the provisions of the 'Acquired Rights' Directive to ensure that this is the case.[40]

Management–Labour Dialogue: New Forms

The drive to create the SE Regulation was such that compromises had to be reached in relation to employee involvement. Leaving that particular legislation aside, increasing employee participation through improved dialogue has been a favourite theme of European social policy over the years. Legislation such as Directive 75/129/EC attempts to encourage dialogue, communication and co-operation in the context of plant closures and layoffs. This legislation has been described in a previous section. In many ways this kind of legislation is very unlike traditional labour legislation in that it attempts to achieve broader aims which are more aptly described as social aspirations. Thus this legislation can be contrasted with what would be regarded in European terms as the more traditional 'floor of rights' legislation such as the legislation described in the last chapter, which seeks to protect the employee from unjust termination of the contract of employment, or uncompensated lay-offs. For this reason this kind of legislation is often derided by the more traditional labour lawyer and by realists alike as being ineffective. It is argued here that this inclusive approach is extremely challenging and exciting in that it offers the opportunity to restructure the corporate model in a very positive way.

European Works Councils

In response to the resistance being experienced in some European countries to the implementation of worker directors, the European Council of Employment and Social Affairs Ministers then turned their attention to the implementation of the European Work Council Directive. This Directive was adopted in

[39] Clause (5) Council Directive 2001/86/EC.

[40] Council Directive 77/187/EEC which is amended by Council Directive 98/50/EC. See the current Directive, Article 13.

September 1994.[41] The implementation deadline for domestic legislation was September 1996. It is estimated that over one thousand firms operating in Europe including 450 German firms, 220 French firms and importantly, 250 American firms are affected.[42] EWCs are intended to deal with cross-border issues and will therefore add an additional layer to existing management structures in most cases. Interestingly, although the UK had again derogated from this Directive under its derogation from the Maastricht Treaty, over 100 British firms were required to create a European Works Council for their employees based in other member states. Labour MEPs from Britain also objected at that time to the fact that the Conservative British government had successfully 'designated British workers as the underclass of Europe', although this situation has changed with the election of the Labour government and the full participation of the UK in the social programme. Nevertheless, the position of American companies and UK companies highlights the point made by Horst Guenther, the German Deputy Labour Minister that in a market without borders, worker's rights do not stop at the border. In a global context it is interesting to consider the fact that employees of American companies operating in Europe are the beneficiaries of a whole bundle of rights not available to their American-based counterparts. This point is developed in chapter ten. The French Labour Minister; Michel Girau pointed out that at least 29 multinational groups have already adopted such practices including Mercedes Benz, Volkswagen, Airbus Industrie, Continental Can and Nestle. The Directive provides that in all multinational groups of over 1,000 employees, including at least 150 employees in at least two Member States, procedures must be established for the provision of information to, and consultation with, wage earners at a European level. The Works Council will be composed of three to 30 members and will meet at least once a year 'to discuss transnational business.' The emphasis is on the provision of information by management to employees and encouraging dialogue and consultation between these groups. This information according to Marginson *et al*, will cover 'economic, financial and social/employment issues.' Where plant closures or changes in location are contemplated which 'will have serious consequences for employees' welfare' a committee of the Council will meet to talk with the management of the multinational group (not the local or national level

[41] Council Directive 94/45/ EC 1994 OJ (L 254).

See further the Europe Information Service bulletin on European Social Policy of 13 October 1994. For example in Ireland this directive has been enacted in the Transnational Information and Consultation Act 1996. For an excellent treatment of the European Works Councils see Marginson, Michaels, and Sisson, *The European Works Councils: Planning for the Directive* (Kluwer Law International, The Hague, 1994). For a discussion on the implementation of the directive in the UK in 1999 see Mark Carley and Mark Hall, 'The Implementation of the European Works Councils Directive' (2000) 29 *Industrial Law Journal* 103.

[42] Figures given by Marginson *et al*, *ibid* relating to multinationals not headquartered within the European Economic Area (which includes members of the EU in addition to Austria, Finland, Iceland and Norway) based on Fortune 500 companies state that of those companies, 76 will be affected including 48 US companies. They also state that the Directive will cover many medium-sized multinationals, although these would not be in the Fortune 500 list.

management). Interestingly, the Directive provides for the representation of individual plant executives on the Council as wage earners, but with somewhat different interests.

Before the passing of the legislation, there were over 41 multinational European companies where works councils had been introduced on a voluntary basis or under the domestic laws of the particular country (in particular in France and Germany[43]). In many cases there was an agreement forming the basis of the works council and this agreement specified issues which would be discussed. These issues are of the type described above but it was usually stated that the issues must be of a general nature and of strategic importance. Usually the agreement excluded discussion of issues relating to specific countries or plants only. The purpose of excluding these kinds of issues is to ensure that local collective bargaining structures are not overtaken or supplanted. Marginson *et al*[44] state that in relation to existing works councils the reaction of management is 'almost universally positive' with management identifying a number of important benefits. These include the following:

—information benefits (opportunities to dispel rumours and fears among the workforces, exchanging information, and receiving information and opinions from employee representatives);
—communication and contact benefits (in particular the opportunity for direct contact with employees for group, as distinct from subsidiary, management);
—and finally, group and transnational benefits (the encouragement of a fuller understanding of the group situation, 'suppressing national sentiment' and encouraging a sense of group identity).

Employees perceive the same benefits, and whilst research into employee reaction seems more extensive, more problems are perceived by employees, including most importantly problems with the 'variable quality and quantity of information' provided: the fact that information may be too general, too superficial and overly targeted at encouraging corporate spirit.[45] In concluding this section it is also worth noting that existing formulations of the works council arrangement do not follow any rigid pattern and that many issues are open to negotiation and agreement. Thus Marginson *et al*[46] state:

> The diversity of the existing EWCs means that employers and employee representatives/trade unions have before them a range of approaches and options from which they might draw ideas for their own EWC, or identify 'best practice' for which they themselves might wish to aim. Furthermore the generally positive experience of the voluntary EWCs may ease worries about the functioning and impact of such structures.

[43] Such companies include well known multinationals such as Nestle, Volvo, Schering, Danone, BP Oil (Europe) Bayer and the US food processing company CPC.

[44] Marginson *et al*, above n 41 ch 4.

[45] Marginson *et al*, above n 41 ch 4 p 23.

[46] *Ibid* ch 4 p 24.

By 2000 a number of empirical studies have indicated that 'the initially foreseen information was not carried out in most EWCs' although it is acknowledged that it is still very early in this project to make a clear assessment of the workings of EWCs.[47]

From the US perspective, even though many US companies will be affected because of European based investments, at home, theoretical and practical resistance to this type of approach to management issues is rooted in a number of powerful factors prevalent in the US. Firstly, there is the traditional and persisting structure of corporate ownership in the US which is conducive to increased pressure from shareholders not to include employee participation of this kind. Secondly, there is the still dominant conceptualisation of the employment relationship as a contractual one with parties bargaining at equal levels. Thirdly, there is continued corporate resistance to the inclusion of the corporation in public discourse as a public actor in the context of employee welfare. Finally, at present, traditional US labour law presents a legal obstacle to worker participation or any other form of worker representation under the terms of section 8(a)(2) of the Labor Management Relations Act 1947.[48] In contrast there is a dominant theory that the corporation is a private actor, similar to a private individual and as such should be as free from regulatory and legislative intervention as possible, insofar as corporate actions affect employees.

It is argued here that such resistance emanating from a traditional understanding of corporate functions and structures is increasingly resilient and will prove to be so in the future, as it is at this point that the most obvious challenge to management prerogative will take place. On the other hand the conceptualisation of the labour–capital exchange as a freely entered into contract with equal bargaining power has been almost completely eroded in European labour market theory. This conceptualisation, therefore, no longer serves any useful purpose other than to justify a laissez-faire attitude to regulation of the labour market.

THE TRADE UNION MODEL

At present the US corporate governance debate largely ignores the Trade Union as a viable alternative, having it seems, accepted the prevalent view that trade unionism is in irreversible decline.[49] A small number of commentators have

[47] Peter Kerckhofs, *20 Years of European Works Council Dynamics* (European Trade Union Institute, Belgium, 2001). See Charlotte Villiers, 'The Rover Case (1)—The Sale of Rover Cars by BMW—the Role of the Works Council' (2000) 29 *Industrial Law Journal* 386 for a description of the failure of the Works Council to deliver on its functions in that case.

[48] See further the following chapter.

[49] Clyde Summer, 'Labor Law as the Century Turns: A Changing of the Guard' (19988) 67 *Nebraska Law Review* 7; see in particular pp 15–16; in considering the concept of trade unionism as the vehicle of protection he is of the opinion that trade unionism has failed. Nevertheless he recognises that there is still a need for employee protection, and argues that some other form of protection is needed. In particular he argues that individual labour law can be used as a guard to protect employees.

argued that collective empowerment and not an individual rights approach will be more effective in the long run in protecting employee interests.[50] Although not really coming from quite the same perspective, advocates of share ownership as a means of providing voice and control have accepted the idea of collective empowerment in principle. In contrast, in modern times, European social policy initiatives always include European Trade Unions at a consultative level as 'social partners'.

It should be appreciated that trade unionism in Europe is also experiencing some of the same kind of decline as in the US in terms of membership and presence in many sectors, yet European social policy has perceived the existing collective organisation structure manifested in trade unionism to be a potentially vital tool in achieving its goals. For example, the social partners had a very important role in the enactment of the European Works Council Directive referred to above. The European Trade Union Confederation, ETUC, has described the establishment of European Works Councils as

> essential to the achievement of democracy in the workplace which will at the same time enhance the efficiency of companies in line with a modern vision of industrial relations.[51]

ETUC has proposed improvements to the Works Councils Directive which include a lowering of the threshold of applicability in terms of numbers of workers, adding additional subjects to the areas of discussion including equal opportunities, health and safety and environmental matters, the provision of written, comprehensible information and most importantly the addition of a penalty providing that any measures taken in contravention of the directive would be null and void.

Trade Unions are also recognised as a useful vehicle for identifying the concerns of employees as a group and as a means of enabling input to management decisions from this constituency. The Social Charter annexed to the Maastricht Treaty specifically mentions, in Articles 3 and 4, the possibility of the social partners contributing at Commission level to the further implementation of the Social policy. It is thus envisaged that there may be consultation, negotiation and agreement at extra-national level in the same way that there is national bargaining at present in many European countries, in addition to industry wide or plant bargaining.

> At a time when unions appear to be in an almost irreversible state of decline in the United States, and when many American liberals and conservatives alike have

[50] Stone, 'The Adequacy of Stakeholder Contractual Protection', above n 5. Stone, almost a solitary voice in the corporate governance literature, considers the traditional collective bargaining approach as good a vehicle as any other to encourage and support employee empowerment. See also Stuart Schwab, 'Realigning Corporate Governance: Shareholder Activism by Labor Unions' (1998) 96 *Michigan Law Review* 1171.

[51] Europe Information Service: Bulletin on European Social Policy: October 1994.

> declared collective bargaining a failed or irrelevant experiment, Europe's endorsement of the institution seems nothing less than extraordinary.[52]

A distinction has already been made between devices, which simply protect employees in pathological situations, and those structural alterations which go beyond this reactive approach to accord voice to employees. Trade union membership is in decline, that cannot be argued with, but this does not necessarily mean that trade unionism has failed entirely. In particular, if we consider the argument that many labour lawyers[53] have been making over a period of time; that the law's hostility to collectivisation has contributed to its decline, it is plausible that if the law were to create a more conducive environment to foster new directions for trade unionism, this decline could even be reversed, with positive benefits for all.

There is also an identifiable and important role for trade unionism in relation to the growth of institutional shareownership and increased activism.[54] Whilst organised labour participated in the founding of the Council of Institutional Investors, which has become a reasonably powerful lobby group in Washington DC, it has been the case that this role was limited.[55] In fact the role of institutional investors generally, and the role of organisations such as the Council for Institutional Investors is in itself quite limited. Nevertheless there is potential for organised labour to play a more active role in influencing managerial decisions through the medium of institutional investment. In pointing out this potential, it is not intended to ignore the problems discussed below in relation to the influence of institutional investment, nor is it intended to undermine the primary role of trade unions as industrial relations negotiators.

Recent figures indicate that, given current trends, trade union membership within the US will continue to decrease to five per cent of the workforce by the turn of the century as compared with one-third of the workforce being unionised in 1955. Paradoxically studies have shown that strong union representation in innovative, high performing firms tends to yield positive results in terms of growth in the firm. It has also been shown that unions and secure

[52] Thomas C Kohler, 'Lessons from the Social Charter: State Corporation and the meaning of subsidiarity' (1993) 43 *Toronto Law Journal* 621.

[53] See for example James Carey Pope, 'Labor and the Constitution' (1987) 65 *Texas Law Review* 1076: 'For decades the labor movement argued passionately that human labor is not a commodity. This philosophical debate neatly coincided with the proper place of labor in the constitutional order. If labor is a commodity, then the constitutional principles that govern the commercial marketplace also govern labor. For the past century judicial acceptance of the commodity conception has cut against constitutional protection for labor protest . . .' and William E Forbath, 'History of the American Labor Movement' (1989) 102 *Harvard Law Review* 1111.

[54] Teresa Ghilarducci *et al*, 'Labor's Paradoxical Interests and the Evolution of Corporate Governance' (1997) 24 *Journal of Law and Society* 26.

[55] Ghilarducci *et al*, *ibid* p 28 note that 'its role was very limited until recently.'

unionised workers tend to add value through co-operation.[56] Yet neither of these models necessarily imply shareholder wealth maximising outcomes.[57]

It is clear that the currently dominant demands of shareholder wealth maximisation has led to the sacrifice of other goals. Evidence[58] from the writings of business and industrial relations analysts seem to suggest that there are deep concerns that over-emphasis on one purpose of corporate function has led to a serious imbalance between competing claims. Lost growth in productivity, coupled with rising inequality of wages (which is now regarded by some as an acute problem compared with wage disparities in Europe), are referred to in literature as particularly American issues. In turn responses to international competition which focus on cost reduction measures rather than quality and skill improvements, (a response described by others as a 'low road' response) and a general failure to deal adequately with the pressures brought to bear as a result of international or global competition have exacerbated the imbalance struck between shareholder wealth maximisation and employee welfare.[59] This is an issue which will be returned to in chapters nine and ten. Interestingly two of the most influential writers in this area seem to regard trade unionism as a possible source of renewal in relation to these problems.[60]

In the European structure a new and more progressive role for trade unionism has been identified which also contains positive echoes of the past. US labour lawyers have similarly argued that US trade unions need to move away from an adversarial approach to particular sectoral or firm based issues, to a different more macro-oriented approach:

> . . . [Unions] . . . need to find a way to serve their members' interests which also serves the interests of capital and (precisely because it serves both) enables labor to claim to advance a general will that stands above the special pleading of any particular group.[61]

[56] Ghilarducci *et al*, *ibid*. The authors refer to a number of works to support these claims including JK Galbraith, *American Capitalism: The Concept of Countervailing Power* (ME Sharpe, White Plains, NY, 1956) and E Appelbaum and R Batt, *High Performance Work Systems* (1993); C Brown, M Reich and D Stern, 'Becoming a High Performance Work Organisation: The Role of Security, Employee Involvement and Training' (1993) 4 *International Jounral of Human Resource Managment* 247.

[57] See further Joel Rogers, 'Reforming US Labor Relations' (1993) 69 *Chicago-Kent Law Review* 97 Professor of Law, Political Science and Sociology, University of Wisconsin-Madison.

[58] Joel Rogers, 'Reforming US Labor Relations' *ibid* p 114. Here Rogers refers to Richard Freeman whose work with Rogers is cited throughout the article. Rogers notes that 'In real purchasing power parity terms . . . the wages of the bottom decile of American workers are now only one half of those of their counterparts in Europe.' Rogers argues that consistent employer resistance to trade unionism and the changing characteristics of the workforce have rapidly 'disappeared' (sic) unions as 'a presence in national life' yet the law prevents any other forms of worker participation or representation to flourish in their absence. Here Rogers refers to s 8 (a)(2) of the Labor Management Relations Act 1947.

[59] Rogers refers to an impressive range of labour law writers who support this proposition, *ibid* p 100 n 8.

[60] See references to Richard Freeman and Robert Reich in ch 10.

[61] Above n 57 p 123.

Whilst this sentiment is admirable one can see that it might easily be misunderstood by those currently involved in organised labour. It is very difficult to convince such groups or individuals that serving the interests of capital, as presently articulated, is something worth doing. It is clear that whilst such arguments reflect very much the modern experience of trade unionism in many European firms, it should be emphasised again that this co-operative approach is supported by a legislatively mandated floor of rights agreed to by capital for the benefit of workers. Without this background of quid pro quo it is difficult to envisage this new trade unionism gaining much credibility.[62]

In conclusion therefore, it is argued that collective action through the trade union movement does have real potential to answer some of the corporate governance issues raised regarding employees as stakeholders. This involves acceptance by management of a new view of the purpose of trade unions, a view emphasising partnership rather than conflict. Trade unions must be prepared to change their perspective on this issue also. Nevertheless such an expectation is not realistic without the provision of some *proprietorial interest* protection. A combination of models is not only desirable from a pragmatic perspective but also it seems clear that in fact new directions require the support of other legal reforms. A revamped collective bargaining paradigm must be augmented by worker participation models, and mandated job security of some sort.

[62] Paul Weiler is another writer who sees the advantage of collective bargaining as a means of answering many of the issues raised in this thesis regarding the position of the American worker. In his latest work: *Governing the Workplace: The Future of Labor* Weiler canvasses a number of options for workplace governance such as government regulation; managerial autonomy; employee ownership; or collective bargaining, mirroring in part the issues raised here under the term corporate governance. Paul C Weiler, *Governing the Workplace: The Future of Labor* (Harvard University Press, Cambridge, Mass, 1990) 317. Interestingly Weiler seeks to defend collective bargaining as the best option and has been criticised by others for not taking a more pragmatic approach to resolving the issues raised by opting for a combination of the options raised:

'Not only does Weiler fail to consider pragmatic combinations of the various modes of workplace governance, but he sets up the comparison of the different models so as to show collective bargaining at its best and all rivals to collective bargaining at their worst.' Alan Hyde, 'Endangered Species: A Review of Weiler: Governing the Workplace: The Future of Labor Relations' (1991) 91 456 (book review).

5

US Models for Improved Governance

These proposals have everything to do with labor relations and nothing to do with corporate governance.[1] James Allen, vice president at Consolidated Freightways Inc (1994)

EMPLOYEE SHARE OWNERSHIP

In US academic literature many commentators have considered employee share ownership as a solution to some of the vexed questions raised by the corporate governance debate in relation to management accountability to employees. Essentially those in favour of structures providing for employee share ownership see these mechanisms as providing a closer link between employees, as providers of firm specific labour and skills, and the functions of management. Employee share ownership increases the ability to control the direction of the firm and to benefit from risks and rewards regarding the firm's success or failure.[2]

The Firm Distinguished From the Corporation

The focus of this work is the role of employees as stakeholders within the large corporation. This is reiterated to underline the fact that many observations by those considering ownership of *firms* by employees are not directly relevant insofar as these commentators are considering *other forms of business organisation*. Thus, for example, comments made extolling the virtues of entrepreneurial sized firms, franchising agreements and partnerships, although providing valuable insights into questions of motivation and incentive, are not directly in point. Such examples simply do not address the problems faced by many employees of publicly quoted companies who are experiencing, or have

[1] Wall Street Journal report on labour unions taking a more pro-active stance in relation to voting of shares at corporate shareholder meetings in 1994.

[2] For a very brief but clear description of the introduction of employee shareownership schemes in the US see Robert Monks and Nell Minnow, *Corporate Governance* (Blackwell, Cambridge, MA, 1995) 253.

experienced, the effect of management practises entered into and adopted in the name of shareholder wealth maximisation. Thus questions as to whether different forms of business organisation ought to be encouraged through different public policy and legislative strategies as preferred forms of business organisation will be left aside. Many writers have pursued this question including Blair,[3] Monks and Minnow[4] and Hyde[5] but the positing of alternative types of business organisation misses the central question. How can we improve corporate governance structures so that there is increased accountability by corporations and management to those who are currently employed by large corporations? How can corporate structures be adapted so that employees enjoy more voice and control within those structures? To adopt a quotation from George Bernard Shaw, 'Why can't a company be more like a collective?'[6]

Writers who have considered different forms of business organisation identify key elements which present attractive alternatives to structures within the large corporation. Particularly significant is the ability to relate risk and reward with control in a closer way. Most importantly these characteristics, shared by co-operatives, partnerships and entrepreneurial firms, are viewed as adding considerable value to the firm.

Blair for example discusses the three forms of business organisation mentioned above ie the entrepreneurial start-up firm, the partnership and the franchising agreement as three forms of organisation which in her opinion 'appear to put risk, reward and . . . control rights much closer to those who supply . . . critical firm specific inputs.'[7] In Blair's view 'risk, reward and control rights' are 'bundled together' in ways which are 'conducive to encouraging and protecting investment in the corporations reputation.'[8] Hyde makes similar observations. He cites empirical examples of successful employee-owned firms such as plywood manufacturing co-operatives, professional partnerships such as law firms and accounting firms, taxi cab collectives, artisanal manufacturing and the co-operatives at Mondragon in Spain.[9] However, examples of other types of business organisation are not directly relevant but may provide us with the ability to consider how elements from these successful examples can be imported into the corporate form.

The adoption of employee share ownership schemes (ESOPs) are considered as a means of bringing employees closer to elements of risk and reward within the firm.

[3] Robert Monks and Nell Minnow, *Corporate Governance* (Blackwell, Cambridge, MA, 1995) 253.

[4] Monks and Minnow, above n 2. In particular see the discussion therein of the model of governance presented by the Mondragon co-operative system at p 258 ff.

[5] Alan Hyde, 'In Defense of Employee Ownership' (1991) 67 *Chicago-Kent Law Review* 159.

[6] *Pygmalion*.

[7] Margaret M Blair, *Ownership and Control* (Brookings Institute, Washington DC, 1995) p 278.

[8] Blair *ibid* p 279.

[9] Hyde above n 5 p 168.

'Revolution or Rip-Off?'[10]

Although having acquired much popular currency since their recognition in the US through the creation of a tax friendly environment in 1974 it seems clear that ESOPs have not met with universal approval.[11] Opinion is strongly divided as to whether ESOPs in fact serve to advance the position of employees at all. Borrowing the title of an important work by Blasi[12] it seems that ESOPs can operate either as a 'rip-off' or in a revolutionary way. This division of opinion has been described as the 'always' and 'never' schools of thought, those who are of the opinion that employee ownership[13] always works and those who think it never works.

Although not everyone would agree with the rather dramatic use of the term 'rip-off' it seems clear that there are two main areas of potential 'rip-off'. Firstly there is the potential for a financial 'rip-off' where we see employees trading traditional employee benefits, ranging from pay rates to paid lunch breaks, for shares in the company which may ultimately yield more benefits to management than to employees! The price paid for the establishment of ESOPs should certainly present concern for those traditionally concerned with advancement of labour interests. Thus for example Monks and Minnow describe the fact that the Polaroid ESOP was funded by the 'deferral of raises and bonuses by employees' and point out that in this case, and in the case of Carter Hawley Hale, 'corporate management has used the ESOP form to protect itself from prospective hostile acquirers.'[14] A number of reasons have been identified as to why companies sponsor or encourage employee share option schemes.[15] Some of these reasons clearly seem to primarily serve management aspirations or goals. These include using share option schemes as a means of fighting a hostile takeover bid.[16] Indeed many commentators see this as the prime motivating force for corporate sponsorship of employee share option schemes. In addition

[10] JR Blasi, *Employee Ownership, Revolution or Rip-Off?* (Ballinger, Cambridge, MA, 1988).

[11] Caver notes that Louis O Kelso , a San Francisco lawyer and banker is usually credited with presenting the advantages of employee share ownership schemes to the US public. In 1958 he assisted the employees of a newspaper to buy out their company. In 1974 Senator Russell Long of Louisiana guided this tax legislation through Congress. Paul Caver, 'Employee Owned Airlines: The Cure for an Ailing Industry?' (1996) 61 *Journal of Air Law and Commerce* 641, 642.

[12] Blasi, above n 10.

[13] Hyde, above n 5 p 162. Note that Hyde is referring to employee ownership of firms in this regard and not to employee shareownership.

[14] Monks and Minnow above n 2 p 254.

[15] See further Caver, above n 11 p 642.

[16] See Caver *ibid* who refers to other commentators to support this view including Corey Rosen and Michael Quarrey, 'How Well is Employee Ownership Looking?' (1987) *Harvard Business Review* 126. Monks and Minnow, above n 2 p 254 conclude that 'some substantial questions remain as to whether ESOPs will carry out their authors' intention of making owners out of employees. Their status as trusts under ERISA and their use as financing devices for the fundamental benefit of management or outside entrepreneurs have severely restricted their utility as ownership vehicles for employees.'

ESOPs are used as financing vehicles because a company can borrow on foot of a leveraged ESOPs and deduct contributions used to repay loans. Finally, management may see opportunities for using ESOPs as a bargaining tool in union negotiations. The identification of these advantages for management inherent in ESOPs naturally encourage a more sceptical view of these schemes. Similarly in relation to one of the most well known ESOPs involving United Airlines the employees exchanged control of the company for approximately $5 billion in wage and work-rule concessions which would have occurred over a six year period from 1992. In the words of Monks and Minnow the employees of United Airlines 'To stay employed, . . . were willing to take pay cuts of 10 to 17 percent. In addition, there were other concessions, like unpaid lunch breaks and reduced pension plan contributions.'

Secondly there is a more conceptual aspect to the 'rip off', which relies on claiming reality for the myth that share ownership increases voice and control when this very issue has been central to mainstream governance debates concerning more usual shareholders all along. Monks and Minnow state that ESOPs allow employees to acquire 'meaningful ownership interests in the firms in which they work'. But it is not at all clear exactly how meaningful ownership of even relatively large blocks of stock actually is, in any event. In fact much of the theory discussed in this work illustrates that in a large corporation, the usual bundle of rights associated with ownership does not present itself, even when one is considering the group normally described as the owners of the corporation, namely the shareholders. The next section will discuss the role of institutional investors generally and will cast some light on this claim to meaningfulness. Where the ESOP does not represent a substantial block of stock ownership, the rights of the employee shareholders, as with all other shareholders, are not meaningful in terms of voice and control.

Nevertheless meaningfulness may be intended to describe the claim that share ownership amongst employees leads to added commitment to the corporation on the part of employees, but this is intuitively difficult to accept for a number of reasons. Firstly, in view of the usually insignificant percentage of shareownership held by each employee, it is hard to accept that even if ownership does lead to a correlative improvement in productivity on the part of the individual, that this in turn has a significant impact on overall corporate performance. Secondly, it is difficult to accept that an individual employee could decide on the appropriate level of input or increase in productivity which would enable him or her to achieve the relevant gain as shareholder. This problem would prevent an employee from being fully motivated by such ownership. Thirdly, there are obvious free-rider problems presented by this argument, ie an employee may well decide to shirk and rely on his colleagues to increase their output to add to share value. Moreover as described by both Hyde and Caver employees are adopting elements of risk which they normally do not adopt.[17]

[17] See below.

It is equally possible that employee share ownership of corporations may work to salvage a company from financial disaster and operate to improve efficiency and productivity in certain situations. However commentators are loath to extrapolate any given set of circumstances guaranteeing success in this area.[18] Case studies including studies of Rath Packing Co; Wierton Steel Corporation, and Avis-Rent-a-Car;[19] companies familiar to those interested in this area as representing moderately successful employee share ownership schemes, do not present convincing arguments in favour of ESOPs. The employee shareownership scheme did not serve to rescue Rath Packing in the long-term and the other two companies continued to experience other difficulties which employee ownership could not redress. It seems from these studies together with an analysis of the airline industry made by the same author,[20] that to maximise the benefit of employee share ownership to the corporation generally, employees must actively participate in the company and must not simply be confined to the normally passive role of shareholders. This point will be considered further in the conclusion of this chapter. In fact the problems surrounding the lack of success of ESOPs are largely attributed by this study to lack of participation by employees in management structures, lack of consultation of employees by management, and to what would seem to be almost acute levels of secrecy on the part of management with regard to financial disclosure.[21] In addition, employee share ownership cannot, of itself, redress many of the problems which a corporation may experience. In the case studies cited, these problems ranged from higher fuel and landing costs and costs in relation to the expansion of United Shuttle experienced by United Airlines, to $1 billion of debt in TWA, to high interest rates and 'outdated plant and marketing strategies' in the case of Rath.[22]

Again it seems that, in a manner analogous to the previous analysis of works councils and worker participation on boards of directors, the advantages of employee share ownership to employees are minimal without substantial levels of employee participation in traditional management structures. If corporate structures are reformed to improve management-labour dialogue, such measures must be supported by mandated security of tenure. Similarly it seems that commentators who have studied ESOPs in detail are of the view that to be successful, good management structures must also be put in place. Without this participation employees are taking on additional firm-specific risks without the necessary control over such risks. In other words one structure will not work without the other.

[18] See Caver, above n 11; Monks and Minnow above n 2; Hyde above n 6.

[19] See Caver, above n 12 p 654–59.

[20] *Ibid.*

[21] Caver, above n 11; Blair, above n 7 p 316 referring to JR Blasi and J Kruse, *The New Owners: The Mass Emergence of Employee Ownership in Public Companies and What It Means to American Business* (1991) indicating that where employee ownership has occurred through ESOPs 'employees . . . have not typically gained commensurate access to the boardroom.'

[22] Caver, above n 11 p 655.

The issue of risk presents us with a particular problem in relation to ESOPs. Assuming that most employees are risk-averse they have already made a considerable investment in the firm which becomes more firm-specific and location-specific over time. Share ownership adds to the element of risk and to the firm-specific nature of an employee's investment, in contrast to ordinary wage remuneration. In addition the American worker is more tied to his or her employer in terms of health benefits and retirement benefits, compared with his European counterpart.[23] Risks for the employee are compounded by relatively little control rights where management dominate the Board, short-term shareholder wealth maximisation is the driving conceptual force, pay and other labour benefits are regarded as costs rather than investment in human capital and where there is very little by way of mandated employee rights coupled with hostile trade union laws. Internal structures do not, therefore, create a friendly environment in which an active ESOP could thrive. There are further complicating factors which are, to some extent, external to the actual employment relationship but relate to benefits which, as it happens in the US, are uniquely related to employment, rendering the US scenario even more difficult. Hyde underlines this fact in the following passage:

> Still, imagine that a good fairy could present working people or their leaders with a choice: a risk-free environment in which a welfare state or employers provided iron-clad promises of health, unemployment, disability and retirement security; or, on the other hand, an economy in which all enterprise was owned and controlled by employees, but there were few public benefits providing a floor, and few opportunities for diversifying investments. Of course the votes would divide, but who is confident that the second alternative would be decisively preferred?[24]

The question therefore remains as to whether within the corporate form, employee shareownership will answer any of the governance issues raised here.

In the absence of considerable consolidated share ownership blocks we can only assume that the employee share owner experiences the same sorts of problems regarding voice and control as experienced by the ordinary shareholder. Thus all the original problems raised by the corporate governance debate are still present. More significantly arguments are made that these sorts of schemes simply serve to confuse the motivations and decision-making ability of employees. Given the present dominant paradigm where management view shareholder wealth maximisation as the primary goal and that this is pitted against all costs including labour, it is impossible for the employee shareholder, even if they had any significant decision-making powers, to respond coherently to these competing demands.

[23] Hyde, above n 5 p 168 has stated that in the context of ensuring access to health benefits and retirement security American workers are reliant on their employers 'To an extent unique in the industrialised world, [T]heir access to health care and retirement security will also be a function of their employer's health.'

[24] Hyde above n 5 p 205. A good European fairy provides most of the benefits and securities mentioned by Hyde but ESOPs are not generally common in European companies, although initiatives have been taken to increase their adoption.

INSTITUTIONAL SHARE OWNERSHIP

A distinction must be made then between ESOPs involving direct share ownership on the part of individual current employees and share ownership schemes where the shares are held institutionally through a pension fund or, as in some cases, in the US by a trade union. According to the Brancato Report on Institutional Investment[25] in 1994 the top five institutional shareholders held 10.5 per cent of all shares in the top 25 largest firms. Similarly Blasi[26] predicted that on the basis of current levels, employee share ownership would continue to grow to the point where by 2000 more than 15 per cent of the stock in more than a quarter of all US stock market companies would be owned by employees. In a different study[27] it has been estimated that ownership of the 10 largest US corporations by the 30 most active institutional shareholders will range between 22 per cent and 29 per cent.

The rise of the activist institutional investor in relation to corporate governance in the US has been viewed by some as a move away from the market for corporate control model of governance to what has been described as the 'political model of governance.'[28]

> Seen in an historical context, what is happening within the corporate governance arena is simple, yet dramatic. It is the reassertion of a 'political model' of corporate governance over a transactions-and market based one. By 'political' I mean an approach in which active investors seek to change corporate policy by developing voting support from dispersed shareholders.[29]

Distinctions must be made between different types of institutional investors however. There are a number of different categories of investors including public pension funds, corporate pension funds, union pension funds, retail mutual funds, banks and thrifts, insurance and annuity companies and private foundations.[30] The perception of what is in the interest of investors represented by mutual funds, or other types of investment trust funds, might not coincide or parallel the perceptions of institutional investors such as CalPERs representing the interests of retired employees. It is also probable that because the trustees of these funds and their in-house administrative staff 'enjoy job security largely

[25] See Teresa Ghilarducci *et al*, 'Labor's Paradoxical Interests and the Evolution of Corporate Governance' (1997) 24 *Journal of Law and Society* 26, 31.

[26] J Blasi, 'Employee Ownership and Participation: the Facts and the Trends, the Problems and the Policy Options; Analysis for the Clinton Transition Team' referred to in Blair above n 7 p 303.

[27] Millstein, The Institutional Investor Project at Columbia University—Progress to Date in 22nd Annual Institute of Governance Symposium, September 1996.

[28] See J Pound, 'The Rise of the Political Model of Corporate Governance and Corporate Control' (1993) 68 *New York University Law Review* 1003. This article is considered further in ch 10.

[29] *Ibid* p 1004.

[30] J Barnard 'Institutional Investors and the New Corporate Governance' (1991) 69 *North Carolina Law Review* 1146.

unrelated to fund performance' and 'because of their social and organisational loyalties,'[31] they are likely to identify with management rather than with shareholders. Even if trustees of funds do not positively identify with management, it is sufficient that they are not proactive in advancing shareholder interests. The most important question here however is whether any of the trustees of any type of investment fund are likely to consider the interests of *current union members as well as retired employees.*

Thus from the employee perspective, it would seem that, on the face of it, very little will be gained by the participation of institutional investors, for the simple reason that the primary motivation of most of the active institutional investors is not to protect or advance the interests of current employees. The interests of retired employees may not always be similar to current employees. Similarly, in April 2000 California Public Employees Retirement Systems (CalPERS) one of the most significant institutional investors in the US, issued a policy statement underlining that it would not invest in corporations where employee welfare issues were not given serious consideration by management. It could be argued further that the input of executives of institutional investors would be even further removed than management's view of the welfare and needs of employees. This is particularly true of corporations which foster and benefit from good management-labour relations. In fact such 'long-distance' management tends to emphasise different requirements than those considered to be important by employees.

On the question of whether institutional investor activism is likely to advance the interests of *current employees,* overall one can only conclude that at present it is rare to find the interests of current employees being advanced by institutional investors. One exception was the initiative by the United Mine Workers Union in 1989 where it formed a group called the Pittston Independent Shareholders Committee. This group presented shareholder proposals challenging the company's poison pill, advocating the introduction of confidential proxy voting and the establishment of a shareholder committee. Although obviously concerned primarily with shareholder issues, it has been argued that the real purpose behind these initiatives was to gain additional strength in relation to a strike, which was ongoing in the company at that time.[32] Two further initiatives referred to by Ghilarducci are a 1994 decision by construction industry trade unionists to work with CalPERS colleagues to bring pressure to bear to restrict investment by CalPERS in construction projects that did not meet explicit labour standards, and resolutions passed at a 1996 Steelworkers and AFL-CIO conference in Pittsburgh calling for investment by pension funds in medium sized firms to encourage regional economic growth.[33] But examples

[31] J Barnard 'Institutional Investors and the New Corporate Governance' (1991) 69 *North Carolina Law Review* p 1156.

[32] *Ibid* p 1169. It is interesting to note that Ghilarducci *et al*, above n 25 p 38–39 refer to the same incident at Pittston as one example of shareholder advancement of employee interests and do not seem to be aware of many other examples.

[33] Ghilarducci *et al*, above n 25 p 38–39.

such as these seem to be quite rare. This is not a cause for criticism as there is no reason to suppose or expect that institutional investors would not be primarily concerned with the advancement of shareholder interests per se.

Furthermore there are many complex reasons why companies will resist activist institutional shareholder governance in the short term and even possibly in the long-term. Firstly, data to date does not indicate that the presence of activist institutional shareholders through the implementation of ESOPs or otherwise actually improves firms productivity or profitability.[34] Secondly, activist institutional investment in corporations may compound many of the problems experienced by the corporation because of its own institutional structures. In law and economics terms there is no reason to suppose that institutional investors do not suffer from their own agency costs which will impact on corporations. Put another way it has been argued that active participation by institutional investors in a number of different corporations will lead to over-simplistic analysis of a particular corporation's performance using criteria applicable across a wide range of sectors.[35] Lack of expertise in relation to the particular industry or sector may also present a threat to the particular corporation.

Even if this problem is solved by the institutional investor hiring appropriate expertise, there is no reason to suggest that such expertise could not equally be hired by incumbent management. More to the point, neither option will serve to further the interests of current employees. It is interesting to note that proposals for shareholder advisory committees have not generally been successful and indeed it has been argued that shareholder advisory committees may not be an effective governance measure specifically because such committees will lack expertise, that their function might simply duplicate the function of outside directors or amount to a sort of 'shadow cabinet' and be 'unlikely to perform well any unique function which would warrant the cost involved.'[36] Similarly the Council of Institutional Investors (CII—an independent representative body which works with institutional investors in US companies), although continuing to take an activist role in governance issues seem to be more concerned with what could be described as 'high profile issues' such as the issue of executive compensation at very large US corporations[37] and challenging new initiatives in

[34] See Blasi, *Employee Ownership, Revolution or Rip-Off?* above n 10; Barnard, above n 30 p 1163.

[35] See Graves and Waddock, 'Ownership at a Distance: Implications of Activist Institutional Investors' *Business in the Contemporary World* (Spring 1990) cited by Barnard, above n 30 at p 1163. Thus Barnard states that 'corporate pension fund trustees, union pension fund trustees, and mutual fund executives are seldom themselves experts in corporate strategic planning'.

[36] Barnard above n 30 p 1168. Barnard is of the opinion that rather than duplicating the functions of the board and increasing the number of decision-making fora it might be better and the same results would be achieved through placing institutional shareholder representatives on the Board.

[37] Of the approximately 300 shareholder initiatives made by CII in 2002 over 57 related directly to executive compensation. http://app.cii.org although with little effect and little support. In contrast only 24 initiatives related to workplace standards and most of these referred to practises in overseas locations, such as the use of child labour.

a high profile and rather negative manner,[38] rather than being concerned with any ongoing and sustained analysis of corporate and management accountability, least of all corporate and management accountability to employees. In fact even as the CII was busy engaging in all sorts of shareholder initiatives throughout 2002, the scandals looming on the horizon escaped them until after they had occurred. Furthermore no statements as to employee welfare are contained in their set of stated policies.[39]

Even if institutional investors were to attempt to advance the cause of current employees such attempts could face difficulties, both in relation to objections from other shareholders, and from current legal and regulatory obstacles. Thus a Wall Street Journal report noted that a somewhat more pro-active stance taken by labour unions in the proxy season of 1994 caused alarm amongst other institutional investors. The Journal noted that

> While most of these proposals call for the same corporate governance reforms that public pension funds have long championed, a growing number seek to push controversial union agendas. That worries some shareholders-rights advocates, who fear that labour's new activism may subvert, not advance, their own goals . . .

The alarm would seem somewhat misplaced when one considers that most of the time, most of these shareholders express the same concern as other shareholders. Secondly, it has been noted that the US Federal Securities and Exchanges Commission (SEC) has 'generally not been sympathetic to union-backed proxy proposals that appear to be more about labor relations than corporate governance' and notes that 'In particular, the SEC has ruled against union sponsored proposals when it viewed them as part of campaigns to win higher wages or other contract improvements.'[40]

Conclusion on Employee Share Ownership

To conclude this section let us bear in mind that institutional investors representing retired employees will not have the same interests as current employees. Even if one accepts a different understanding of the corporate function ie a function embracing the interests of many constituencies, there is no reason to suppose that even within this paradigm different constituencies are not entitled

[38] *The New York Times*, 12 July 2002, 'Commitment of WorldCom's Latest Chief is Questioned'.
The New York Times, 10 July 2002, 'Corporate Conduct: The Reaction'; A Talk on Corporate Integrity Heard in the Street and the Suite, where the CII Executive Director expressed disappointment in reaction to President Bush's statements on corporate integrity, but does not expand as to what would have been expected.
The New York Times, 25 July 2002, 'Bill Addresses Business Fraud is seen as First Step', where the CII Executive Director states that the bill is better than she feared although also states that 'it probably won't make a huge difference . . .'

[39] www.cii.org. Not that this should necessarily be expected, given current understandings of corporate function.

[40] Blair above n 3 p 318.

to advance their own interests. The question remains as to how to mediate between the interests of these constituencies and who should be charged with striking the balance. Management or government authorities?

These facts reiterate the very basic point that the workers' interests often conflict with interests of shareholders and management in the current dominant paradigm of corporate governance. ESOPs do not present a conceptually clear tool for redressing the imbalance between different assertions of these competing interests. Nor, as a matter of reality and experience, have these schemes served to protect workers' interests all the time. More invidiously, these schemes cannot even claim to be harmless, in situations where workers are not served, because of the fact that, as indicated by Monks and Minnow and others, such schemes can be manipulated by incumbent management to protect themselves.

In summary, even in the context of ESOPs it would seem that the overall absence of any governmental or legislative authority charged with the task of considering the social role of the corporation places a huge pressure on the worker to accept very difficult terms.

The only conclusion seems to be that voice and control for employees in large publicly quoted companies must seek a different vehicle or mouthpiece other than through share ownership.

THE MULTI-FIDUCIARY APPROACH

A further form of internal restructuring of the corporation which, it is claimed, would give protection to other stakeholders including employees is the concept of expanding the traditional rules on the director's fiduciary obligations. The starting point is the set of fiduciary obligations which directors owe to the company and consequently to the shareholders. Some US academic writers[41] have argued that the extension of these obligations to include other stakeholders might be an appropriate device to enable recognition of the contribution and importance of other stakeholders to the life of the corporation.

The consideration of the extension of fiduciary obligations received particular impetus, it seems, from the enactment in many States in the US of what are called 'other stakeholder statutes'. These statutes allow directors to consider the

[41] Marleen A O'Connor, 'Promoting Economic Justice in Plant Closings: Explaining the Fiduciary/Contract Law Distinction to Enforce Implicit Employment Agreements' (1995) *Progressive Corporate Law* 219, Lawrence E Mitchell (eds); Marleen A O'Connor, 'A Socio-Economic Approach To The Japanese Corporate Governance Structure' (1993) 50 *Washington and Lee Law Review* 1529; Marleen A O'Connor, 'The Human Capital Era: Reconceptualizing Corporate Law To Facilitate Labor Management Cooperation' (1993) 78 *Cornell Law Review* 899; Marleen A O'Connor, 'How Should We Talk About Fiduciary Duty? Directors' Conflict Of Interest Transaction And The ALI's Principles Of Corporate Governance' (1993) 61 *George Washington Law Review* 954; Marleen A O'Connor, 'Corporate Malaise—Stakeholder Statutes: Cause or Cure?' 21 *Stetson Law Review* 3; Marleen A O'Connor, 'Restructuring The Corporations Nexus Of Contracts: Recognizing A Fiduciary Duty To Protect Displaced Workers' (1991) 69 *North Carolina Law Review* 1189.

interests of employees, suppliers and customers when making management decisions.[42] It is widely accepted that these statutes were enacted to give directors more discretion in defending takeover bids by permitting them to legitimately respond defensively to hostile bids using the interests of employees, suppliers, customers and other constituents as criteria by which to make their decisions. Such decisions were thus permissible, in theory at least, even where defending the takeover would not have yielded the optimum result for the shareholder. In essence however, all of the statutes, with only one exception are permissive and do not therefore mandate consideration of stakeholders' interests.[43]

Proponents of the 'multi-fiduciary approach' view it as a good solution to the problems presented for workers interests by certain types of management strategies based on an exclusive commitment to shareholder wealth maximisation. The following outcomes have been identified as possible by proponents of the multi-fiduciary paradigm: Firstly, whilst not imposing an obligation on directors to maintain a plant or to maintain non-cost effective employment relationships in the face of a proposed plant closure, such an extended duty is regarded as obliging directors to ensure that the corporation would pay 'severance benefits according to the employees' years of service' and would similarly oblige directors to ensure the continuance of 'health care insurance for a period of time.'[44] The fiduciary duty would also include an obligation to maintain pension funds, to assist employees to find replacement work, to assist in retraining workers and to provide workers with 'transfer rights' and 'relocation pay'. It has also been argued that the fiduciary duty approach would ensure that employees were fully informed and consulted in relation to proposed redundancies or closure. In further cases a corporation would be obliged to attempt 'to provide unions with successorship protection for their collective bargaining agreements' and severance packages would be pre-planned. Proponents of the multi-fiduciary approach would see these outcomes as desirable. In addition the extension of fiduciary duties is viewed as the best way to ensure these outcomes.

It is important, therefore, to note that all of these enumerated outcomes are legislatively mandated under the European social policy, and so the need to consider this approach in a European context is not as compelling.[45] Nevertheless, flexibility seems to be a desirable aspect to the multi-fiduciary approach. It seems to be envisaged that not all of these issues or outcomes would arise in all cases in relation to all employees. It is clear that within this structure a central

[42] Marleen A O'Connor, 'Restructuring The Corporations Nexus Of Contracts: Recognizing A Fiduciary Duty To Protect Displaced Workers', *ibid*. In her article in the North Carolina Law Review, O'Connor presents two alternative models for protecting workers in relation to plant closures: these are described by her as the fiduciary duty model and the legislative solution.

[43] A somewhat similar provision is found in the Companies Consolidation Act (UK) 1985 and in the Companies Act (Irl) 1990 which provide that directors are entitled to take into account the interests of employees when making decisions regarding the best interests of the company. Again both provisions are permissive and not mandatory.

[44] Above n 42.

[45] See ch 4.

role for the courts is proposed whereby they would enforce some or all of these obligations on a case by case basis. One commentator has stated that 'recognition of a fiduciary duty to employees would empower courts to police corporate restructuring events to determine whether the corporation treated displaced workers fairly.'[46] Before considering the issues presented regarding the manner in which the courts would 'police corporate restructuring events' a number of arguments against the implementation of the fiduciary duty approach will be made in the following paragraphs.

Questions Raised but Not Answered by Proponents of the Multi-Fiduciary Approach

Firstly the issue of enforcement presents fundamental difficulties. It is accepted as a fundamental principle of corporate law that a director's fiduciary obligations are owed to *the corporation* and through this entity to the shareholders. The significance of this principle is that the proper plaintiff in relation to the enforcement of fiduciary obligations is the corporation, in most cases. The ability of individual shareholders to enforce the fiduciary obligations of the directors is, therefore, severely limited.[47] This basic principle presents acute problems to any claims for the extension of a positive fiduciary duty benefiting other stakeholders. How would these fundamental rules apply in relation to employees? For example, commentators have suggested that a fiduciary duty is owed to creditors of the corporation in certain circumstances, and indeed, it has now been accepted in a number of common law countries that corporate directors owe fiduciary obligations to creditors in certain situations.[48] However it is common for the courts when enunciating this concept to state that the directors do not owe these duties to the creditors individually, or directly, but owe obligations to *the corporation* which, in bankruptcy situations, enure to the benefit of the creditors rather than the shareholders.[49] Thus again the obligations would be enforceable by the corporation initially and through that by some representative of the corporation, in the case of liquidation (bankruptcy) by the liquidator (bankruptcy trustee). This point is mentioned simply to illustrate that when

[46] Above n 42 p 1255.

[47] This is also the case in other Anglo-Saxon corporate law systems where even the availability of the derivative action is more restricted than it is in the US. See further LS Sealy, *Company Law: Cases and Materials* 6th edn (Butterworths, London, 1996) who reiterates that the position in England is very restrictive regarding the availability of derivative or representative actions, although Sealy does point out that the restrictive approach enunciated by the English courts has not been followed in Australia. See further p 527 *et seq*.

[48] *Kinsela v Russell Kinsela Properties Ltd* (1986) 10 ACLR 395, *Winkworth v Edward Baron Development Co Ltd* [1987] I All E R 114, *Re Frederick Inns Ltd* [1994] ILRM 387.

[49] See for example the following passage from Street J in *Kinsela v Russell Kinsela Properties Ltd* (1986) 10 ACLR 395: 'Once it is accepted, as in my view it must be, that the directors' duty to the company as a whole extends in an insolvency context to not prejudicing the interests of creditors . . . the shareholders do not have the power or authority to absolve the directors from that breach.'

the courts have tried to grapple with the enforcement of specific fiduciary duties the conceptualisation of this action has not been straightforward.

Accordingly, there is a conceptual flaw in the analysis of O'Connor as an example of an advocate of the multi-fiduciary approach. Although reference is made to the fact that some commentators 'suggest that *a corporation* (sic) owes a fiduciary duty to creditors'[50] and O'Connor refers to *the corporation* owing duties to creditors,[51] '*directorial fiduciary responsibilities*' are mentioned in the same passage.[52] Thus the issues raised by the corporate entity doctrine are ignored completely. Similarly, whilst discussing the specific problem of 'how to enforce the director's fiduciary duty to employees'[53] it has been acknowledged that 'Legislation avoids these problems by providing clear rules about *the corporation's liability*.' The basic questions such as who will owe these obligations to the employee, the corporation or the directors individually and against whom will the action be taken, the directors or the corporation, persist. Secondly, there is the question of to whom these obligations will be owed, to each individual employee depending on his or her circumstances or to the employees collectively or to some groups of employees? Thirdly, how will these duties be enforced, by each individual employee or by some employees in a class action? A trade union? The logic of the multi-fiduciary argument, seems to indicate that every employee will be owed this duty. Cases from other areas of commercial activity where the courts have imposed a fiduciary obligation have been cited to illustrate that the courts will usually look for something more than parties 'having confidence that the other party will keep its explicit promises and carry out specific tasks in a competent manner.' Fiduciary trust evolves through some type of personal involvement 'face-to-face contact' that promotes compassion which allows an 'ethic of care to mature and prosper.' Indeed this must approximate to 'a close personal tie encompassing a moral commitment.' In the employment context, such ties must exist on a personal and individual level, if at all, leading one to conclude that multi-fiduciary advocates would not shy away from a claim that an individual employee would have a legal cause of action enabling him or her to enforce a fiduciary duty. A further question remains in relation to liability. It seems to be assumed[54] that the corporation would be liable for breaches of this fiduciary obligation, although it is the director who owes such duties. Not only are these statements unrealistic, but the legal rules which would be necessary to reflect these propositions are clearly unworkable.

[50] See further O'Connor, above n 42 at p 440. O'Connor refers to McDaniel who has made this argument elsewhere.

[51] Above n 42 p 1248.

[52] Above n 42 p 1248.

[53] *Ibid* p. 1254.

[54] Marleen A O'Connor, 'Restructuring The Corporations Nexus Of Contracts: Recognizing A Fiduciary Duty To Protect Displaced Workers', above n 42, p 1255.

Criticisms of the Fiduciary Approach

All of these questions might simply mean that more work has to be done. Yet there are further substantive criticisms of the fiduciary approach. All of the outcomes described above as desirable and attainable through the fiduciary approach are mandated outcomes through legislation in all member states of the European Union as described in the previous chapter. European legislation therefore mandates a common standard of behaviour for all directors or management of the same type or size of company throughout the European Union in relation to all employees. This has the advantage of certainty. In contrast, the multi-fiduciary approach presents possibilities of endless and multiple litigation arising from the fiduciary approach imposing additional costs on both employees and management. Not only that, the fiduciary approach would place an intolerable practical burden on the courts obliged to consider individual claims from employees attempting to enforce alleged fiduciary obligations.

A further, and probably the most difficult issue, would be how the courts could mediate between the enforcement of different obligations in relation to different constituencies, particularly where the interests of both or more conflict. Although it has been argued that it will not be usual for these interests, specifically the interests of employees and shareholders to conflict, this is clearly not the case. Admittedly plant closure represents the competing interests of workers and shareholders most acutely, but many decisions made by management of corporations regarding labour benefits such as wage rises, leave entitlements and other benefits, are characterised as the protection of the goal of shareholder wealth maximisation against over-demanding employees, or indeed vice versa. As we have seen from the discussion in chapter one, adverse decisions made by management in relation to employee demands are all too often justified by reference to cost, profit and shareholder welfare. There are two possible criteria for the courts to employ: the business judgement rule or the fairness test. The business judgement rule would simply provide even greater leeway to directors in exercising discretion, which might in turn 'increase agency costs by facilitating inefficient managerial behaviour and encouraging excessive risk aversion by management.' Instead a 'fairness test' is advocated to avoid these sorts of problems, which, it is argued, would subject management decisions to a degree of 'substantive review' by the courts. This begs the question as to whether this approach would in fact yield substantively different outcomes. The analysis of how each rule would or would not operate in practice is wholly inadequate.

The analysis proffered to date in relation to the adoption of a multi-fiduciary approach in any positive or rights conferring manner fails completely to address the interface between such an approach and fundamental principles of corporate law. Instructive on the many corporate law issues which might arise in this regard, is the discussion of competing models of corporate governance provided by Dooley.[55] Here two alternative models characterised as the Authority model and the Responsibility model, are considered. The position of the shareholder in relation to the enforcement of directors' duties which, in both models, include the primary obligation to consider 'the best interests of the corporation' is considered. In describing the delimitation of the small category of situations where a shareholder may sue for failure to meet this obligation, a number of fundamental principles which place substantial obstacles in the way of the shareholder are considered.

The first of these is the business judgement rule as set out in the Delaware Supreme Court decision in *Aronson v Lewis*,[56] entrenching the concept of management prerogative. Here the courts have consistently followed the principle that 'absent an abuse of discretion' the judgement of the directors 'will be respected by the courts'. In addition, the second principle of the Aronson test provides that the presumption of good faith and honesty inherent in the business judgement rule will only be displaced where there is a reasonable doubt created about the independence of the board, or where the board was grossly negligent.[57] It is not at all clear how this could possibly be reconciled with the current test enunciated in *Aronson*. A second device employed by the courts to delimit the availability of shareholder actions is the adoption of the distinction between what has been described elsewhere[58] as 'ownership claims' and 'enterprise issues', the latter being excluded entirely from judicial review on foot of a shareholder action. Finally, the availability, or lack of availability of the derivative action, the procedural device by which a shareholder can adopt a cause of action on behalf of the corporation, must be mentioned. In most cases involving directors' fiduciary duties it is the corporation which has the cause of action. This excludes all 'ownership claims'—claims by shareholders involving an assertion of their own property rights. However, these claims are not usually understood in corporate law terms as involving an action relating to the breach of fiduciary duties owed by a director to a corporation. The ability of a shareholder to take action against a director on behalf of the corporation is thus severely limited:

> Thus the supply of claims that can be brought derivatively under existing law is constrained by the courts' deference to the institutional role of the board, particularly as that deference is implemented by the screening function of the business judgement rule.[59]

[55] Michael P Dooley, 'Two Models of Corporate Governance' (1992) 47 *Business Law* 461.

[56] *Aronson v Lewis* 473 A 2d 805 9Del (1984).

[57] The business judgement rule is also adhered to in other common law jurisdictions. See Sealy, above n 47.

[58] Bayliss Manning, 'Life in the Boardroom After Van Gorkom' (1985) 41 *Business Law* 51.

[59] Dooley, above n 55 p 496. It should be noted that Dooley argues that the ALI Governance Project proposals should increase the availability of derivative suits. Interestingly in the UK the view is that the trend is in the opposite direction. See further the UK DTI Company Law Reform project which considers, inter alia, reform of the derivative action. www.dti.gov.uk.

Conclusion of the Discussion of the Multi-Fiduciary Approach

If individual shareholders find it difficult to assert or to enforce a directors' fiduciary duties requiring the director to act in the best interests of the corporation, a difficulty which is clearly intentionally created through principles of corporate law, then this will be even more the case in relation to employees, even if the courts were to recognise the existence of such a duty. The commentary to date has given us no guidance as to how to resolve these issues.

However, even if the argument is for a specific fiduciary duty to be owed by directors to employees, individually or collectively in a manner which is separate and distinct from duties presently owed to the corporation, such a proposal ignores the agency relationship that is the basis for the fiduciary duty presently imposed. It would also effectively mean that this new fiduciary duty owed *on a personal basis* by directors to employees would in fact provide a stronger cause of action to employees than that which shareholders currently possess. This would mean that directors' actions and decisions would be more readily 'policed' by the courts for failure to consider employees interests, than for failure to consider the welfare of individual shareholders or groups of shareholders.

Thus, although perhaps a useful tool for prompting us to think about employees interests in a theoretical way, from the perspective of a corporate lawyer the multi-fiduciary concept is fraught with so many difficulties that it is unworkable.

6

The Theoretical Debate

Ownership also has always implied responsibility for the harms that one's property can inflict on others, but by and large, this has been a minor consideration in most people's thinking. Those who flagrantly abused or neglected their property might, at worst, lose it. In the late twentieth century, however, as a result of unprecedented growth in our technological capabilities and the scope of business activities we have entered another realm.[1]

INTRODUCTION

THERE IS A growing appreciation of the need to 'redefine corporate law.'[2] At present there are two main schools of thought. The first, and most prominent, described as the contract theory, is informed and underpinned by a law and economics analysis. The contract theory firmly places each constituency in the corporation within a contractual paradigm, where only bargained for rights are recognised. Thus the shareholder, whose contract recognises him as the residual claimant, has primacy. The purpose of the corporation is to maximise shareholder wealth within the limitations already contracted. In this paradigm limitations on management include fiduciary duties owed to the corporation. These duties are balanced against the business judgement rule,[3] which protects management prerogative. Finally the capital markets theory of accountability provides a further monitoring function.[4] Other constituencies such as employees, bondholders and other creditors are protected by contracted-for rights.

[1] Ronald M Green, 'Shareholders as Stakeholders: Changing Metaphors of Corporate Governance' (1993) 50 *Washington and Lee Law Review* 1415. Green goes on to explore liability in relation to environmental damage and continues from this to consider the question of corporate liability to other stakeholders generally. 'As any banker can attest in a world of Superfund toxic clean-up legislation, property can be a dangerous and expensive liability. In a host of industries, including pharmaceutical, chemicals, energy, and transport, the misuse of corporate property and technologies can kill or maim hundreds or thousands of people and cause damages in the tens of billions of dollars. The record of the past two decades is littered with disasters of this magnitude: AH Robins and the Dalkon Shield; Union Carbide and Bhopal; Johns-Manville and asbestos; Exxon and the Valdez oil spill; and most recently, Dow Corning and silicone breast implants'.

[2] From David Millon, 'Redefining Corporate Law' (1991) 24 *Industrial Law Review* 223.

[3] See further ch 5.

[4] See ch 3.

The second, but less well defined school, is described as the communitarian school. Here the purpose of the corporation is less well defined and the claims of other constituencies are recognised to varying degrees.

Margaret Blair[5] offers a variation on the traditional, and currently dominant paradigm, which is derived from neo-classical firm theory, but which takes us closer to a more inclusive understanding of the role of the corporation. This variation, offers a reconsideration of the wealth creating function of the corporation. While rooted in a law and economics theoretical approach, Blair's analysis offers exciting possibilities for a reconsideration of the role of employees as stakeholders. This analysis is considered in the context of the work of communitarian writers and thus, in referring to both schools of thought, an even stronger case than that offered by the communitarians on their own for the reconsideration of the purpose of the modern corporation will be developed.

CORPORATE LAW SCHOLARS AND THE REAL WORLD

At present academics in the communitarian school vary widely as to their aspirations and so it is difficult to describe their work as representing one unified school of thought. For example, those writers who seem more specifically concerned with the welfare of employees vary in their views on practical solutions to this issue. Such solutions vary from attempts to reconstruct the power relationship through the use of tort and property doctrines,[6] to arguments for worker participation on boards of management based on a European model,[7] to more recent proposals for a neutral referee model.[8] Others argue that a collective model, based on the use of a more traditional trade union model, is more satisfactory.[9]

However, at present the writers who have explored these issues from a theoretical perspective, have presented more useful insights. Although not presenting any specific solutions, their arguments raise the issues which a new model must

[5] Margaret M Blair, *Ownership and Control* (Brookings Institute, Washington, DC, 1995).

[6] Singer, 'The Reliance Interest in Property' (1987–1988) 40 *Stanford Law Review* 713 p 611 ff. See also Singer, 'Jobs and Justice: Rethinking the Stakeholder Debate' (1993) 43 *Toronto Law Journal* 475.

[7] See further the work of Marleen O'Connor referred to extensively in ch 5.

[8] *Ibid*. O'Connor's work on the multi-fiduciary is discussed in ch 5.

[9] Stone, above ch 4 where the sort of collective bargaining argued for 'places primary emphasis on union-participation in strategic level corporate decisions', a collective bargaining rather different from that which exists in American management–labor relations at present. However this does resonate with certain initiatives of EU social policy discussed and described in ch 4.

address. Interestingly many of the most persuasive writers in this category are not legal academics but hail from the business schools.[10]

In an article in 1993[11] Chancellor Allen of the Delaware court entered into the contractarian versus communitarian debate on the conception of the purpose of the corporation. It is interesting that Chancellor Allen identifies the 'managerialist' conception of the corporation, (the conception of the function of the corporation prevalent amongst managers), which resonates more with the understanding of the function of a corporation emanating from communitarian writers, than with the more rarefied version emanating from the law and economics corporate law scholars. Allen described the two opposing schools of thought which have been identified in this section and considered the philosophical roots of both.

According to Allen, the first school of thought is the Liberal–Utilitarian Model grounded in the work of Hobbes, Locke and Smith and shaped by the work of Bentham and Mill. He states that under this model

> the law creating and protecting property rights and the law enforcing contracts is the law of greatest importance to our welfare. The legal value of the highest rank in this classical liberal view is . . . human liberty, and the greatest evil is oppression by the State.

[10] Green, above n 1 who argues that the present model of corporate governance does not permit managers of corporations to act as moral agents or even to balance in any moral way the competing interests of different constituencies. Professor Green is a faculty member at Dartmouth College and the Amos Tuck School of Business. Millon, in 'Redefining Corporate Law', above n 2 argues that management should not seek short-term gains that frustrate legitimate constituent interests. However, in his view of balancing competing interests constituents would only be protected against 'abrupt, unfair disruption of relations' in the name of profit maximisation. It is my view that this will not be sufficient to protect employees from current demands of profit maximisation. Moreover, this resolution of the problems represents an unnecessarily conflictual view of the interests of the various corporate constituents. (Professor of Law and Director of the Frances Lewis Law Center at Washington and Lee University School of Law). See also David Millon, 'New Directions in Corporate Law' (1992) 50 *Washington and Lee Law Review* 1373. See also Alan Wolfe, 'The Modern Corporation: Private Agent or Public Actor' (1993) 50 *Washington and Lee Law Review* 1673. Professor of Sociology and Political Science at the University of Boston. See also Eric W Orts, 'The Complexity and Legitimacy of Corporate Law' (1993) 50 *Washington and Lee Law Review* 1565. Professor of Legal Studies at the Wharton School, University of Pennsylvania. This work is discussed below. Elizabeth Wolgast, *Ethics of an Artificial Person* (Stanford University Press, Stanford, 1992) who asks how artificial persons can have moral responsibility for decisions when these decisions are made by collectivities of individuals where the decision-making and thus the responsibility is diffuse and therefore untraceable. The diffuse nature of the decision-making also means that there is little moral connection between the decisions and the consequences. Lawrence E Mitchell, 'Groundwork of the Metaphysics of Corporate Law' (1993) 50 *Washington and Lee Law Review* 1477. Alan Wolfe, 'The Modern Corporation: Private Agent or Public Actor' (1993) 50 *Washington and Lee Law Review* 1673. Professor of Sociology and Political Science at the University of Boston. See also Eric W Orts, 'The Complexity and Legitimacy of Corporate Law' (1993) 50 *Washington and Lee Law Review* 1565. Professor of Legal Studies at the Wharton School, University of Pennsylvania.

[11] William T Allen, 'Contracts and Communities' (1993) 50 *Washington and Lee Law Review* 1. The discussion of Allen's views and quotations are all derived from this article.

He then describes the evolution of the law and economics analysis of corporations beginning with Coase, through Alchian and Demsetz and on to Easterbrook and Fischel in their work: 'The Economic Structure of Corporations':

> The dominant legal academic view does not describe the corporations as a social institution. Rather the corporation is seen as the market writ small . . .

This has led to the nexus of contracts paradigm.

The second school of thought described by Allen is The Social Model grounded 'in the dominant concepts of continental Europe and a yet earlier age.' Allen refers to Durkheim as a philosophical influence:

> This alternative paradigm describes the world as populated not by altruistic rational maximizers, but by persons of limited rationality who lead lives embedded in the social context, in a community. . . . Those holding this perspective are more willing to regulate and define the legal institutions of property and contract in service of social values. The pragmatic or managerialist view can be loosely categorized as part of this school.

Allen points out that the liberal-utilitarian model is not necessarily 'conservative' or 'right'. This model has both a (classical liberal) right of centre school and a left of centre (left liberal) school. The social model also has a left (communitarian) and right (moral majority). In concluding he states that:

> In the United States the liberal utilitarian account of and prescription for corporate law is the dominant legal academic model and will remain so for some time. The coherence and power of the economic model . . . have for many an all but irresistible appeal. Moreover, in our pluralistic society, it may be especially difficult to formulate any alternative comprehensive theory of corporations that takes its animating power from a conception of human connectedness and responsibility.

In identifying the philosophical roots of both approaches Allen provides an important insight which is particularly apt in relation to the comparisons between US corporate governance theories and European theories. Allen's attempt to trace the lineage of current corporate law theory ties in very strikingly with the fact that EU corporate regulation seems to be deeply embedded in predominant philosophical views in Europe, whilst the predominant paradigm in the US is also still embedded in the historically dominant philosophical and political culture of the United States.

OWNERSHIP

Drawing primarily on communitarian theory, the argument is that shareholders enjoy a rather weak claim to ownership of the corporation's assets and wealth. Furthermore it is argued that employees have a better claim to certain incidents of ownership of the corporation than shareholders. Incidents of ownership include, amongst other things, control, or the ability to exercise control, reliance on the continuance of the value of one's investment in the property, the possession of a bundle of rights exercisable to protect one's property or investment from erosion or dissolution. These rights are mentioned here as examples because they include some of the rights of shareholders which have been the focus of the 'mainstream' corporate governance debate. Here, in the context of employee welfare, these rights could also refer to rights exercisable by employees in relation to the values of their investment over time in the corporation.[12] In addition specific legislative measures adopted by the EU seem to protect these sorts of rights.

To talk of the shareholders as owners is not an accurate description of reality. If the use of the word 'owner' is intended to convey the notion of full ownership with which we are familiar when we consider ownership of other types of property, such as land or houses, then in many cases shareholders are not owners in that sense. Although it is true that some shareholders in some corporations are owners in that sense of the word, we should confine that understanding of ownership through shareholding to shareholders of close corporations. Leaving the close corporation the description of the shareholder as owner where the shareholding is diverse and publicly traded describes no *ab initio* entitlement to other incidents of ownership such as control or voice. Thus the division of ownership and control as described by Berle and Means does not present cause for concern in the present corporate world. Rather, the Berle and Means description is simply a description of reality, of surrendered claims rather than the basis for a claim to more control.[13] Berle and Means raised the issue as to whether shareholders should be accorded the same property rights as other owners of other kinds of property and arrived at a negative conclusion. The shareholder was described as a passive owner, who had surrendered control.[14]

However, the most persuasive argument against according the usual incidents of ownership to the passive shareholder emanates from the typical behaviour of the investing shareholder. This is the shareholder who has his eye on profits translated into dividend and on earnings per share, rather than long term development; who will exit where there is no satisfaction level with dividend yield, or where there are other perceived defects in the property, such as management function. Rather than attempting to exert influence as a true owner would

[12] In effect this moves away from the old paradigm of the employee's relationship to the firm or employer, away from the commodification of labour, the fitting of the employment relationship into a contract model with all the baggage of freedom of contract doctrine, equal bargaining power which that entails.

[13] It is not intended to cavalierly ignore the significant body of governance literature on the issue of shareholder power which exists. This issue of management accountability to shareholders has particularly been the focus of much of the discussion on governance in the UK. However, the focus of this work is on other stakeholders and therefore the purpose here is to clearly state the arguments relevant to that issue.

[14] 'At the same time, the controlling groups, by means of the extension of corporate powers, have in their own interest broken the bars of tradition which require that the corporation be operated solely for the benefit of the owners of passive property.' Berle and Means, *The Modern Corporation and Private Property* (Commerce Clearing House Inc, New York, 1932) 355.

to remedy defects in one's property, the shareholder simply leaves. He or she simply translates his property into another type of asset without any real commitment to the corporation. It is important to note that these patterns of behaviour are already documented and accepted by finance model theorists such as Fama, Jenkins and Meckling,[15] and in fact are central to the claims that they make for the capital markets as a monitoring device. This behaviour in fact discredits the claims of ownership rights which shareholders have, leaving the way for others to claim these incidents of ownership. In some ways this is nothing new. It is why shareholders are described as 'residual claimants'. Here however, the implications for others are considered. Thus our understanding of property ownership usually implies some type of commitment or, using law and economics language some type of 'firm-specific investment.' The shareholder as a constituency member lacks this characteristic in publicly held corporations. Their position, in this regard, is in stark contrast to the employee and even management. When we talk of employee ownership here it should be clarified that the argument is not that the employee exercises a full complement of ownership rights, but that as the shareholder exercises only *some* of the incidents of ownership, the employee should be entitled to exercise *others*, for example, some property rights recognising and protecting their investment, even if this simply amounts to protection of their job. The question however remains as to the extent of the employee's ownership rights. The employee may be very easily described as having ownership rights in their employment or job, but are we willing to make more extensive claims? Does the employee have some rights of ownership in the corporation's profits, in the wealth created as a whole and so on?[16]

Berle and Means also recognised that there were further implications once the shareholder is identified as a 'residual claimant.' They were concerned with the position of the control group and go on to state that even though the shareholder is identified as a passive owner this does not imply that the controlling groups' interests should triumph. Rather they argue:

> [T]he control groups have . . . cleared the way for the claims of a group far wider than either the owners or the control. They have placed the community in a position to demand *that the modern corporation serve not alone the owners or the control but all society*. (my emphasis).

In this section, drawing heavily on communitarian writers, it is argued that *employees, above all other stakeholders,* have a prior claim to certain incidents of ownership as we normally understand them.

[15] See ch 3.

[16] Berle and Means, above n 14 at p 355–56. See also Blair above n 5 at p 205.

STAKEHOLDING AND OWNERSHIP

> To assume that we can know who property owners are and to assume that once we have identified them their rights follow as a matter of course is to assume what needs to be decided.[17]

Blair, in her work,[18] adopts a definition of property already canvassed by communitarian writers and supported here. Property consists of a bundle of rights such as the right to possess, rights to use, the right of disposition, right of exclusion of others and the right to management and control. This 'bundle of rights' can be distributed differently amongst different owners. Some owners may choose not to exercise all of these rights. The law already facilitates this sort of behaviour, particularly in relation to the use of trusts, similarly present in our understanding of how corporations operate. Blair goes on and states that 'when property rights have been broken up in this way trying to identify one party as "owner" is neither meaningful nor useful.' I would agree with that view. Within the corporation shareholders exercise some of these rights, management exercise others, but employees have a claim to the exercise of many. 'In modern corporations, by definition all stakeholders have some stake and moral interest in the affairs of the corporation . . .'[19]

We will return to the sorts of claims made by communitarian writers such as Singer , Donaldson and Preston and others. These are claims for other stakeholders emanating from concepts of social and distributive justice; concepts such as the idea of a moral claim based on contributions of effort, investment of skill over time and sacrifice.

CORPORATE FUNCTION: 'TOTAL WEALTH CREATION'

The concept of firm-specific investment in an enterprise emanating from workers has already been considered. Pragmatically, legislation which ensures continued job tenure, except where there is just cause for dismissal, and legislation which compensates workers for loss of jobs in the context of corporate restructuring,

[17] Joseph William Singer, 'The Reliance Interest in Property' (1987–1988) 40 *Stanford Law Review* 713.

[18] Blair, above n 5 at p 224 refers to Votaw as having originally coined this definition of property. D Votaw, *Modern Corporations* (1965). Further Blair refers to Donaldson and Preston who argue that property rights are based on some 'underlying concept of justice, especially distributive justice' . . . notions of distributive justice are based in turn on . . . who has a moral interest in the use of the asset—who has contributed what effort or made what sacrifice. . . .' Interestingly Donaldson and Preston draw a specific link between contemporary theories of property rights, which they describe as pluralistic in nature, and theories which recognise the claims of other stakeholders in corporate law. Blair, above n 5 at p 225. See further Thomas Donaldson and Lee E Preston, 'The Stakeholder Theory of the Corporation: Concepts, Evidence and Implications' (1995) 20 *Academy of Management Review*, 65.

[19] Blair, above n 5 at p 225.

recognises this investment. Such investment is considered to be worth protecting as a strategy to encourage commitment on the part of workers, productivity and competitiveness. Blair's analysis provides us with similar reasons why we should protect and foster firm-specific investment.

Rethinking the finance model Blair[20] takes issue with the presently accepted view that 'the primary goal of corporate endeavours should be to maximise value for shareholders.' Boards and management of corporations should view their function as maximising the 'total wealth creating potential of the enterprises they direct.' Stakeholders can be identified by inputs contributed to the enterprise, those who therefore have, at risk, investments which are specific or 'specialised to the enterprise.'[21]

Claims to inclusiveness, even for employees, are based on a notion of total wealth creation—the function of the corporation is to create total wealth and to do that, one strategy is to encourage firm specific investments from employees who will then become more committed to the corporation. Labour economists have pointed to three kinds of evidence showing that employees accumulate valuable, firm-specific skills if they stay with the same employer for an extended period.[22]

Firstly, that wages rise with tenure by more than is proportionate to employees' experience. Secondly, that job turnover rates fall with length of tenure and so these employees are more valuable to the firm but also very importantly and significantly 'the jobs are more valuable to the workers'. (Here,in itself, is the basis from which I would argue for a moral claim). Thirdly, lay off costs are larger for workers with tenure.[23] Thus in a general way economic analysis demonstrates that firm-specific investments are recognised by many US corporations through increased wages and salaries commensurate with length of tenure. In addition it has already been mentioned in the context of the discussion on 'just cause protection', that many US corporations also recognise firm

[20] Blair, above n 5 p 239.

[21] *Ibid* p 209.

[22] *Ibid* p 263.

[23] *Ibid* p 265. This part of her text is supported by reference to Topel, R, *Specific Capital and Unemployment: Measuring the Costs and Consequences of Job Loss in Studies in Labor Economics in Honor of Walter Y Oi*, AH Meltser and CI Plosser (eds) (Amsterdam, North Holland, 1990) pp 181–214. These assertions are supported by Blair's reference to Topel's analysis of the effect of layoffs and job losses on workers. Above n 5 p 266. It was found that on average the pay reduction suffered by these workers in their next jobs was about 14%. From this Blair posits that as 'much as 14% of total wages and benefits paid to employees . . . in the US may represent a return to firm specific human capital.' Thus firm specific investment is already recognised in compensating terms. Most importantly Blair then goes on to point out that in 1993 US corporations paid a total of $2.26 trillion in compensation to employees. In the same year total pre-tax profits were calculated at 293 billion. (See The Council of Economic Advisors' Report of the President 1994 Table B–88) In her analysis Blair is of the opinion that if all accounting profits are counted as rents or quasi rents and only 10% of labour costs are treated as rents and quasi rents (which she calls a conservative estimate) then accounting profits represent only 57% of the total rents and quasi rents generated by US corporations. The rest of the rents in Blair's view then go to employees to reward specialised human capital and firm specific investments.

specific investments in a pragmatic way by not availing themselves of the employment-at-will doctrine as much as they might.[24] If firm specific investments are already recognised in this way then why not in others such as rights to job security, mandated leave rights, rights of voice and participation and rights in regard to plant closure? However if the law is to recognise the claim of employees as stakeholders, this recognition cannot be confined to certain groups of workers with certain types of skills. Nor can the recognition of such claims vary significantly with length of tenure. These issues will be further discussed below.

CORPORATE FUNCTION: LABOUR AS COST

If we argue that the function of a corporation is not only to create wealth for shareholders, but to create wealth in the community generally, the 'total wealth creation' function, then there is something wrong with a corporate governance model where compensation of workers is treated, according to accepted management accounting principles, *as costs to be reduced* (my emphasis) 'rather than as one part of what the corporation as a whole should be trying to maximise.'

> The accounting system that US corporations use . . . provides no information about the return a company can earn on other kinds of investments, such as investments in the skills of its employees or in organisational capabilities. The system also fails to measure and count as wealth creation the share of rents generated by the firms that are captured by employees (or other stakeholders).[25]

Blair also refers to David Levine who has identified the same bias in corporate accounting system which 'treats investment in people as costs, biasing managers away from human capital.'[26] There is an inherent bias within corporate governance structures (the acceptance of the shareholder as residual claimant and owner) and consequent accounting practices, away from encouraging investment in human capital and skill. Not only that but the present system places considerable obstacles in the way of management who may instinctively understand that investment in human capital and skill is important to the success of the business enterprise.

[24] Ch 5.

[25] In the course of presenting this argument Blair refers to Henry P Hill, *Accounting Principles for the Autonomous Corporate Entity* (Quorum Books, New York, 1987) who has criticised current accounting practises based on the 'illogical and unsustainable' assumption 'that shareholders are the only owners of corporations and that all other contributors of capital are outsiders.' Hill has put forward an argument for an entity theory of accounting which would take into account all sources of capital. According to Blair 'Hill's entity concept seems a good starting place to rethink the way wealth creation is measured in publicly traded corporations.' Blair above n 5 p 327–328. Blair also refers to David Levine to support her arguments here.

[26] D Levine, *Reinventing the Workplace: How Business and Employees Can Both Win* (Brookings Institute, Washington DC, 1995); Blair, above n 5 p 327.

> Thus even directors and managers who understand their jobs to be maximising total wealth creation and who are well motivated to pursue that goal are generally receiving partial and misleading information about the sources of wealth in their firms.[27]

Wages, salaries and the level of other benefits extended to labour should not always be regarded as a cost which should be minimised wherever possible. This argument gives us a different perspective on a number of issues to be considered. It is true that emphasis on shareholder wealth maximisation leads to focus on pre-tax distributable profits. By viewing labour payments and benefits as costs, shareholder welfare is inevitably pitted against labour or employee welfare. Labour market flexibility in its turn allows for a reconfiguration and extensive manipulation of these costs. Furthermore, it is an accepted part of corporate culture to overtly manipulate labour costs (compared with, for example, overtly manipulating costs of compliance with EPA regulation or consumer safety requirements). Although such statements are greeted with dismay on the part of workers' organisations and communities, nevertheless these claims have a currency of respectability in other sections of society.

Furthermore the role of globalisation is also overtly addressed in relation to labour. Again this compares unfavourably with how management deal with environmental issues.[28] Thus managers often claim proudly to be locating in low labour cost countries. On the other hand no modern company would ever claim to be relocating so that they can pollute at liberty. There are some possible explanations for this distinction. Clearly environmental protection is presently regarded as a public good, indeed a global public good in which everyone regardless of social standing and wealth has an interest. Unfortunately worker protection and welfare is not so clearly regarded. But this is only because the issue is more complex. In contrast the most popular and generally accepted argument is that worker welfare and protection involves the imposition of extensive costs on countervailing interests. I would argue that this kind of argument results from a fundamental conceptual failure in relation to the proper purpose and role of a corporation. In contrast, those interested in broader public policy issues have argued on the contrary that to ignore questions of worker welfare and consequently community welfare imposes extensive social costs in the long term. The failures of the former perspective are redressed in both the view of corporate function at European policy level (to a certain extent) and in the communitarian view of the corporation in the US. A view, which in essence claims that employee protection and welfare, is beneficial to the community as a whole.

The exaggerated pitting of shareholder welfare against labour in terms of the cost of labour is going to be more acute where managers are responding to the capital markets theory of accountability and governance. So where managers

[27] Blair, above n 5 p 328.

[28] Blair above n 5 at p 327. See also Eric W Orts, 'The Legitimacy of Multinational Corporations' in Lawrence E Mitchell (ed), *Progressive Corporate Law* (Westview Press, Boulder, Co, 1996).

see and accept that their main goal is to maximise shareholder wealth in terms of profit and dividend then these problems will be accentuated. In contrast, if there was a greater emphasis on the job-creating function of a corporation and on the quality and type of jobs created, both in terms of security and benefits, management would have greater discretion in answering the claims of more than one constituency. In smaller close corporations where the capital markets theory of accountability will not operate, the sacrificing of labour welfare will not be demanded on a theoretical level in the first instance. Therefore the accountability issues regarding other stakeholders will also not be as acute.[29] In addition, in small entrepreneurial corporations, the role of shareholder, employee and manager will often become conflated, thus giving rise to less conflict amongst stakeholder claims.

Protecting Labour as a Stakeholder

However, even if we accept that at present there is an emphasis on the cost elements of labour, in both management accounting practices and management practices generally, it is difficult to answer immediately how that balance should be altered. The emphasis on shareholder wealth at the expense of labour benefits has led to the distribution of corporate wealth in a manner which does not seem acceptable to all. Wealth in this context does not simply indicate a distribution of profits. The emphasis is more on the question of how corporate wealth should be deployed to improve the quality of life for all. Getting the balance right between the generation of profits for shareholders and the creation of quality jobs for workers is however, a hard, not easy question to answer.

> Nor does this chapter call for a focus on employees to the neglect of other stakeholders. Such a distorted focus combined with generous lifetime employment contracts may in fact have contributed to the adjustment difficulties Japanese and German companies seemed to have had in the recession of the early 1990s. I do not advocate governance changes that are intended to disenfranchise shareholders or give total control to employees or to any other stakeholders. Instead I stress that the goals of directors and management should be maximising total wealth creation by the firm.[30]

Nevertheless, the important point is made at a theoretical level. That employees, as *stakeholders ie with firm specific investments* have a claim in economic terms to corporate wealth. The wealth generated by corporations can legitimately

[29] This is why, contra Landauers the writers in *Progressive Corporate Law*, above n 28, address the accountability problems presented in large publicly owned corporations only and rightly so. In chs 9 and 10 when considering possible reforms we will do this through the perspective of two problems which are experienced acutely by management and employees of large corporations, plant closure through 'downsizing' or other similar strategies and the related problem of pressures experienced from global competition. See Carl Landauers, 'Review of Progressive Corporate Law' (1996) 84 *California Law Review* 1694.

[30] Blair above n 5 p 328.

be deployed for the benefit of workers, even where this may not yield the optimum benefit for shareholders. In a later work in the Virginia Law Review, Blair has developed, with another writer, the Team Production Model (TPM), further elucidating themes referred to in this chapter. The Team Production Model has been described as a 'sophisticated economic argument for rejection of shareholder primacy' which emphasises the role of the board of directors as an independent mediator between stakeholder interests.[31] Although it might, therefore, seem that Blair's work seems to support the extension of incidents of ownership to non-shareholder stakeholders, this is not the case. At this point it is important to note that Blair in both her earlier work described in detail here and the later TPM work does not acknowledge any claim which employees might have as of right, or if you will, as a matter of social or distributive justice. Others have described this as an ethical claim.[32]

> Aside from these efficiency questions, from a progressive perspective, TPM's most troubling aspect is its distributional implications. If the board's rent allocation decisions are to be solely a matter of political power and its existing distribution among workers and shareholders, there is no reason to believe that workers would fare any better under TPM than they are able to do now. . . . Despite the apparent appeal of its rejection of shareholder primacy, TPM therefore does little to advance a progressive agenda for corporate law.[33]

In conclusion arguments emanating from concepts such as efficiency, productivity and total wealth creation, coupled with a broader understanding of the role of the corporation based on distributive justice, leads to an inescapable conclusion that employees should certainly be placed nearer to centre stage in corporate America than they currently are. The focus on well-being, property rights and a voice for employees has been the focus of EU social policy for nearly 30 years.

Finally, one problem with economically modelled theories on corporate governance is that, generally, such theories do not generate any normative responses applicable across the board to all or most firms, or at least to a category of firms which can be easily identified by reference to size or number of employees. So, for example, there will only be some firms where firm-specific human investments are more likely to be valued, firms which are 'reliant on

[31] See Margaret M Blair and Lynn A Stout, 'A Team Production Thoery of Corporate Law' (1999) 85 *Virginia Law Review* 247. Millon has criticised the model developed by Blair and others described as the Total Production Model on the basis that it would generate new inefficiencies of its own and would not improve distributional outcomes for non shareholder stakeholders over what is 'currently available through market interactions'. David Millon, 'New Game Plan or Business as Usual? A Critique of the Team Production Model of Corporate Law' (2000) 86 *Virginia Law Review* 1001.

[32] See further inter alia, Allen, above n 11. William W Bratton, 'Confronting the Ethical Case against the Ethical Case for Constituency Rights' (1993) 50 *Washington and Lee Law Review* 1464. Ronald M Green, 'Shareholders as Stakeholders: Changing Metaphors of Corporate Governance' (1993) 50 *Washington and Lee Law Review* 1415.

[33] Millon, above n 30 p 1043–1044.

technology intensive or service oriented enterprises where most of the value added comes from innovation, product customisation or specialised services.'[34] However valid this analysis may be,[35] these elements are not easily identifiable a fortiori and moreover may change as characteristics over time. Therefore although firm specific investment provides a justification for recognising some stakeholder, and even *some* employee claims in *some* organisations, this analysis does not lead to workable solutions capable of being translated into legal principles.

CORPORATE FUNCTION: THE COMMUNITARIAN VIEW

The economic model analysis, is insufficient to take us through an analysis of present corporate governance structures and provide us with logical conclusions and definite proposals for reform. An analysis based on concepts such as distributive justice, moral claims, effort and sacrifice will take us even further. Communitarian corporate governance scholars have tried to formulate appropriate legal responses to such issues. In the unusual litigation arising from the closure by United Steel of their Youngstown plant in Ohio, Lambros J considered the issue of whether there were any obligations incurred by the corporation towards either the community or its employees in respect of such closure. He was of the opinion that there were possibly some property rights enuring to the employees, which could be considered for protection. Unfortunately, for corporate law scholars, even though moral claims can be articulated in this way the law presents us with very clear obstacles to establishing any coherent set of property rights for employees. It is clear that Lambros J recognised these legal obstacles to his view of what might be the most just result in this case. For example if employees do have property rights in the corporation, what sorts of rights are involved and to what property?

Lambros J goes on:

> Perhaps not a property right to the extent that can be remedied by compelling US steel to remain in Youngstown. But I think the law can recognise the property right to the extent that US steel cannot leave the Mahoning Valley and the Youngstown area in a state of waste, that it cannot completely abandon its obligation to that community because certain vested rights have arisen out of this long relationship and institution.

A further issue, which unfortunately again is not necessarily amenable to the language of legal rights, is adumbrated by the views of Lambros J. This issue is

[34] Blair above n 5 p 238.

[35] In fact it could be argued that technology-intensive firms depend on a relatively high turnover of employees in a highly competitive labour market where new skills are constantly being developed. Thus it is difficult to identify which employees in which types of business can be identified in Blair's terms.

really the crux of the matter and that is that US Steel cannot do all this and ignore these vested interests unless it has a very good reason for doing so.

On appeal, the sixth circuit, while voicing sympathy and concern for the community interest, also concluded there was no property right. Unfortunately all that the Youngstown workers were left with was the recognition of their commitment by some lawyers whilst being informed that the law could do nothing to help them.

In an article considering this litigation, which has been subsequently described as a 'pathbreaking article on plant closings' which ' eloquently articulated communitarian perspectives on the problem of nonshareholder vulnerability,'[36] Singer[37] argues that employees have a property interest in job security which is based in part on the doctrine of reliance interests in property which is a feature of modern property law theory. This theory rejects the traditional view that property interests are created solely through contract. He attempts to construct a paradigm in which such property rights could be recognised arising from the closure, arguing that employees in these cases should be accorded certain rights through use of the doctrine of the reliance interest in property. He mentions the

> wide variety of legal rule[s which] can be justified in terms of . . . reliance interest in property: for example the doctrine of adverse possession; the recognition of prescriptive easements and of public rights of access to private property. The whole body of law dealing with tenants' rights; division of property after divorce and State welfare rights.

It is true that responsibility is already imposed on corporations through legislation recognising obligations regarding consumer welfare and environmental protection. Thus legal mechanisms have been found to oblige corporations to act responsibly in the community in relation to consumer welfare and in relation to the environment but not in relation to workers. It could be argued here that environmental wellbeing is a public good and that therefore the protection of the environment is a matter which concerns the entire community. This may well be so, but as previously observed employee welfare and the effect of job losses on communities are also public goods, admittedly in a more complex way. Furthermore consumer welfare is no more a public good than the wellbeing of employees. In addition, it is recognised that employers have certain obligations in relation to certain employee welfare issues, such as the protection of employees from discrimination and harassment, so this argument is not a logically seamless one.

In this vein the conceptualisation of the United Steel problem by the court represents to Singer a conceptualisation of the problem which placed the free

[36] Described as such almost 10 years later by David Millon. See further David Millon, 'Communitarianism in Corporate Law: Foundations and Strategies' in Lawrence E Mitchell (ed), *Progressive Corporate Law* (Westview Press, Boulder, Co, 1995) 1.

[37] Singer, above n 6 p 713.

market and market autonomy centre stage with the 'public sphere of state regulation and the sphere of the family . . . as peripheral and supplementary.' Singer argues that this conceptualisation is faulty. It is incorrect to associate property ownership with freedom to act in relation to that property because, according to Singer,[38] this conceptualisation presupposes or assumes strong property rights.[39] But Singer points out that owners are hardly ever given complete freedom to act as they wish with their property. Ownership is not a simple issue nor are incidents of ownership allocated in a simple fashion, even in relation to more simple types of property such as land or other real property. Ownership of property is a more complex story and the ability to assert the incidents of ownership such as control, the ability to dispose and the ability to prevent disposal may not, in all cases, be clearly underpinned by concepts of individual freedom or market autonomy.

Other communitarian writers support this view that property carries with it responsibilities and obligations.[40]

Two issues need to be distinguished here: Firstly, who can rightly be regarded as the owner of corporate wealth and property? Some of the writers we are considering are of the view that shareholders are not the only owners of corporate wealth and property. Here Singer seems to recognise that the shareholder is the rightful owner but the exercise of the property right is limited and constrained and this ought to be the case. Furthermore Singer argues that in the context of modern property law this is not an unusual claim. Thus in this analysis the exercise of the shareholders' property rights is offset by a bundle of rights constraining their actions. Developing Singer's analysis we can arrive at the second issue, whether, even if the shareholder should be regarded as owner, should the shareholder possess the usual bundle of rights accorded to property ownership. This 'bundle of rights' has been previously referred to as 'incidents of ownership'. Within the corporation incidents of ownership are splintered. Employees should be accorded some of these incidents of ownership, including elements of voice and control over the disposal of corporate property, and property rights in their employment, which in turn would lead to protected job security and other related claims on the corporation, such as claims to leave and so on. In fact the employee ought to have a bundle of rights stemming from his investment and commitment to the corporation. This would not amount to formal ownership but a claim to property rights of some sort.

Reflecting Allen's analysis, Singer attempts to build up a bundle of rights by adopting a 'social relations' as distinct from a 'free market model' of property

[38] Singer, above n 6 at p 641.

[39] Singer, above n 6 at p 638.

[40] Green, above n 1 at p 1415. This point is made by Green with particular reference to liability imposed on corporations in relation to Superfund toxic clean-up legislation and product liability. Here Green cites instances where liability has been imposed on corporations for huge disasters such as those involving AH Robins and the Dalkon Shield; Union Carbide and Bhopal; Johns-Manville and asbestos; Exxon and the Valdez oil spillage and Dow Corning and silicone breast implants.

rights. In the latter model we see people as autonomous individuals. Our understanding of the type of social relations relevant to legal analysis are set by focusing on voluntary agreements or contract and entitlements defined a priori. So rights are characterised as being fully articulated and we focus on two issues: Who is the owner? And what did the owner promise? In my view if we adopt this kind of model the law experiences a crippling inability to adapt and develop over time in response to varying situations. In the social relations model posited by Singer this model encourages us to see people in relationships continuing over time. These relationships are not limited to contractual relationships. It is argued here that this model allows us to accommodate our intuitive understanding that contractual bargains are not always entered into with full information and with equal bargaining power. Moreover that whatever the starting point might have been at the time a contract was agreed the relative position of the parties may have changed. Thus as Singer argues we can view rights as emerging over time and we are entitled to ask questions about relationships between the parties; questions about the balance of power, inequalities and so on.[41]

In conclusion, the failed approach of Lambros J does not leave the employee in a particularly strong position. Yet we now have a different understanding of ownership which may well fit the corporation more accurately than the finance model of the corporation which focuses on the shareholder as the sole claimant of property rights. Ownership rights in the corporation are splintered. Other stakeholders have claims to the wealth of the corporation and these claims may yield specific benefits over time.[42]

[41] Singer makes the point that economic analysis is fine because it may provide useful information about which legal position to choose but it leaves us with the problem of how we count costs and benefits. How confident are we that we are measuring costs and benefits properly? Thus foreshadowing Blair's much more practically oriented reassessment of management accounting practices.

[42] United Steel Workers, above n 34 p 1280.

7

The Ethical Corporation

> Although situations of combined economic stagnation and international economic integration would seem to make the question of the public role of the corporation more salient than ever, a good deal of contemporary economic and legal theory attempts to define the corporation as little more than a large bunch of private actions lumped together.[1]

BUILDING ON THE reconceptualisation of the corporation, the work of other communitarian writers may give us some idea of how such theoretical claims might be expressed in legal terms. At this point two primary approaches have been considered: the multi-fiduciary approach[2] and the property interest approach.[3] However, approaches such as the multi-fiduciary model seem unsatisfactory, partly because they rely on the extension of rights by the judiciary on a case by case basis. Other communitarian writers have expressed doubts about the efficacy of such private law approaches to 'the problems of nonshareholder vulnerability.'[4]

> I therefore find it very difficult to accept the view that so-called private law approaches to the problem of nonshareholder vulnerability are fully adequate.[5]

The communitarian conception of corporate law has been described as having three elements. Firstly, it challenges the premise that even if it is acknowledged that other stakeholders need protection they can negotiate and bargain for self-protection. Secondly, it includes the argument that even if self-protection is possible through contract, the disparities in bargaining power render this difficult. Finally communitarians offer a view of the corporation as a community in society rather than a mere aggregation of self-seeking individuals

[1] Alan Wolfe, 'The Modern Corporation: Private Agent or Public Actor' (1993) 50 *Washington and Lee Law Review* 1673 Professor of Sociology and Political Science at the University of Boston.

[2] See the discussion of this in ch 5.

[3] Discussed in ch 5.

[4] David Millon, 'Communitarianism in Corporate Law: Foundations and Strategies' in Lawrence E Mitchell (ed), *Progressive Corporate Law* (Westview Press, Boulder, Co, 1995) 1. Millon criticises writers such as O'Connor, who has focused primarily on the multi-fiduciary model and Daniels who used a 'hypothetical contractual approach to protect non-shareholders'. See Ronald Daniels, 'Stakeholders and Takeovers: Can Contractarianism Be Compassionate' (1993) 43 *University of Toronto Law Journal* 315. Millon seems to also include Singer under this title, although this categorisation is not entirely clear.

[5] *Ibid* p 22.

whose relationships are defined solely by contract. On a theoretical level this will raise many questions about the role of the corporation in relation to its constituents. If the corporation has a role in society how should we judge this role and what legal responses should there be? Is the corporation a public or private actor in this regard?[6] In pragmatic terms this view of the corporation will include the possibility of Blair's total wealth creation paradigm and of course is reflective, although accidentally so, of the European understanding of the role of the corporation.[7]

An over emphasis on the contract paradigm has led law and economics scholars to ignore the real fact of inequality of bargaining power. Arguments which focus on the employee as a rational wealth maximiser operating in the labour market with full information and full choice are counter intuitive and do not stand up to close scrutiny. The important point is that even though statements regarding inequality of bargaining power may be applicable to a range of stakeholders they apply most specifically to employees. Thus a specific claim for protection can be made for employees only. This sort of clarity is important or there is a danger that the consequent conclusions of the communitarian approach raise more problems than are answered.

TRUST

> In our legal and social system as manifested in the structure of corporate law, contract is king.[8]

Trust is also an important concept in our legal system for communitarians. It has been argued[9] that in the context of corporate law two institutions; procedural fairness and the law of contract have eroded trust in our society. There are two separate, but ultimately related legal causes of erosion of trust in our society: 'an over-reliance in our legal system on procedural fairness and an increased reliance on the law of contract.' But what do we mean by contract in this context? A number of competing models of contract have been offered, from what has been described as the 'so-called Chicago School'[10] which treats contract as a means for individuals to maximise their own goods, and at the other end of the

[6] This question is considered below.

[7] It is interesting that in many ways the communitarian scholars in the corporate law field reflect on a theoretical level the sorts of policy initiatives which are present at EU policy making level, yet very little, if any reference is made to this fact in the communitarian literature. Conversely, but somewhat similarly no theoretical justification is offered, in the context of EU policy for this view of the corporation in society.

[8] Lawrence E. Mitchell, 'Trust, Contract, Process' in Lawrence E Mitchell (ed), *Progressive Corporate Law* 185 (Westview Press, Boulder, Co, 1996) 185. 'To the extent that interacting parties can rely upon legally enforceable promises enforced by the coercive power of the state the need for them to trust one another is diminished.'

[9] *Ibid* p 185.

[10] *Ibid* p 196.

spectrum, a model 'of relational contract, which casts contract in a light almost (but not quite) approaching fiduciary obligation.'[11] Regardless of which model of contract is used an over-emphasis on contract according to some communitarians displaces trust as an important concept. Trust becomes limited in its role to ensuring that the parties have sufficient trust in the contract model and in each other's mutual dependency to achieve their goals.

Trust is identified by communitarians as the morally superior alternative to contract and process. Some practical examples of how trust might alter our understanding of corporate law and its application have been provided. For example in relation to self-dealing it is argued that current corporate law in fact countenances an element of self-dealing on the part of corporate directors. By doing this

> it encourages fiduciaries to self-deal up until the point at which the costs outweigh the benefits, that is, the point at which stockholders sue. This state of affairs leads stockholders to be less trusting, and results in litigation on the suspicion of misconduct in the hope of forcing directors to settle even unmeritorious suits.[12]

In contrast a

> system in which the substantive laws err at the margins in favor of the trusting party [which] . . . will lead the trusted party more carefully to examine her actions in light of the expectations and interests of the other.[13]

Thus breaches of trust per se should be sanctioned rather than the results of such breaches. Accordingly if directors as a result routinely avoided any opportunity of self-dealing, they in turn would be rewarded with more trust from the stockholders and less litigation initiated as a result of a lack of trust.

' A system based on trust gives us confidence in dealing with others whereas contract and process-based systems lead to mutual superstition.'

These concepts can be extended to the relationship between management and workers and can be used to argue that a legislative framework ought to encourage not only trust as between management and shareholders, but even more so trust between management and workers. For example, interesting points are made about the relationship between trust and communication which can easily be transposed on the relationships experienced by employees and management. 'Lack of trust can impede communication between individuals.' These concepts are underlined in light of comments made previously regarding a 'floor of rights' model being necessary to support more sophisticated structures for management-labour dialogue.[14]

However, some of the arguments made by communitarians regarding trust are extremely theoretical in nature, whereas this work aspires to yielding some

[11] *Ibid* p 197.
[12] *Ibid* p 203.
[13] *Ibid* p 203.
[14] See ch 4.

pragmatic results, inspired as it is by the rhetoric and achievements of EU social policy in comparison with the predominant US approach. These arguments are based on the premise that legal models can create a society where it is 'part of the value system of such a society that the members treat one another fairly, or consider the effects of their actions on the other members.' Such a statement can only be regarded with a healthy scepticism, not least because it expects too much of the function of law in our society. Trust is viewed as an overriding legal principle which renders specific laws unnecessary. This view leaves us with unrealistic expectations as to the power of law to achieve something, which in many cases is almost impossible, even on a moral level. In fact it could be argued that the precise role of law is to fill important gaps where our sense of fairness is faulty and that therefore law tends toward the specific rule.[15]

Finally, even if we are attracted to the communitarian view of trust, contract is nevertheless the dominant paradigm. I do not see trust as providing a practicable answer. Even a limited experiment with extending our understanding of trust through extending the concept of fiduciary obligations to employees, yields results which are unsatisfactory.[16]

Criticising the existing contract paradigm from the communitarian perspective concerning bargaining inequality provides a more realistic opportunity to reconsider our present understanding. To conclude, those who support the free market model often ignore an important feature of corporate bargaining. Here the issue of trust does provide us with a new perspective on the corporate contract. A contract where a corporation is one of the parties, is very different from contracts between individuals. A fundamental part of reliance on contract has been the acceptance of the contract as being legally enforceable and binding for all, the acceptance that my contract is as good as yours. But as it turns out my contract with the corporation is not as good as the corporation's contract with me because of the fundamentally different nature of the corporation as a party to the contract. The corporation is the beneficiary of two legal doctrines, that of limited liability and corporate personality which in fact act as a 'social subsidy.'[17] Here there is no long-term reliance and understanding that the contract will last or that as with other contracts, certain terms continue even into its breach. Disastrous events involving corporations, whether these involve product liability, devastating environmental pollution or the tragic abandonment of workers and communities through plant closure, illustrate the ultimate futility of contracting with the corporation which can voluntarily remove itself from the consequences of a breach of contract through dissolution of the corporation.

[15] See Rafael La Porta, Florencio Lopez-de-Silanes, Andrei Shliefer and Robert W Vishny for the interesting hypothesis that law, in a related area, has been a key determinative force in the development of corporate financing patterns and thus corporate governance and performance. This hypothesis has been developed in a series of articles referred to in the bibliography, although outside the scope of this work.

[16] This is illustrated in detail in a consideration of O'Connor's work in ch 5.

[17] See further Steven Bainbridge, 'In defense of the shareholder wealth maximization norm: A reply to Professor Green' (1993) 50 *Washington and Lee Law Review* 1423 discussed in the next chapter.

There is in fact a fundamental incoherence in the contract paradigm. This insight is important to understanding a fundamental tenet of the communitarian critique of corporate law which is also a fundamental tenet of EU social policy and that is inequality of bargaining power.

> After all it is at least theoretically possible to structure a regime of contract that is more protective of entrusting parties than our current concept of that approach, or to develop strict procedural models that favor the entrusting parties by placing the heavier burdens of justification on power holders. While these approaches will not, as I earlier suggested, entirely eliminate the need for trust, they would significantly reduce those areas of our lives to be governed by the more indeterminate concept of trust.[18]

THE ROLE OF ETHICS

The question of whether ethics has any role in the corporate governance debate must be addressed—a question worth asking only in the light of the current dominance of the law and economics school of thought in corporate law theory. 'The present custom of restraint'[19] in relation to ethics arises from concerns about the meaning of justice, and a certain 'philosophical scepticism.' In my view this restraint has led to a devastating philosophical impoverishment in considering the question of corporate responsibility and accountability. The present 'custom of restraint' in relation to ethics complements the current emphasis on an economic analysis of corporate function where concepts such as efficiency and cost, not only seem particularly apt, but also dominate the analysis of many. In addition connections are made between the current restraint about ethics and the emphasis on individual autonomy and the private market as the dominant paradigm.[20] However, the triumph of individual autonomy may have given rise to many more questions about the corporate function in society than it has answered. Ethics is a very important member of the set of concepts we might use to consider corporate function. In fact, not least because the actions of corporations can have such powerful effects, both beneficial and detrimental, an ethical consideration of corporate actions is almost imperative. Actions of corporations, which have led to devastating results, both environmentally, and in relation to effects on communities in terms of employment, have provided an impetus for communitarian writers in this area. Often the most vulnerable have been employees.[21] The workplace is a 'quasi-community'

[18] Mitchell, above n 8 at p 198.

[19] William W Bratton, 'Confronting the Ethical Case against the Ethical Case for Constituency Rights' (1993) 50 *Washington and Lee Law Review* 1464.

[20] *Ibid.*

[21] *Ibid* p 1465. 'Reference to ethics adds an element of urgency to the story of stakeholder injury. Moral intuitions instruct us in how best to behave in situations in which it is in our power to counteract the extreme vulnerability of others by being considerate. Ethics function as a safety device, compensating for the vulnerability built into life in society. Thus described, ethics have a tie to the satisfaction of social needs, a tie not dissimilar from those of economics and law.'

which shapes the employees identity, particularly in a long-term employment relationship.[22] The worker invests substantial personal elements in his work. This is an important additional dimension to the commitment we have hitherto been describing in economic terms as 'firm specific investments.'

From the ethical perspective it is also acknowledged[23] that shareholder primacy has its own ethical imperative linked as it is to wealth maximisation, and consequent overall wealth creation. Yet clearly this ethical imperative is based on a particular view of wealth creation. A different understanding of wealth creation, informed for example, by the understanding that the creation of high standards of living and good quality jobs is a worthwhile corporate function, may well change our view of this ethical imperative. It is central to the formation of EU policy, which continuously stresses the need to balance corporate and economic competitiveness with high standards of living and good working and social conditions.

In considering the heated debate between the two schools of thought summarised neatly by Allen, it is clear that in the predominant legal theory of the corporation derived from a law and economics understanding of the corporation, the legal actor has been conflated with the purely self-interested rational actor of microeconomics. So, for example the usual argument that a law and economics scholar would make in favour of the doctrine of limited liability can be summarised in the following terms:

> By providing the rule that the parties would choose if they could bargain, society facilitates private ordering. To be sure, this benefits shareholders, but is also benefits the firm's other constituencies. Because society benefits as well . . . [L]imited liability is less a social subsidy than a social contract supported by consideration.[24]

And so the argument here is that '[T]he nexus of contracts model treats corporate law as doing little more than providing a standardized form contract' ie a set of desirable default rules. Thus limited liability is not a privilege granted by society, it is just a default rule 'nothing more and nothing less.'

We have seen the same sort of analysis applied by corporate law scholars to issues of corporate governance. So the argument goes that the shareholders in a corporation have the only claim to corporate wealth, *because* they are the residual claimants and that this residual claim *should be* protected. In the context of employee welfare this calls for the continued corporate prerogative in deciding where and when plants and subsidiaries should be located to *maximise profits* regardless of the impact on employees and communities. In addition, such an

[22] William W Bratton, 'Confronting the Ethical Case against the Ethical Case for Constituency Rights' (1993) 50 *Washington and Lee Law Review* p 1465. 'The case for employees must be distinguished from that of other constituents. Employee dependence is more than economic. A work place is a quasi community. Some element of identity will take shape in connection with a long term employment relationship. A bondholder in contrast does not invest substantial personality in the relationship . . .'

[23] *Ibid.*

[24] Bainbridge, above n 17 p 1431.

analysis calls for continued corporate prerogative in deciding when and how corporate wealth should be shared with employees.

In essence this sort of reasoning ignores totally choice of law problems and ignores the function of law in our society. Even if rational maximisers do choose a law limiting their liability or indeed governance structures which suit them we might well have decided to prevent this as being undesirable in some cases.[25] The law and economics scholar will tell us about how limited liability benefits shareholders and also society as well. This is the classic argument made in favour of the status quo, defined as the shareholder wealth maximisation view of the function of the corporation. In other words shareholder wealth maximisation is a good thing not only for shareholders but for everyone else. Although often couched in complex terms, this argument and its variants is basically a sophisticated version of the 'what comes round goes round' school of thought. Regardless of course as to how long this cycle of well-being and wealth creation might take. Here we must refer again to Bainbridge who tells us that:

> The rule (*ie limited liability*) has helped produce an economy that is dominated by public corporations, which in turn has produced the highest standard of living of any society in the history of the world.

and that he also tells us that he personally feels good about this. *(sic)*[26]

This statement is really striking in view of OECD figures which report that of a number of industrialised countries such as Japan, Germany, Belgium, Finland and Canada, the US has the highest proportion of low-paid workers. The figures are that 25 per cent of all US workers are low-paid workers where low-paid workers are defined as those earning less than two thirds of the median weekly earnings.[27] Sometimes these workers are referred to as the 'working poor.'[28] Is this appropriate for a society which enjoys, as Bainbridge states 'the highest standard of living of any society in the history of the world'? The vast inequalities occurring within American corporations in terms of executive compensation as compared with employee benefits and compensation are a source of concern to a number of US commentators, who have also concerned themselves with other related societal problems.

Nevertheless and despite the clear philosophical impoverishment of the law and economics paradigm it has been observed that:

> as a practical matter, the solution of these problems and the [legal] mandate [for such a solution] itself can come to corporate law only as a result of a broad sustained political process . . . The prevailing version of the corporation as a wealth creating mechanism has a powerful ethical presupposition. In a world of scarcity and physical suffering it is central to what 'should be' respecting production organization. This leaves the

[25] For example the rule in both Ireland and the UK that lawyers may not operate as incorporated limited liability companies.

[26] Bainbridge above n 17 p 1446.

[27] OECD National Reports, 1997.

[28] See further chs 9 and 10 on competitiveness and productivity.

proponent of an expanded definition of the firm with an extraordinary burden. It really will take a theory to beat this theory—a prospective theory of wealth creation that includes constituent rights rather than a theory of equitable allocations of an existing quantum of wealth.[29]

THE USE OF THE MULTI-FIDUCIARY APPROACH TO ACCOMMODATE THE ETHICAL CORPORATION

Writers in the field of business ethics have debated issues which are similar to issues which have been raised in part by the corporate governance debate conducted by corporate law scholars. Within the ethics field, a multi-fiduciary approach has been identified as a possible solution to resolving competing ethical claims. Thus 'stakeholder' and 'multi-fiduciary' theories of the firm have been advanced as ways of recognising the potentially devastating impact corporations can have on their internal and external constituencies. Such approaches are viewed as a way of empowering senior managers and directors sometimes to subordinate shareholder interests to those of employees, communities, or other groups affected by corporate activities.[30] This resonates with the managerialist concept of the corporation referred to by Allen. It is argued that a multi-fiduciary approach allows directors the discretion to consider the well-being of a number of constituencies. The multi-fiduciary approach has been viewed alternatively as a broadly sketched business judgement rule.[31] The question has also been raised as to whether either a multi-fiduciary approach or a broadly sketched business judgement rule would in fact yield a different set of solutions to what is currently presented.[32] It has been argued by Green that the traditional approach:

> does not permit . . . managers to respect even their strongly felt moral obligations when acting on them clearly fails to augment the value of shareholders' holdings or when such actions may reasonably be construed as tending to damage shareholders' long term positions.

So, for example, in the context of the Bhopal disaster Green states that:

> within the traditional model of fiduciary responsibilities these managers would be in the difficult position of arguing that slight risks to human life and health justify incurring relatively high and unreasonable costs.[33]

[29] Sentiments echoed by Ross Grantham, 'The Doctrinal Basis of the Rights of Company Shareholders' (1998) 57 *Cambridge Law Journal* 554. See also Gavin Kelly and John Parkinson, 'The Conceptual Foundations of the Company' in Andrew Gamble, Gavin Kelly and John Parkinson (eds), *The Political Economy of the Company* (Hart Publishing, Oxford, 2000). These issues are considered in more detail below.

[30] Ronald M Green 'Shareholders and Stakeholders: Changing Metaphors of Corporate Governance' (1993) 5 *Washington and Lee Law Review* 1415.

[31] Green *ibid*.

[32] See further ch 5.

[33] Green, above n 30 p 1220.

However, they could possibly within the framework of the business judgement rule have defended decisions 'for investing in plant safety as a way of protecting the long-term interests of the corporation.'[34] Furthermore, any balancing of shareholders' interest in profit maximisation in an unfavourable manner against the welfare of employees is even more indefensible under the traditional model, particularly where there are no life or death issues at stake. So here we can see that it is inevitable that under a traditionally framed paradigm of corporate purpose it is impossible to justify actions which would increase employee welfare.[35] This is why it is imperative that we fundamentally change the way we view the purpose of the corporation. A change in political views of this kind would provide legitimacy to the enactment of legislation supporting employees' claims to incidents of ownership.[36]

A number of arguments against the multi-fiduciary approach have already been considered.[37] Here, in the context of resolving competing ethical claims two further arguments are considered. Firstly, there is the argument that fiduciaries cannot coherently serve two beneficiaries with conflicting interests.[38] However the argument that criteria for setting reasonable and defensible priorities can be established for managers ought to be considered.[39] Also the point is well made that there must be cases in trust law generally where the trustee has to deal with conflicting interests amongst the beneficiaries. Moreover the reconciliation of competing claims on corporate wealth and power has been addressed in a very clear way in EU policy documents. Whether such policies strike the absolutely correct balance is largely irrelevant. The fact is that there is a workable balance struck with reasonably acceptable results.[40]

A more powerful and important argument against the multi-fiduciary approach is that endowing managers with social responsibilities will give them too much power.[41] Why should the resolution of these issues rest solely with a group or class who it is often argued exercise too much control over

[34] The relationship between fiduciary duties and the business judgement rule is further considered in ch 5.

[35] See further William T Allen, 'Inherent Tensions in the Governance of US Public Corporations: The Uses of Ambiguity in Fiduciary Law', *NYU School of Law*, 23 September 1998 papers.ssrn.com. Allen argues that managerial actions cannot, with any specificity, be dictated by a pre-existing legal rule and that in the open-textured governance environment of the large publicly financed corporation, ex-post constraints do present one plausible means of resolving governance issues, however such an approach which is exemplified by the fiduciary rule will be pragmatic and imperfect.

[36] Chs 4 and 5 survey the type of laws currently in place which are designed to achieve particular goals in relation to the advancement and protection of employee interests.

[37] See ch 5.

[38] This question is considered by Frank H Easterbrook and Daniel R Fischel, 'The Proper Role of a Target's Management in Responding to a Tender Offer' (1981)94 1161.

[39] Green, above n 30. Bratton, above n 19 agrees with this and refers in support of this to Patrick Ryan, 'Calculating the "Stakes" for Corporate Stakeholders as Part of Business Decision Making' (1992) 44 *Rutgers Law Review* 555.

[40] See further chs 9 and 10 for more on comparative competitiveness and productivity.

[41] This argument was first presented by Berle in a warning to Dodd. AA Berle, 'For Whom Corporate Managers are Trustees: A Note' (1932) 45 *Harvard Law Review* 1365.

corporate wealth and power as matters stand? Who will monitor these decisions and how?

Finally this argument against the idea of the competing claims being resolved in a private sphere through the exercise of management power raises an important issue concerning the role of the state. In this work various themes considered throughout are drawn together to indicate that the preferred forum for the resolution of competing stakeholder claims must be a public one. In other words there is a legitimate role for the state and legislation in the resolution of these claims in a uniform policy driven manner, reflected in legislative outcomes.

THE CORPORATION AS PUBLIC ACTOR

The debate over the nature of the corporation—the contract or communitarian debate—has been described as really a debate over whether the corporation is a public or private agent.[42] Historically, the corporation has presented itself as a private actor. This view has now been underlined by the theoretical analysis of the law and economics school. In the ethical context the microeconomic paradigm sees the primary ethical problem as 'the threat that state regulation poses to individual autonomy and private wealth creation' and 'the very articulation of an ethical component of the constituents' case is associated with the statist threat.'[43] I would certainly be of the view that the public role of the corporation in the context of employee welfare and consequent social issues has not been considered as extensively as it might have been. This is particularly borne out when comparisons are made with the view of the corporation and its role expressed in policy documents of the EU. The public role of the corporation in European society is so clearly assumed that whether or not the corporation is a public actor is not seriously debated. In that sense the European view is more pragmatic and interestingly reflects a pragmatic response to this question. In my opinion, within the debate in the US, this view has its nearest equivalent in what has been characterised by Allen as the managerialist conception of the corporation. Good managers and their corporations understand the value of employee investment and will often act where they can to protect this investment. Yet the absence of legal responses to this understanding means that in other cases a short-term, short-sighted approach to questions of employee welfare, benefits and costs is often imposed on the corporation.[44]

[42] AA Berle, 'For Whom Corporate Managers are Trustees: A Note' (1932) 45 *Harvard Law Review* 1365.

[43] Bratton, above n 19.

[44] David Millon, 'The Ambiguous Significance of Corporate Personhood' (Washington and Lee Public Law Research Paper No 01–6) argues that the important questions raised about internal corporate relations and the relationship between internal participants and the state are not answered by reference to issues relating to the nature of the corporation.

One of the attractions of the currently dominant view in the US of the corporation as a private actor in the social sphere is its coherence,[45] even if this coherence stems from a rather limited view of the corporation. In contrast those who would tend to the alternative view of the corporation as having a public role have 'no developed theory to which they can turn.' Problems have been identified with the multi-fiduciary approach and with the ethics paradigm. It has also been argued[46] that if the lines between the corporation's role as a private actor and as a public actor are simply redrawn to include labour we may again be presented with a coherent model but will sacrifice the principal reconceptualisation of the corporation as a fully public actor. Nevertheless as an intermediate step is this not an attractive option? Some commentators argue[47] that the public function is already understood. What is good for GM is good for the US. This statement presents us with the paradox of corporate culture. Everyone agrees with this statement, whether it is made in Europe or the US, but when it comes to the identification of the needs of workers and their community in a broad sense, there is a varied acceptance of the consequent obligations incurred by the corporation. This is the same sort of point Chancellor Allen made regarding the more pragmatic view abroad amongst business people which can be contrasted with the discourse amongst legal academics. Nevertheless even if there is an intuitive understanding of the corporation's public role recognising the connection is not the same as mandating certain legal consequences as a result. A conceptual framework must be developed to accommodate this intuitive understanding of the corporation's role.

[45] Alan Wolfe, 'The Modern Corporation: Private Agent of Public Actor' (1993) 50 *Washington and Lee Law Review* 1673.

[46] *Ibid.*

[47] William H Simon, 'What difference does it make whether Corporate Managers have Public Responsibilities?' (1993) 50 *Washington and Lee Law Review* 1673.

8

Comparative Ownership Structures

INTRODUCTION

ANOTHER ASPECT TO the consideration of the role of the employee as stakeholder is that the ownership structures of European and US companies historically is very different. The primary difference is that European companies in general do not display the same diversity of share ownership as US companies do. However, this is not true of the UK and to a lesser extent Ireland, where companies which are quoted on the London or Dublin stock exchange display characteristics similar to US quoted companies in terms of ownership. Interestingly these countries share a common law heritage with the US. Overall, the public equity markets are not in general the primary source of capital for many European companies. Recent data has shown some evidence of convergence for both trading blocs. In Europe a trend towards privatisation has added to the 'phenomenal growth' of equity markets in a number of OECD countries in Europe. This has been further fuelled by 'a growing process of disintermediation in the financial markets, shifting savings from the banking sector to equity (and bond) markets.'[1] On the other hand, growth in institutional shareholding has probably led to a decrease in diversity of shareownership in the US, with latest figures showing that 'less than 100 large non-bank financial institutions hold approximately 20% of the top 20 more liquid markets in the world.'[2] Despite evidence of convergence, it must be emphasised however, that figures for stock exchange turnover show a marked difference between the level of stock exchange activity in Europe overall (32, 500 m Euro for 1998) and the US (13 bn Euro for 1998).[3]

Three hypotheses are presented here. Firstly, it is now accepted that the different ownership structure of continental European companies in particular, (ie excluding the UK and Ireland) compared with the ownership structure of US companies, determines how monitoring of management takes place. If we accept the capital markets theory of management accountability,[4] which is put

[1] Stilpon Nestor, International Efforts to Improve Corporate Governance: Why and How? OECD 2002.

[2] *Ibid.*

[3] Stock Exchanges: Basic Economic Data, 2000 CESifo: DICE.

[4] See further ch 3.

forward in relation to US companies, it is clear that in view of the fact that European companies are not subject to the same sort of activity on the equity markets this theory will not readily apply in the European context. Thus these markets could not be described as a forum in which management performance could be assessed. Similarly most European companies do not operate in a market which allows or indeed permits an active take-over culture of the sort which dominated US corporate culture, particularly in the 1980s. Thus the question of how management are accountable and to whom will yield different answers.

A second hypothesis, and a more complex argument, is that different ownership structures have had a profound impact on the acceptability of including other constituencies as stakeholders. The argument is that ownership structures of European companies have facilitated a more tightly controlled type of governance system, which allows, for example, close monitoring by creditors as stakeholders. This, in turn, has allowed for a more open acceptance of some level of monitoring by other stakeholders such as employees.

Thirdly, it is argued that the more tightly or closely held ownership of European companies has, in a political sense, facilitated a corporate culture which is more open to the influence of centralised planning by government authorities, whether this is at national level or at EU level. Present governance structures in European companies have a significant impact on the acceptability of the type of planning evidenced by EU policy documents considered in chapter four. This is reflected in legislation protecting employees as stakeholders. If we consider the position of an employee within a typically European corporate structure with that of the US employee, it is clear that European companies have accorded incidents of ownership, such as voice and some degree of control to employees, by allowing for employee representation on Boards of Directors and by providing for further fora for management-labour dialogue.[5] In addition the European employee enjoys legislatively mandated employment rights such as protection from dismissal without cause, mandated leave rights and so on.[6] Thus when we consider the position of the European corporation in terms of shareholder wealth maximisation we can see that this may mean something quite different in the European context where other interests, such as the interests of labour, are protected, albeit in a limited way, from the more rigorous pursuit of this goal.

US commentators[7] on European governance systems tend to assert the advantages of the market for corporate control governance model over the institutional governance model represented in European corporate structures.[8] The

[5] See ch 4.

[6] These sorts of rights are described in ch 4 under the heading of the Proprietorial Interest Model.

[7] See also ch 3.

[8] Mark Roe, 'A Political Theory of American Corporate Finance' (1991) 91 *Columbia Law Review* 10. See also Mark Roe, 'Some Differences in the Corporate Structure in Germany, Japan and the United States' (1993) 102 *Yale Law Journal* 1927. Ronald J Gilson and Reinier Kraakman, 'Investment Companies as Guardian Shareholders: The Place of the MSIC in the Corporate Governance Debate' (1993) 45 *Stanford Law Review* 985. Jonathan R Macey and P Miller,

preference for arm's length monitoring over relational monitoring seems overall to be the one preferred by a report issued by the World Bank in relation to the development of emerging economies, driven in part by research conducted by La Porta *et al.*[9] This would seem to be a rather meaningless exercise because of the fundamentally different structure of ownership in both systems. Rather than seeking to establish the merits of one model over the other it is argued therefore that the models have sprung from different political and social contexts and tend to address different problems.[10] Furthermore these models will continue to reflect, and in turn influence, political and social developments in both systems. Commentators such as Macey and Miller[11] who argue that the German and Japanese corporate governance models are not preferable to the American model because these systems 'reduce risktaking among borrowers and retard the market for corporate control' miss two fundamental points. Firstly, whether the primary assertion regarding the reduction of risk-taking is true or not (and it does not seem to be true in any strong form[12]) it is accepted in European corporate culture that management prerogative in the strong form indicated by Anglo-American corporate theory simply does not and should not exist. Whatever this may mean in terms of reducing the taking of unacceptable risks at the expense of labour or other stakeholders' interests is exactly the desired end rather than being an accidental by-product of the structures involved.[13] Thus the following statement from Macey and Miller, misses the point completely:

'Corporate Governance and Commercial Banking: A Comparative Examination of Germany, Japan and the United States' (1995) 48 *Stanford Law Review* 73.

[9] MR Iskander and N Chamlou, *Corporate Governance: A framework for Implementation.* (The World Bank, Washington DC, 2000). See also the Corporate Governance in OECD Member Countries: Recent Developments and Trends (OECD Steering Group on Corporate Governance April 2001). See also Rafael La Porta, Florencio Lopez-de-Silanes, Andrei Schleifer and Robert W Vishny, 'Legal Determinants of External Finance' (1997) 52 *Journal of Finance*, 1131 'Law and Finance' (1998) 106 *Journal of Political Economy*, 1113, 'Corporate Ownership Around the World' (1999) 54 *Journal of Finance*, 471.

[10] See further David Charny, 'Workers and Corporate Governance: The Role of Political Culture' (Sloan Project on Corporate Governance: Employees and Corporate Governance, Columbia Law School, 22 November 1996).

[11] Macey and Miller, above n 8 p 73.

[12] Theodore J Baums, *Takeovers versus Institutions in Corporate Governance in Germany* in D Prentice and PJR Holland (eds), *Contemporary Issues in Corporate Governance* (Oxford University Press, Oxford, 1993) 174, addresses this issue and argues that risk aversion may be a problem where banks are not shareholders. However, in most instances in Germany they are. Secondly he questions to what extent profit maximisation is pursued in the first instance and refers to the 'managerialists' who claim that size maximisation is the priority for management. (Although, see ch 5 for a slightly different understanding of managerialism as described by Chancellor Allen of the Delaware Supreme Court). If the size maximisation hypothesis is true, then Baums argues that banks and management will be able to mutually agree objectives at the expense of shareholders. However, Baums is also sceptical about the managerialist argument as he describes it, referring to the fact that debt is usually viewed as a means of disciplining management: See further Michael Jensen, 'Agency Costs of Free Cash Flow, Corporate Finance and Takeovers' in *The Modern Theory of Corporate Finance* (Smith, ed., 1990) and asks if this is so 'why should management yield to its alleged incentives for growth maximization with the help of credit finance?' (Professor of Law, University of Osnabruck in Germany).

[13] Macey and Miller, above n 8 at p 89.

> The German bank's dual role as creditor and shareholder creates a significant conflict of interest. Banks have an economic incentive to vote against risktaking at firms to which they have lent money. However, from the perspective of shareholders on whose behalf the banks vote, banks reduce the aggregate risktaking to a suboptimal level and thereby transfer wealth from shareholders to themselves. Furthermore, labor interests on the supervisory board are unlikely to oppose banks' efforts to reduce aggregate risktaking because they, too, are fixed claimants, their interests are aligned with those of the bank.

Secondly, statements to the effect that the 'Japanese and German bank-dominated systems of corporate governance actually prevent the development of robust markets for corporate control in those countries'[14] display lack of understanding of the public choices made against the latter model and ignorance of the fact that many of the laws of European continental countries governing equity voting rights and take-overs discourage an aggressive take-over culture deliberately. Baums,[15] in quoting the observation by Cosh, Hughes and Singh[16] that the bank-based or institutionally driven approach to corporate governance is preferable to the market for corporate control model found in Anglo-American corporation, makes a similar point and argues that both systems address different problems. Baums suggests exploring the possibility of combining elements of both models rather than considering each as a 'contrasting and incompatible approach'. This work seeks to do that in relation to employee interests.

COMPARATIVE OWNERSHIP STRUCTURES RELEVANT TO STAKEHOLDING IN THE ANGLO-AMERICAN AND EUROPEAN CORPORATION

Germany

In Germany,[17] there are 2,682 Aktiengesellschaft (only one of a number of types of German business organisation, representing that which is most like the listed Anglo-American corporation) and only 551 of these corporations were stock exchange listed.[18] Figures show 1,043 domestic German companies listed for

[14] Macey and Miller, above n 8 at p 76.

[15] Baums, above n 12 p 151.

[16] A Cosh, J Hughes and A Singh, 'Analytical and Policy Issues in the UK Economy' in A Cosh, *Takeovers and Short Termism in the UK* (Institute for Public Policy Research, Cambridge, 1996).

[17] See generally The Control of Corporate Europe, Fabrizio Barca and Marco Becht (eds), (Oxford University Press, Oxford, 2001). See also E Wyermeesch, 'The Corporate Governance Discussion in some European States' in D Prentice and PRJ Holland (eds), *Contemporary Issues in Corporate Governance* (Oxford University Press, Oxford, 1993). Theodore Baums 'Takeovers versus Institutions in Corporate Governance in Germany' in *Contemporary Issues in Corporate Governance*, *ibid* p 151.

[18] Note that Robert Monks and Nell Minnow, *Corporate Governance* (Blackwell, Cambridge, MA, 1995) 288 writing in 1995, state that there are 'fewer than 700 quoted companies in Germany' the difference being possibly accounted for by changes after German unification.

1999, although this figure is probably reflective of some multiple listings in one or more stock exchanges of the German Federation of Stock Exchanges.[19] Of these companies 90 per cent are majority-owned by one or more active controlling shareholders, leaving only about 70 companies which were really publicly traded companies.[20] In addition in Germany only 39 companies have 75 per cent of their shares in public ownership and these may be held by foreign investors.[21] However, as in other countries, the role of institutional investors has increased. Over the period of 1960–1990 ownership held by institutions, in particular insurance companies and pension funds increased from 3 per cent to 12 per cent, and increased again in 1990–2000 to 17.8 per cent.

The most important feature of the German ownership system, which has equivalents elsewhere, most notably in Japan, is the role of the banking sector. In Germany the role of institutional investors is limited compared with the role of banks which exercise a dominant influence disproportionate to their actual ownership. Bank ownership is stated to be about 10 per cent of quoted companies. The reason for this dominance is the fact that German banks are the beneficiaries of a type of proxy system whereby shareholders delegate voting to the bank through which their brokerage business is conducted. The voting process in German companies is entirely different from the Anglo-American model. In Germany there is no proxy system whereby management exercise the voting power of shareholders. Shareholders vote their own shares or these shares are voted by institutions, mainly banks, as 'custodians' for their shares.[22]

[19] Above n 3.

[20] See Marco Becht and Ekkehart Boehmer, 'Ownership and Voting Power in Germany' in Fabrizio Barca and Marco Becht (eds), The Control of Corporate Europe, n 17 above, which illustrates that these figures have remained reasonably constant since the mid 1990s. See also Benn Steil *et al*, *The European Equity Markets: The State of the Union and an Agenda for the Millennium* (Kluwer, London, 1996) note that whilst data on ownership in European firms are still 'rather poor' the concentration of ownership in Continental European and Scandinavian firms compared with the United Kingdom and the United States is striking. Considering only quoted companies, Steil *et al* note that 79% and 85% of companies in France and Germany respectively had one shareholder owning more than 25%. They also note that in the United Kingdom this was true of only 16% of quoted companies:

'In effect, the overwhelming majority of listed companies on the European continent are closely held. Comparisons over time are not always available, but evidence from France, Germany and Sweden shows an increase in ownership concentration over the 1970s and 1980s.'

[21] Schneider, 'Auf Dem Weg Des Pensionkassenkorporatismus (1990) 35 AG 317.

[22] See generally, Wyermeesch, above n 17. This relationship seems to be akin to a discretionary trust relationship. Shares are deposited with banks under what is described as a custodial relationship where banks require written authorisation to vote the designated shares. This power can be delegated for a maximum period of 15 months and is revocable at any time. Before a shareholders' meeting banks have to recommend to their clients how to vote and must ask for instructions. However, in the absence of instructions (and that would be the usual case according to Baums) the bank may vote as it recommends. Finally there is no limit on the percentage of shares held by banks so any bank may hold considerable power in the shareholders' meeting. In a study conducted by Gottschalk, Der Stimmrechtsteinfluss Der Banken in Der Aktionarsversammlungen von Grossunternehmen (1988) Wsi-Mitteilungen 295–6 it was shown that voting rights are highly concentrated in the three largest German banks: Deutsche Bank, Dresdner Bank and Commerzbank. These 3 banks were shown together to have voted on average approximately 45% of the stock represented at the general

One commentator, writing in 1993[23] noted that the issue of take-overs was not a debated issue in Germany where companies are not taken over through the generation of public market activity but only, if at all, through private agreement such as in the take-over of Continental by Pirelli[24] and the attempt by Krupp to take over Hoesch. This characteristic, which has not changed since the early 90s is consonant with the closed structure of ownership in Germany, and is significantly different from the Anglo-American model. The two-tier board system is operated for all stock corporations (Aktiengesellschaft AG) and for limited liability companies employing over 50 employees (GmbH-Gesellschaft mit besachränkter Haftung). Employees are represented on the supervisory (as distinct from executive management) board and the number of labour representatives depends on the number of employees. This figure will vary between one third and a half.[25] The management board of the two—tier system is appointed usually for a five year term and is controlled in terms of ability to dismiss by the supervisory board. However, the management can only be dismissed prematurely for cause. This is viewed as being one factor in the unpopularity of hostile take-overs as a form of management control.[26] Secondly, the shareholders' meeting has a different role in the large German corporation than in the Anglo-American model.[27] The power of the shareholders' meeting is limited to

meetings of 32 companies. Note that under German law an individual shareholder, in contrast to the position of the banks, may only exercise votes in relation to a maximum of 5% of the capital of any company regardless of the size of the actual shareholding.

[23] Wyermeesch above n 17 p 19.

[24] The takeover by the Italian company, Pirelli, of Continental AG illustrates some interesting aspects of the German system in contrast to the Anglo-American system. Here Pirelli approached the takeover through contact with the chairman of the supervisory board of Continental, Ulrich Weiss of Deutsche Bank, who was also in charge of Italian affairs at Deutsche Bank. The chairman of Continental's executive board, Horst Urban, decided to resist the bid and hired Morgan Grenfell as Deutsche Bank's merchant bank to mount a defence campaign. However, those within Deutsche Bank who supported the takeover eventually persuaded the anti-takeover group that the takeover was in the best interests of Continental and the chairman of the executive board was forced to concede the agreed takeover. See Monks and Minnow, above n 18 p 292–93.

[25] NG Maw, *Corporate Governance* (Dartmouth, Aldershot, 1994) 121. However, in relation to employee representation which takes place at supervisory board level only, AGs employing over 500 employees are now required to include employee representatives, an exemption having been introduced in 1994 for smaller AGs. See further Adriaan Dorresteijn *et al*, European Corporate Law (Kluwer, Deventer, The Netherlands, 1994) 112. See below for a more detailed discussion of the role and impact of the supervisory board.

[26] Baums above n 12 p 151. Other factors described by Baums include corporate statutes which provide typically that a shareholder cannot vote more than 5% of stock irrespective of the total number of shares held and the fact that corporate statutes, even of publicly held companies grant a discretion to management to register an acquirer's shares. The exercise of shareholders' rights are dependent on registration and thus a shareholder may be powerless in the face of the exercise of such discretion. Under British and Irish company law rights are dependent on registration but directors may not exercise this discretion in publicly held companies.

[27] See further AF Conard, 'Comparative Law: The Supervision of Corporate Management: A Supervision of Developments in European Community and United States Law' (1984) *Michigan Law Review* 1459 FF and Christian J Meier-Schatz, 'Corporate Governance and Legal Rules: A Transnational Look at Concepts of International Management Control' (1980) 13 *Journal of Corporation Law* 431–80.

decisions regarding changes of statutes, approval of accounts, distribution of half of the annual balance sheet profits, election of half the members of the supervisory board and decisions regarding specific structural changes. These features are substantially different from the Anglo-American model

France

A similar pattern exists in France where studies have shown, for example, that over the three year period from 1987–1990 share ownership of French companies remained fairly stable in terms of structure with approximately 36 per cent of all quoted shares being held by individuals, with 26 per cent–21 per cent held by institutional investors and 24 per cent held by industrial commercial enterprises. By 1998 this had increased to 30 per cent. Most importantly the 36 per cent of shares held by individuals tend to be concentrated in individual companies within family members and groups. The biggest change over this period was a relatively small decrease in the holdings of institutional investors and a similar increase in foreign shareownership, which varied from 10 per cent to 17 per cent between 1987 and 1990.[28] It should be emphasised, however, that many commentators have stated that there is very little information available on share ownership in many companies. French corporate ownership is even more concentrated than in Germany.[29] In addition French laws reflect a policy which safeguards restricted ownership of major French companies even after some of these companies, which had been state owned, were privatised in the 1980s.[30]

In France[31] the basic Company Law Code in operation at present was enacted in 1966. French Company Law allows for a one or two-tier management board. Labour representation is mandated for state enterprises but not for private enterprises. If a Societe Anonyme employs more than 50 a works council must

[28] Wyermeesch above n 17 p 7.

[29] Monks and Minnow above n 18 p 299 give the following figures taken from a study of corporate governance in the G7 countries conducted by Oxford Analytica consulting group:

'The top 50 industrial, commercial and service companies of France break down as follows:
12 state controlled/owned
17 management controlled
14 family controlled and managed
3 family controlled but with outside management
4 subsidiaries'

Little has changed in the intervening period. Laurence Bloch and Elizabeth Kemp in a recent study, 'Ownership and Voting Power in France' in F Barca and M Becht (eds), *The Control of Corporate Europe* above n 17 state that 'Families seem to play an important role in ownership and voting power, both in unlisted firms and in the CAC 40 firms. Around 40% of unlisted firms have, as first shareholder, individuals owning directly more than 50% of the capital. For the CAC 40 firms, individuals are not the largest blockholder, but when they effectively are present as blockholders, they hold around 30% of the voting rights and have the control in facts. (sic)'

[30] See further Monks and Minnow above n 18 p 300 ff.

[31] Wyermeesch, above n 17 p 16–18.
Maw, above n 25 p 124–28.

be established[32] whose members are elected by employees. The works council is entitled then to send two of its members to meetings of either the management or supervisory board as non-voting observers. However, it is common[33] for companies with works councils to have preliminary board meetings without the representatives of the works council. This inherent problem in co-determination arising from essential differences between employee and management constituencies has been recognised as a difficulty with employee representation.[34]

In relation to the market for corporate control, reform of the basic 1966 Company Law Code has led to an amendment in 1992 of the rule requiring a two thirds bid upon acquisition of a third of the shares[35] on foot of protests from minority shareholders in particular arising from the Pinault take-over of the department chain Le Printemps. In relation to contested take-over bids the Conseil des Bourses de Valeurs has extra powers regarding valuation of offers, for example the Conseil has the power to reject a price as an inadequate one even if above market value.[36] It also has considerable powers to investigate possible abuses. It functions as a quasi-judicial body.[37]

Belgium

A similar profile emerges in relation to Belgian companies where ownership is even more tightly held amongst individuals, who, very significantly, are usually part of a group of controlling shareholders or the only majority controlling shareholder. Institutional investors hold 22 per cent of all Belgian shares. Again, however, commentators have noted that the 'figures are unfortunately not very reliable, as little detailed public information is available.'[38] In addition it is important to note that there seems to be a very close relationship between these institutional investors and banks or other financial institutions that 'dominate the Belgian economic scene'. The Belgian Company Law Code dates from 1935 but has been reformed on a number of occasions to comply with European Company law directives. In relation to take-over bids, a number of issues are worth noting. Firstly, most Belgian stock exchange listed companies are owned by a small group of majority shareholders. Secondly, a big fear expressed in

[32] See further EC Directive on Works Council described in ch 4.

[33] Maw, above n 25 p 127.

[34] Ch 4. But note that this does not seem to be a problem in relation to the German system described in detail by Baums.

[35] Art 5–3–1 of the regulation approved Decree 28/09/ 1989 as modified by Decree 15 May 1992. D Carreau and J-Y Martin, 'La Reforme du Régime des Offres Publiques', (1992) *Rev Sociétés* 451.

[36] *Ibid* 356, 675.

[37] Wyermeesch, above n 17 p 16.

[38] Wyermeesch, above n 17 p 7–9. See Marco Becht, Ariane Chapelle and Luc Renneboog, 'Shareholding Cascade: The Separation of Ownership and Control in Belgium' in F Barca and M Becht (eds), *The Control of Corporate Europe* above n 17 who state that of the 140 listed Belgian companies there is a high degree of ownership concentration with holding companies, families and, to a lesser extent, industrial companies being the main investor categories.

Belgium is the increasing prevalence of foreign ownership of interests in the Belgian economy and accordingly this has given rise to proposals 'for better linking the leading enterprises to local ownership, including institutional investors and indirect state ownership.'[39] The response to these expressed fears is to restrict opportunities for take-overs and this makes for a striking contrast to the US approach which would not countenance such restrictions to fluidity in the stock market and consequently in the market for control. Thirdly, take-over rules in substance are concerned primarily with two issues: as in France the requirement of a mandatory bid, in this case mandatory acquisition of a controlling share at above market price;[40] and secondly the rule prohibiting directors using defensive mechanisms once the bid is disclosed.

The Netherlands

In the Netherlands, company law issues of governance were considered during the 1970s. In 1996, after discussion and agreement between the Amsterdam Exchanges and the association of listed companies, a Corporate Governance Committee was established with a view to increasing shareholder voice, in particular that of minority shareholders.[41] Subsequent recommendations depended on voluntary adoption by companies of structures which would increase shareholder voice, although it seems that little changed. Of the companies listed on the Amsterdam Exchanges, the average stake of the largest blockholder is 27 per cent and that of the top three is 41 per cent. These holdings seem to be held through what are termed in one study 'administrative offices' and are generally viewed as a means by which control is tightly held.[42] In a manner similar to the other European countries considered here, the market for corporate control is not a significant monitoring device and there is evidence to support the view put forward by Wyermeesch that Dutch companies have actively used many protective techniques regarding take-overs. In contrast to the position of shareholders per se, a major feature of Dutch law is the recognition of other stakeholder interests as a relevant constituency where directors are making corporate decisions. Wyermeesch observes that the regulation of take-overs and mergers is accordingly influenced by this feature. Decisions of directors in this context are regulated by the Social Economic Council which is composed of representatives of employers, employees and the State.

[39] Wyermeesch refers here to the King Bedouin Foundation—Konig Booudeijnstichting Onze Welvaart: Zelf Belissen, Mee Belissen? (1992).

[40] In the case of Wagon Lits the Brussels Court decided (6/08/1992) that because of pre-existing undisclosed share transfer agreements, French Accord acquired control of the company without disclosing it to the Banking Commission. Accordingly the court decided that the company was obliged to bid for the plaintiffs shares at the same (high) price at which Accord had bought.

[41] See Abe de Jong, Rezaul Kabir, Teye Marra and Ailsa Roell, 'Ownership and Control in the Netherlands' in F Barca and M Brecht (eds), *The Control of Corporate Europe* above n 17. See also Wyermeesch, above n 17 p 22. See further RP Voogd referred to at n 82 in Wyermeesch.

[42] *Ownership and Control in the Netherlands, ibid* p 205.

THE MARKET FOR CORPORATE CONTROL: A EUROPEAN PERSPECTIVE

It is clear that there are 'quite substantial factual differences existing between the different national settings.'[43] There is evidence of some convergence in ownership structures of large listed corporations between 1990 and 2000 which is largely driven by the growth, on both sides of the Atlantic, of institutional ownership. Nevertheless, in conclusion of this survey it is clear that only a minority of European companies possess the characteristics of the Berle and Means corporation. Essentially this type of company exists only in relation to publicly quoted companies on the Stock Exchange of the UK and Ireland. In contrast in Germany, Belgium, the Netherlands and France even listed companies are closely held and often minority controlled either by a founding family, a financial institution or institutions, or other interests acting together. Ownership and control can often be traced to an identifiable person or group. Thus whilst there are some differences between the company law codes of these European countries they share characteristics which are significantly different from the US or 'Anglo-American system'. On the other hand problems of monitoring of corporate conduct including a discussion of the appropriate role for institutional investors has not received much attention, in contrast to problems presented by the large-small shareholder conflict. This lack of interest can be attributed to

> the structure of shareholdings: monitoring has always been strongly organised and assumed, whether by the banks (Germany) or by the controlling shareholders—usually family interests—(France, Belgium, the Netherlands).[44]

In addition the role of take-overs of companies in most European countries is entirely different from the experience of this phenomenon in the United Kingdom and the United States. A recent, but relatively insignificant rise in take-overs (nothing like the take-over rate in the US in the 1980s) has meant that the regulation of take-overs, including defensive techniques, has received attention in these jurisdictions. In most continental European countries the systems contain obstacles faced by a potential bidder which have been described elsewhere as being of both a legal and factual nature.[45] The former are further categorised as pre-bid defences such as voting restrictions which substantially restrict the voting power of even large shareholders. A particular mention is made by Dorresteijn *et al* of the fact that 'the mandatory establishment of a co-determined supervisory board may reduce shareholders' influence in both German and Dutch companies.'[46]

[43] *Ownership and Control in the Netherlands, ibid* n 17 p 22.
[44] *Ibid* n 16 p 24. See also *The Control of Corporate Europe* above n 17.
[45] See Adriaan Dorresteijn *et al*, above n 25 at p 178.
[46] *Ibid* p 178.

Factual obstacles are exemplified by the strong position of German banks described already and the very closely held nature of French and Belgian companies which 'although listed on the stock exchange, are often closely held and controlled by the founding families, financial holdings or indirectly by the State.'[47] This final feature would certainly facilitate the type of centralised planning mentioned in our second hypothesis. Interestingly the same authors describe the UK position in entirely different terms:

> On the contrary, in the UK the number of hostile take-overs has increased enormously since the 1950s. This is due to the different circumstances such as the widespread nature of share ownership, the emergence of 'corporate raiders' and the existence of commercial banks with mergers and acquisitions as a major feature of their activity.

At EU level the Thirteenth Directive on Company law attempted to align the various features of take-over regulation displayed at national level. This Directive included provision for a mandatory bid where a person acquired one-third of the voting rights in the company. Certain notification obligations were also imposed on the offeror. In addition an obligation was imposed on the board of the offeree prohibiting it from taking certain defensive measures. The board was obliged to publicise the views of the board on the offer and the decision of individual members of the board in relation to acceptance or otherwise of the offer in relation to securities held by them. It should be noted that the board was obliged to inform employees of the information provided to shareholders.[48]

Although the authors of European Equity Markets writing in 1996 expressed the opinion that 'initiatives to unify the structure and control of public listed companies, take-over bid procedures and employee rights have effectively been stopped' the European Commissioner for the Internal Market, Mario Monti, revived the legislative process in relation to the Take-over Bid Directive and in November 1997 a new draft directive was prepared for consideration by the Commission. However, the UK Take-over Panel were strongly opposed to any hasty decisions on a mandatory system rather than a voluntary system of the type currently operated by the Take-over Panel. There was also some pressure to alter original statements in the directive relating to the protection of the workforce as a primary concern, to a less radical position, where the consideration of the workforce would be one amongst a number of factors to be considered. After much debate about these and other issues this directive was defeated in the European Parliament in July 2001.

ADVANTAGES OF INSTITUTIONAL MONITORING

From a corporate finance perspective concern has been expressed recently regarding the relatively poor liquidity of the main European stock exchanges.

[47] *Ibid* p 178.
[48] *Ibid* p 62.

Connections are now being made between the issues of liquidity and corporate governance, conceptually similar to the connection made here between the concentration of ownership and governance outcomes regarding employees. In considering the issues of liquidity and governance together, a recent study has stated that: 'Corporate governance is commonly believed to benefit from the concentration of holdings of debt and equity in individual firms.'[49] Steil *et al* conclude that improvements in liquidity of European markets may involve costs 'in terms of less effective monitoring of corporations', although it is also accepted that significant gains in improved liquidity could be achieved in European terms through the elimination of barriers to cross-border acquisitions, ie acquisitions by one company in one member state of companies resident in a second or third member state. The elimination of such barriers and the consequent increase in liquidity would not necessarily impede concentration of ownership.

It is sufficient to note however, that the ownership structures described here are widely accepted in Europe as having significant governance benefits in terms of monitoring generally.[50] Because such firms also display characteristics more favourable to employee representation and participation, it is justifiable therefore to extend this point to include monitoring and accountability in relation to employee interests. A further point is that such close monitoring will assist in resolving the claims of competing interests satisfactorily for all. Where management are closely involved with employee representatives and investor representatives at decision-making levels, this difficult task will certainly be more informed and therefore more meaningful. Outcomes will thus be more defensible, not least because the interests of these groups were represented at the point of decision.

A number of arguments are made regarding the advantages of institutional monitoring, particularly in relation to the role of banks in the German model.[51] Some of these points may be usefully extended by analogy to the inclusion of monitoring by other stakeholders including employees. It is not necessary to assert that one governance model should be adopted wholesale in preference to another, but it is possible to include features from one model in another, specifically incorporating some means of increasing employee voice, control and participation into the Berle and Means type structure. These advantages are described under a number of different facets:

—better access to information for the monitors, in this case the banks;
—influence through advice to management;
—influence through appointment of managers;
—interim and ex-post monitoring.

[49] Steil *et al*, above n 19 p 148.

[50] See generally Klaus Gugler (ed), *Corporate Governance and Economic Performance* (Oxford University Press, Oxford, 2001). In particular see pp 15–20 for a very useful summary of the literature and findings on this issue.

[51] See generally Baums, above n 12.

In relation to the first heading banks will have access to equivalent levels of information as creditors and thus no particular advantages in this regard are presented by the relational corporate governance model. Under German law,[52] board members are under an obligation of secrecy regarding information obtained in that capacity. This would similarly apply to employee representatives. Therefore it is doubtful whether board representation would offer any significant advantages to the employee body as a whole, considering that similar levels of information may be available to employees through other EU representation mechanisms.[53] Indeed board representation does not primarily seem to be constructed to act as a conduit for information from the representatives on the board to their constituencies. Rather it seems the channelling of information is intended to be in the opposite direction and in that direction only, ie from the constituency to the management and that it is intended to improve the quality of management decisions in this way. It is argued that similarly a board would benefit from advice and information presented by long-term experienced employees.

Under the third heading (ie influence through appointment of managers) it is generally considered that the banks role in appointing good managers is very important. This may not be as strong an argument regarding employee representation where certainly it could be argued that employee representatives may not have the necessary information to adequately judge management performance. Yet it can be argued that employee representatives would at the very least have a valuable input into the selection of individual managers most likely to be able to foster good industrial relations:

> all the more important is the question of whether the supervisory board is capable of selecting managers from the beginning who appear capable of doing a good job—because of the pattern of their behaviour in the past, their career, and previous success—even if their efforts cannot be observed on an ongoing basis. This seems, indeed, to be the most important task of the supervisory board, and banks seem to play some role in this respect.[54]

Finally, it is very important to consider the type of monitoring available under the relational model of corporate governance. Here a distinction is made between interim monitoring and ex-post monitoring. Under the relational governance model there are many more opportunities for interim monitoring compared with the market control model where monitors may not have any *proactive or preventative* role through monitoring activities. In the relational model, stakeholders such as investors (banks) and employees may contribute positively to good management decisions rather than being limited, as they are in the market control model, to reacting to *bad* management decisions. In concluding, Baums posits the view that institution-based or relational governance systems and the market for corporate control as monitoring devices focus on different problems and should be considered as 'supplementary rather than

[52] S 116 93(1)Aktiengesetz (Stock Corporation Act).
[53] See ch 4.
[54] Baums, above n 12 p 174. Similarly it is argued that employees would play some role here.

mutually excluding systems.'[55] At the same time it is hoped that this discussion demonstrates that there are profound differences between the two systems. Thus it seems plausible to argue that simple or piece-meal solutions, for example proposing incorporating some elements of one system into the other, such as incorporating a two-tier board system into the Anglo-American model thereby facilitating involvement of employees, will not necessarily fall easily into the Anglo-American structure. Similarly proposals for more employee involvement through share ownership is meaningless in a continental European context but may have some worth in the US context.

It is clear therefore that the nature of the corporate governance debate in continental Europe significantly differs from that in the US and other common law countries. EU directives attempting to harmonise regulation of take-overs at EU level have not focused on the take-over as a monitoring device. Attempts at regulation are based on the recognition of particular problems presented by the drive towards a common market and in particular the perception that economic interests of particular member states may be increasingly owned by foreign interests.[56] In addition, harmonisation of EU company law has bypassed the governance issues presented by diverse share ownership simply because this does not, by and large, exist. Instead harmonisation has focused on a number of specific issues, including the extension of accountability to other stakeholders, in particular employees. A further issue considered at domestic level in a number of member States is the relationship between minority shareholders and majority shareholders and specific problems presented by the presence of large blockholdings in this context.[57] In the European context there is an explicit recognition in many of the domestic codes that employees must be considered by management in making decisions and EU legislation has further advanced this concept. Furthermore acceptance of this legislative movement is conditioned by existing ownership structures which reflect significant stakeholder control and influence, particularly in relation to banks and other financial institutions. The closed nature of ownership in continental European companies reflects a limited 'circle' of ownership which does not embrace the public generally, unlike the US experience.[58] The remaining issue at EU level and within the domestic debates in member states is, to what extent should this power and interest be extended and in particular to what extent can this be achieved through harmonisation.

[55] Baums, above n 12 p 174.

[56] See the case of Belgium and France in particular.

[57] See *The Control of Corporate Europe*, above n 17 p 7.

[58] Although at present it is argued here that the willingness of corporations to extend control and its consequent benefits to employees as stakeholders is reflective of a more socially progressive approach to the distribution of corporate wealth it is possible that, because there has been no substantial change in the structure of corporate ownership in Europe for many generations, the willingness to include employees in this way stems from an older tradition of 'noblesse oblige' in view of the fact that actual ownership of corporate wealth through the holding of shares is almost impossible for the ordinary individual.

THE COMMON LAW WORLD MEETS EUROPE: THE UNITED KINGDOM AND IRELAND

A very important point which emerges from this discussion is that listed companies in those EU countries which have a common law legal system, ie Ireland and the UK, do not have structures which are similar to their continental counterparts and in fact are much more similar to US quoted companies sharing with the latter 'Berle and Means' characteristics.

About 3,000 companies are quoted on the London Stock Exchange compared with approximately 760 for the German stock exchange, 970 on the French stock exchange and 160 on the Brussels exchange.[59] The main issue in Britain has been the poor competitive performance of British companies compared with their continental counterparts and in the context of the continental European experience, the question has been raised whether the use of equity produces 'an unstable and potentially disloyal shareholder body'?[60] However, even if the shareholders are disloyal it is not at all clear whether this has an effect on real performance. It is interesting to note that the corporate governance debate in the UK has been primarily driven by the pragmatic need to examine the causes of British under-performance and these concerns are very much reflected in the tenor of the Cadbury report and beyond, including the Greenbury and Hampel reports.[61]

It is significant that of member States of the EU the UK alone had opted out of further progression of matters under the European Social charter and similarly the UK has been a vociferous opponent to attempts to introduce the two tier board system at EU level.[62] In the European common law countries ie Ireland and the UK, the US approach to corporate governance issues seems more relevant. It has been noted that the ALI project 'provides perhaps the best, widest ranging and most thought provoking analysis and recommendations in the field of corporate governance to us in the UK.'[63] However the US system of having a board consisting mainly of outside, non-executive officers of the

[59] Stock Exchange: Basic Economic Data, 2000 CESifo: DICE.

[60] More cogently Prentice makes the point that if acquisition is vital to the penetration of foreign markets (for example the acquisition of an established distribution network) does this indicate that UK companies (and a fortiori US companies) are at a competitive disadvantage in relation to continental Europe and Japan because hostile acquisitions are much more possible within the UK and US markets than in these other jurisdictions. Prentice goes on to state that in European terms 'the hostile bid is virtually a UK phenomenon'. DD Prentice, 'Some aspects of the Corporate Governance Debate' in D Prentice and PRJ Holland (eds), *Contemporary Issues in Corporate Governance* (Oxford University Press, Oxford, 1993).

[61] See references to this in Prentice *ibid* p 25. See also Adrian Cadbury, 'Highlights of the Proposals of the Committee on Financial Aspects of Corporate Governance (the Cadbury Report)' in D Prentice and PRJ Holland (eds), *Contemporary Issues in Corporate Governance* ch 3. (Oxford University Press, Oxford, 1993). See also Maw above n 24 ch 12. See also the MPR Executive Pay Report 1995–1996 also known as the Greenbury Report (Incomes Data Services (UK) 1995).

[62] Draft Fifth Company Law Directive.

[63] Maw, above n 25 p 121 and p 134 commenting on the ALI Final Draft issued 31 March 1992.

corporation 'equates neither to the two-tier system in continental Europe nor to the UK unitary system, it embraces elements of both.'[64] Nevertheless features of the ALI project which are praised included statements emphasising the role of capital markets as a source of managerial accountability, the strengthening of shareholders activism and the emphasis on the function of the board of directors being 'oversight' rather than direct involvement in management. In addition Section 3.02 of the ALI report describing the function of the board is considered[65] to represent a summary which is both useful and pertinent to the UK experience. Finally the business judgement rule, as developed in American corporate law is considered as a potentially useful qualification of the duties owed by directors under the recommended increased role for shareholder activism which should not be seen as an 'encouragement to litigate'. It has been argued that 'an understanding of the business judgement rule and its judicial adoption here *(ie in the UK)* would be both appropriate and welcome.'[66]

Ownership structures of European companies lends itself to, and facilitates the extension of stakeholder rights to employees. The European ownership structure utilises substantial monitoring mechanisms in any event and therefore including employees as a monitoring stakeholder group seems less intrusive. On the other hand, the ownership structure of US companies has led to a much more private notion of ownership of corporate wealth, with shareholders as the sole and rather passive monitoring group. This environment, it is argued, makes it much more difficult to develop and nurture the concepts of corporate social responsibility, a term used here to indicate a willingness to extend the benefits of management decisions to other stakeholders. Paradoxically it seems that the diverse public ownership of the US Megacorp, has led to an acceptance of the role of the corporations as a private legal actor rather than a public actor, in relation to the 'other stakeholder' issue. This theoretical understanding of the role of the corporation has had a significant impact on the acceptability of legal and government regulation. The converse conditions seem to pertain in the European

[64] Maw, above p 132. Figures provided by Monks and Minnow, above n 17 derived from the Oxford Analytica survey of the G7 countries referred to above state that 'only 42% of all directors are outsiders and 9% of the largest UK companies have no outside directors at all.' In addition 'institutional investors in the UK hold a larger stake in domestic equities than do their US counterparts. In the UK 67% of equity is held by UK institutions; the comparable figure for the US is 46.8%.'

[65] *Ibid.*

[66] It should be pointed out that a form of the business judgment rule has long been recognised as part of British and Irish company law. In *Smith (Howard) Ltd v Ampol Petroleum Ltd* [1974] AC 821 Lord Wilberforce in the House of Lords stated that in considering the exercise of their powers by directors the courts will examine the 'substantial purpose for which it was exercised, and . . . reach a conclusion whether that purpose was proper or not. In doing so it will necessarily give credit to the bona fide opinion of the directors, if such is found to exist, and will respect their judgment as to matters of management.' Similarly in a much older Irish case of *Clark v Workman* 1920 1 IR 107 Ross J stated that it had been 'contended that the Court has no jurisdiction to interfere in a question of internal management. That proposition cannot be disputed. The Court has no right to say how much is to be distributed in dividends, or how much is to be added to the reserve account; what contracts for material are to be accepted, what remuneration is to be paid to their employees, and such like. All these things must be dealt with by the directors, and no Court can interfere so long as they are acting within their powers.'

context. These arguments find empirical support in the fact that of all the European countries it is the UK that has resisted most the further extension of the social policy of the EU.[67] It is interesting that the US publicly-held corporation and companies quoted on the London Stock Exchange seem to share a fundamental distinguishing characteristic ie a wide dispersal of share ownership, the original dispersion described by Berle and Means.[68] There is a consequent resistance to relational monitoring and resistance to state or governmental regulation. European corporations and Japanese corporations do not demonstrate this huge separation of ownership and control. This is significant in terms of how Europeans view ownership and vested interests in the company. The social corporation is in fact more of a reality than it is in either the US or UK.

References in American corporate governance literature to the German experience[69] tend to disregard the fundamentally different nature of corporate ownership in Germany and other continental European countries from that which pertains in the US. American literature has also failed, in the main, to recognise that acceptance of this type of management structure is not confined to Germany but has a wider application in Europe. From a US perspective it is interesting to note that although the experience of the common law countries of Europe are much more similar to the US situation than to the continental European position, the influence of EU law on British and Irish company law and labour law has essentially attempted a type of 'cross-fertilisation,'[70] in some cases with success and in other cases with some difficulties. A consideration of their experience might illustrate the point that one governance model does not necessarily have to supplant the other entirely but that features of one may be imported into the other. This will be of increasing significance in a global economy.

[67] Mark Jeffrey, 'The Commission Proposals on "Atypical Work": Back to the Drawing Board . . . Again' (1995) 24 *Industrial Law Journal* 296. Note Maw, above n 25 p 131 for a fairly typical statement of British resistance:

'No one should compel or exhort national change for the sake of change, or for the sake of an artificial (therefore inevitably unsuccessful) imposed uniformity. In Europe, our structures for and concepts of corporate governance vary, as has been seen, very widely indeed. It would be a lamentable example of empirical and arrogant self- satisfaction for any nation to seek to impose its own systems on its neighbors, even motivated by the best of peaceful and federal objectives.'

[68] Walter Werner, 'Corporation Law in Search of its Future' (1981) 81 *Columbia Law Review* 1611 where the notion that this dispersal of ownership and control is a perversion of the original structure of the corporation is described as the 'erosion doctrine'. Werner disagrees with this doctrine and argues that it was not necessarily envisaged that property and control should remain under a unified possession.

[69] See the work of O'Connor, and Van Wetzel Stone referred to in ch 5.

[70] Monks and Minnow, above n 18 p 270 ff are of the opinion that comparative corporate governance raises vital issues regarding international trade. Stating that 'it is a mistake to attempt to impose one country's corporate governance system on another's' (a view that would be supported here) they nevertheless argue that there are indications that governance practices will 'increasingly converge' in the context of the increased 'globalisation of capital' indicating the availability of international investment opportunities and that certain issues such as dividend policies and disclosure regulations will be decisive in this competition for investment. Given the fundamentally different nature of corporate ownership such convergence seems less likely to this writer. See further chs 9 and 10. In addition see OECD International Corporate Governance Project and in particular OECD Steering Group on Corporate Governance, Recent Developments and Trends, April 2001.

9

Corporate Governance and Responsibility

INTRODUCTION

MANY WRITERS INTERESTED in the area of labour law or employment law are quite clear that there are problems within labour markets.[1] Sociologists,[2] have indicated the many different social problems, which have resulted from demands placed by the corporation on its employees. The position of the European worker seems to be more protected by legislation providing positive rights such as rights against unjust discharge, and positive mandated rights to leave, both vacation leave and family leave. Although these kinds of issues are commonly associated with the study of labour law, there are fundamental issues on the corporate law side of the debate relating to the responsibility of corporations in this area and the accountability of management in this regard. In effect a coherent policy-based approach which in fact yields the individually beneficial outcomes regarding particular labour law or employment law standards, is more likely to be located in our understanding of *corporate function*. Justification for state intervention to constrain corporate actions and in particular to mandate labour standards is ultimately located in our understanding of the range of possible answers to issues raised by the corporate governance debate.

This of course leads to the question: what are the interests of the corporation and what is the function of the corporation? The usual answer provided by the makers of these decisions, and indeed the orthodox answer, is that the interests of the corporation are the same as the interests of the shareholders and the function of the corporation is to maximise the wealth of these shareholders. In the context of the diversity of share ownership under the Anglo-American model it

[1] See for example writers such as Robert Reich, 'The Work of Nations' (Simon and Schuster, London, 1991). Richard Freeman, 'Towards an Apartheid Economy' (1996) *Harvard Business Review*; Paul Weiler, 'Governing the Workplace: The Future of Labor' (??? 1990). See generally Willborn *et al*, *Employment Law: Cases and Materials* (Michie Company, Charlottesville, VA, 1993).

[2] Juliet Schor, *The Overworked American: The Unexpected Decline of Leisure* (Basic Books, New York, 1993); Arlie Hoschschild and Anne Machung, *The Second Shift: Working Parents and the Revolution at Home* (Avon Books, New York, 1989).

would seem that the claim of any one individual shareholder with a diversified portfolio represents a comparatively weak interest or claim on the corporation. Such a shareholder would, in the normal course of events be entitled to only a small dividend as a proportion of corporate profits, as compared with the worker so adversely and profoundly affected by decisions, such as a decision to casualise the employment relationship or to close a plant which has provided employment in a region or community for many years. The second type of gain which a shareholder could make from the sale of shares on a public market raises its own set of governance problems, to which we will return.

The interests of the shareholder as narrowly defined does not always reflect or parallel the interests of the corporation when decisions are being made. For example questions should be raised regarding whether decisions to expand into markets, even particularly difficult attempts at global expansion, such as the growing trend of multinational companies to seek locations in China, or for example, on a smaller scale, the huge amount of assets deployed to sponsor sporting or cultural events are really in the interests of shareholders at all. In these sorts of areas there are continuous difficulties in making any direct correlation between the benefits gained by shareholders and the costs involved in the expansion or sponsorship. This is the original problem presented by the corporate governance debate.

It is difficult to answer the simple question as to what the corporate governance debate really is as it means many different things depending on the interests of the writer and, in fact, on the discipline of the writer.[3] Much of the literature is not at all related to issues regarding workers or employee interests and certainly it has taken some time for this issue to be regarded as one of the issues in the primary debate.[4] Nevertheless it is important to keep the fundamental questions of the corporate governance debate clearly in mind:

> Consequently the participants in a firm must have some governance structure to determine three basic questions. First, what are the general sorts of adaptive decisions that will need to be made over time? Second what general normative principle guides

[3] For an entirely different emphasis on the issues addressed by the corporate governance one need only consider some corporate finance works. Thus for example in Steil *et al*, *European Equity Markets: The State of the Union and An Agenda for the Millennium* (Kluwer, London, 1996) the writers address problems presented by lack of liquidity in the European Equity markets as compared with the US equity markets and consider this from the perspective of unavailability of ready capital. For these writers there is a correlation between this lack of liquidity and good governance. This is referred to and discussed in ch 8.The problem therefore presented is how to increase liquidity without sacrificing elements of governance, which are considered superior to the 'US Megacorp' model. See further ch 8.

[4] Thus those writing in the 1990s were primarily concerned with issues regarding accountability of management to shareholders and in discussion of mechanisms which achieved this. However there were some writers interested in this question early on such as O'Connor and Stone, whereas more recently the issue of employee interests and how these are to be addressed has become more 'fashionable.' See generally the Columbia Law School Symposiums dealing specifically with questions of corporate governance and employees. Sloan Project on Corporate Governance: Employees and Corporate Governance (Columbia Law School, 22 November 1996).

decision-making—that is, for whose benefit are decisions to be made? And, third, who within the firm shall make the adaptive decisions?[5]

THE SAME QUESTION: DIFFERENT ANSWERS

At this stage in the corporate governance debate, it is no longer the case that the usual answer provided to the question of corporate function which focuses on shareholder wealth maximisation is the only acceptable one. On a theoretical level at least this view of corporate function which is informed and supported by an analysis of corporate law from the perspective of the law and economics school of thought, has suffered considerable erosion. Two significant events have occurred in this regard.

Firstly, it is clear that the law and economics analysis of corporate governance issues, even within its own terms, has been losing ground in the face of changing external circumstances. In the 1980s when the hostile take-over era was in full swing in the US the market for corporate control presented a ready answer to the agency problems identified by corporate governance analysts influenced by the law and economics scholars. However as this type of activity has abated there has been a move away from the capital markets theory to a more 'political model of corporate governance'[6] which has placed a greater emphasis on internal mechanisms for control such as activist shareholder participation. In this changing climate, where the focus is on a re-configuration of the role of institutional investors, a greater potential exists to consider structures, which could allow for internal representation of other constituencies, particularly employees. Thus employees can gain access to control and participation opportunities through the use of share ownership structures, placing themselves or their organisations in the same shoes as other activist shareholders. Other opportunities are also offered within the context of internal restructuring to enable employees *as employees* to use the same participatory and control mechanisms used by activist shareholders without being shareholders—for example the election of employee representatives on to boards.

Law and economics scholars seem to confuse two meanings of efficiency. Firstly, efficiency is being used as a term of art, based on Pareto optimality, by law and economics theorists to present an ex-post facto theoretical explanation for why things are as they are, focusing on the individual as a rational wealth maximiser who by definition seeks efficient outcomes. This is the descriptive

[5] Michael P Dooley, 'Two Models of Corporate Governance' (1992) 47 *Business Law* 461, 466. Dooley goes on to provide some answers: 'The answer to the second question is the same for all capitalist firms—decisions are to be made to benefit the interests of the residual claimants because maximising their wealth necessarily maximises the wealth of the coalition. The first and third questions are closely related, but here answers differ depending on the salient characteristics of the type of firm in question.'

[6] See John Pound, 'The Rise of the Political Model of Corporate Governance and Corporate Control' (1993) 68 *New York University Law Review* 1003.

part of the law and economics approach. Secondly, efficiency is being used in the layman's sense to justify present governance structures in the Anglo-American model . . . because the present system has led, the claim goes, to continued economic success stories compared with other structures in other economic regions. I will call this type of efficiency 'practical efficiency'. It should be stated that many law and economics scholars writing on the issues raised in this work point to the European experience as comparing unfavourably with the US in this regard. These two uses of the term efficiency are often confused, or at best compressed, into factual assertions about governance in the US. Thus, statements made by law and economics scholars tend to explain in a theoretical fashion why current legal rules exist but then continue on to conflate the two understandings of efficiency to conclude that therefore these legal rules present the best answers to practical efficiency questions and in this manner conflate the descriptive with the normative.

Secondly, an additional factor which has contributed to the erosion of the dominance of the law and economics analysis is the fact that there has been a huge development in the number of writers offering a different perspective. One commentator has said that it would take a hell of a theory to beat 'this theory'[7] referring to the shareholder wealth maximisation theory, and the many writers who have attempted to describe this theory are closer to that goal. In fact some of the most interesting and thought provoking contributions to the corporate governance debate of the 80s and 90s are provided by those opposing the hitherto dominant view of corporate function. Theorists have provided new ways of considering the question of how we identify efficient outcomes, where such outcomes are no longer identified simply by reference to gains for shareholders, but also by reference to the 'total wealth creating function' of the corporation. A less extreme view of the question of corporate responsibility and management accountability than that posed by law and economics scholars has always been identifiable within judicial pronouncements on this issue.[8] In some ways this would seem to reflect a 'real-world' understanding of the issues involved. This 'real-world' view is also reflected in the writings of academics who are not primarily legal academics but hail instead from business schools or political science faculties.

Nevertheless, despite these developments, in the Anglo-American model, the shareholder wealth maximisation paradigm and the market for corporate con-

[7] See William W Bratton, 'Confronting the Ethical Case against the Ethical Case for Constituency Rights' (1993) 50 *Washington and Lee Law Review* 1464.

[8] For example see Lambros J in *US States Steelworkers v United States Steel* 631 F 2d 1264, 1279 (6th Cir, 1980) . The opinion of the lower court in *Ypsilanti v General Motors Corp* (Cir Ct Washtenaw County, Mich 2.09.1993) referred to extensively in Marleen A O'Connor, 'Promoting Economic Justice in Plant Closings: Explaining the Fiduciary/Contract Law Distinction to Enforce Implicit Employment Agreements' in Lawrence E Mitchell (ed), *Progressive Corporate Law* (Westview Press, Boulder, CO, 1995). See also *Ypsilanti v General Motors Corp* 506 NW 2d 566 (Mich Ct App 1993). See also William T Allen, 'Contracts and Communities' (1993) 50 *Washington and Lee Law Review* 1.

trol as a monitoring device are dominant in the sphere of activity where legal analysis meets actual legislative activity. This phenomenon, particularly in terms of legislative activity, can be contrasted with the European response.

The European Experience

In considering the American worker, it seemed clear that 'incidents of ownership' have been accorded, over time, and through legislation to his European counterpart. The accordance of some degree of job security in this manner is only one of the incidents of ownership which have been argued for. Firm-specific investment of employees should entitle them to property rights such as security from unjust discharge. In addition security or protection should be provided from unjustified or ill-conceived managerial decisions to lay off workers or to close plants entirely. This does not mean that there should be a legislative prohibition on lay-offs or plant closures, but only that such decisions should be reached with more caution. Thus other incidents include rights to voice and the exercise of some degree of control over management decisions. Critically appraising the legitimacy of such decisions can only be done if we reconsider the role of managerial prerogative within the corporation. Specifically, legislation which accords to employees and their representatives information and consultative rights regarding major management decisions which impact on employees amounts to an erosion of the doctrine of managerial prerogative in its strong form. Protection from hasty decisions to close plants could provide security against unjust selection for lay-off, legislatively mandated monetary compensation for job loss, and legislation ensuring that employees are adequately consulted and informed about such decisions. This kind of legislation has been driven by the European Union Social Policy.

Theoretical Perspectives

The concept of firm-specific investment will not be sufficient to justify the accordance of property rights such as those described *to all employees*. Some employees will not possess the same characteristics as others and will be less able to point to firm-specific investment. Thus if we focus solely on firm-specific investment as a justification for protecting employees the difficulty is that we will have to distinguish, practically on a case-by-case basis, between different kinds of employees. In considering the European experience however, it is clear that there are other justifications for protecting employees. The usual argument made to support legislation mandating such rights for all employees is that this redresses an imbalance of bargaining power as between employee and employer. In the European context this is a widely accepted description of the reality of the employment relationship. Arguments, such as those of Alchian and

Demsetz[9] and others that this imbalance does not exist have very little currency in academic or practising legal circles.[10] Perhaps this is one of the greatest differences between the debates on these issues conducted in the US and the EU.[11]

From the perspective of the American academic, arguments for the accordance of property rights to employees in their jobs in a manner which parallels other areas of property law provide an interesting contrast. Areas, such as the division of family property, where the courts have reversed the normal ownership rules because the court considers one party in a relationship to be at a disadvantage to the other, are instructive. The courts have further justified their interventionist approach through acceptance of the argument that such inequality provides opportunities for the exercise of undue influence by one party over another. There is no reason to believe that the same sorts of inequality do not persist in the employment relationship. In fact this inequality in the employment relationship is recognised by legislation in the US and Europe, protecting employees from the effects of various types of discrimination.

The important point is that these kinds of arguments, unlike the arguments regarding firm-specific investment, can be more readily applied across the board

[9] Armen A Alchian and Harold Demsetz, 'Production, Information Costs and Economic Organisation' (1972) 62 *American Economics Review* 777–83. See also RA Epstein, *In Defence of the Contract at Will* (1984) 51 *University of Chicago Law Review* 947.

[10] See, in contrast the considerable body of US literature supporting employment-at-will referred to in J Hoult Verkerke, 'An Empirical Perspective on Indefinite term Employment Contracts: Resolving the Just Cause Debate' (1995) 4 *Wisconsin Law Review* 838. Verkerke adds to this debate by arguing that an empirical study indicated a marked preference for employment-at-will amongst US non-union employees. It is further argued in this article that courts and legislatures should 'reject mandatory rules and reaffirm the at will default.' Verkerke tackles a number of arguments usually made in support of a 'just cause' rule. It is argued here, however, that the extrapolations made from the data are not justified precisely because the data have been collated in the context of an unequal bargaining relationship. The inequality of the employment relationship theoretically underpins most 'just cause' protection in European countries. For example, Verkerke states that contrary to the claim that unequal bargaining power prevents employees from obtaining 'just cause' protection there is no evidence that those employees 'with many alternative opportunities contract expressly for just cause.' However the employees indicated here are not primarily at risk because of inequalities in the power relationship between them and the employer. They are in effect in a 'seller's market'. Laws providing for 'just cause' rules attempt to protect a less fortunate, less powerful group of employees who are vulnerable precisely because there are not many alternatives presented to them. Despite the considerable body of literature in this regard in the US, the employment-at-will doctrine is, from the perspective of a European lawyer surprisingly dominant. For a flavour of the contrasting argument see J Wilson Parker, 'At Will Employment and the Common Law: A Modest Proposal to De-Marginalize Employment Law' (1995) 81 *Iowa Law Review* 347. The author notes that within the debate on employment-at-will both opponents and proponents of the doctrine closely identify the development of the doctrine with capitalist ideology. The author 'eschews purely political explanations' for the doctrine and in my view rightly so. The European capitalist experience demonstrates that 'just cause' legislation is not necessarily derived from any political view.

[11] It is clear from the documents emanating from the EU Commission regarding unemployment that the most trenchant criticism has been received by social security schemes rather than employment legislation per se. So for example unrest in France regarding that country's particularly high unemployment rates of 12% has tended to underline complaints from employers that the cost of competing with social security rates in terms of wage levels and funding social security benefits through taxation have stultified their ability to compete. Importantly the lack of ability of employers to provide employment is not attributed to workers' benefits once employed.

to all employees. In particular these arguments will apply most clearly to the least skilled, least qualified, and least represented employee over others. Thus this theory also serves a secondary purpose in allowing us to extend protection to those most likely to suffer from an abuse of power by the employer. In this way the inequality of bargaining argument allows us to extend these sorts of property rights to employees in a way which accords with our sense of fairness and justice. The consideration of the ethical corporation in this work is pertinent in this regard.

In the context of the corporate governance debate there is however, a third rationale for according the employee property rights in his job. It has been argued here that other incidents of ownership, which could and should be accorded to the employee, include rights of voice and control. This can be achieved by legislation mandating many different kinds of structures facilitating management-labour dialogue, including representation on boards of directors, consultation rights regarding lay-offs and closures, the establishment of works councils and so on.[12] (Interestingly it could very legitimately be argued that both types of concern can be answered by a healthy and responsible trade union movement.) Apart from considering according these rights to employees because they have a moral entitlement to them, it is also clear that there are good reasons for providing such rights to employees from an efficiency perspective. Writers such as Ghilarducci and Craypo referred to in chapter five[13] accept that there is considerable evidence to suggest that such structures contribute to morale, employee loyalty and productivity. However, if any of these arguments persuade the reader that participatory structures should be employed such structures cannot operate without the support of the 'floor of rights' approach, in particular protection from unjust discharge or discharge without cause. Similarly, O'Connor observes[14] that international competition experienced by US corporations has led to a move away from adversarial labour relations to other forms or structures which seek to 'promote innovative shopfloor practices that rely upon flexible, team-based production methods.' O'Connor notes that there is a perception that such practices may increase productivity. However O'Connor identifies the difficulty that:

> At the same time that managers attempt to create co-operative workplace atmospheres, market pressures force managers to implement rapid corporate reconfigurations that threaten job security. This environment of increasing employment insecurity undermines efforts to reform shop-floor practices because workers are understandably reluctant to invest in more firm-specific skills.[15]

Whilst agreeing with O'Connor's analysis I do not agree with her proposals to resolve these issues through the use of the fiduciary principle.

[12] See ch 4.
[13] See ch 5.
[14] O'Connor, above n 8 p 234.
[15] *Ibid.*

Of course it seems that the argument for the accordance of all these rights has effectively been won in the European context. In fact arguments made against the accordance of any of these basic rights do not have substantial support at any level within the fora in which this debate takes place, whether these arguments emanate from the academy or from the business world.

Nevertheless, although a great deal of faith has been placed in the progression of social policy at EU level, doubts have been expressed. Resistance is growing to the continued extension of social policy programmes and this resistance is couched in the same theoretical and pragmatic terms as arguments supporting resistance to any type of legislative interference in the employment relationship in the US. In addition, the continuing problems of unemployment experienced by European countries continue to provide a foundation for doubts about the direction of the social policy. The problem of high levels of unemployment in European countries is referred to in the next chapter.

DIFFERENT FORMS OF CAPITALISM

The question of who actually are the shareholders in a typical European corporation, as compared with the US corporation, was examined on the hypothesis that answers to this question might throw some light on the sorts of ownership claims made by shareholders in each corporation, and on the consequent approaches to the issue of corporate responsibility. Similarly such information could add to our understanding of the issues surrounding management accountability or corporate responsibility to stakeholders other than shareholders. It is clear that the nature of ownership of large EU companies is quite different from that of US companies. Ownership of the EU corporation is much more concentrated, and there is much less ownership diversity. It is hard to see why this fact in and of itself would have any impact on the European understanding of the function of the corporation, or on the claims of shareholders as residual claimants. Surely these claims would be the same regardless of the number of shareholders and the size of their holdings? In other words there is no reason to suppose that the smaller group of shareholders in a European corporation would not make similar demands on management in relation to generating profits as larger groups of shareholders in US corporations. Owners generally would prefer their assets to be put to the best and most profitable use and so we should expect that similar decisions in relation to employee rights of job security and other benefits such as leave, rights to control and voice would be made. It is clear however, that over time substantially different responses to the question of the role of the employee has emerged.

The different ownership structure within the European corporation is present, of course, in tandem with the existence of equity markets possessing substantially different characteristics to those in the US. Thus it would seem that a substantial difference arises in relation to the understanding of the function of the markets in corporate governance. If we accept, for the moment, the hypothesis of the capital markets theory of accountability popular in US literature on corporate governance, it is clear that this same theory of governance could not apply to the European equity markets. It has been demonstrated that the same characteristics of diversity of ownership and investment portfolio are simply not present amongst European investors. Thus Steil *et al*[16] make the distinction between

> two generic approaches to the classic agency problem: either one or more investors are given influence over strategic decisions in the firm (control-oriented finance), or management finds ways of committing to efficient actions and to share in the proceeds from these actions (arm's-length) finance.

They note that under the former model intervention may take the form of vetoing inefficient investment decisions, or ousting incumbent management by using a voting majority. In the case of the latter model intervention 'typically involves some external mechanism such as the market for corporate control, or a court in the case of bankruptcy.' Having noted these differences it is interesting to note that in their work which focuses on many different aspects of the European equity markets Steil *et al* are clearly of the opinion that there is a liquidity/control trade-off in relation to the operation of the markets and that the European system in fact provides the opportunity for better control for the investor.[17]

This comparative exercise leaves us with an interesting question: that is, that if there is a similar class of residual claimants in both the European and US corporate structure and if there are similar opportunities for exercising control, albeit through different mechanisms in both structures, (*with the exception* that the European investor seems to be in a position to exercise even more control than his US counterpart) why do we have these different outcomes regarding the interests of one class of stakeholder—the employee? In fact if there is *more* control exercised by the European investor one would expect to see *less* managerial prerogative on the question of employee interests.

WHAT DO SHAREHOLDERS OR RESIDUAL CLAIMANTS REALLY WANT?

There are two possible answers to the question raised in the last part. Firstly it is possible that shareholders (or perhaps only European shareholders) do not object as strongly as is currently supposed to the accordance of certain incidents of ownership to employees. Perhaps it is understood that according employees these kinds of rights has a positive impact, not only on the corporation, but also on other tangential issues in society. In this vein one might therefore hypothesise that US managers are only second-guessing the views of investors as expressed

[16] Steil *et al*, above n 3 p 154–55.
[17] See further ch 8,

through the markets, and that in fact they are either misreading market signals, or over emphasising the correlation between movements in price shares and managerial responses to employment issues. More bluntly it could be argued that the market is simply an inadequate control device, particularly in relation to management responses to other stakeholder issues. In this regard it is also interesting to note that in my consideration of institutional investor activism managerial responses to employment issues did not seem to be high on the list of issues which activist institutional shareholders have sought to address. In effect there have been no demands placed on management by organisations such as the Council for Institutional Investors to make 'cost-cutting' decisions regarding employment benefits or structures.

The second answer to why there is such a difference in outcomes regarding employee interests within the US and EU corporate structures has to do with governmental policy and state control over the corporation, or put alternatively, to the role of regulation. This issue goes back to the question of whether the corporation should be regarded as a private or public actor. It is accepted in the policy documents of the EU that corporations play a public role in relation to the many issues addressed under the rubric of EU social policy and in relation to other economic policy issues. The corporation is not considered to be simply a private actor in the market place and this is accepted. The acceptance of the corporation as a public actor of course immediately assumes legitimacy for the efforts of the legislatures (both national and supra-national) to regulate corporate activity as it effects many different aspects of life, not least the welfare of EU workers. For example, whilst European corporations are considered to be successful competitors in the global market unemployment is still seen as a persistent European problem.[18] Nevertheless EU policy makers are insistent on advancing the progress of the Social Policy despite the claims of some within Europe that rigidities in the labour market prevent job creation. However it seems that the rigidities caused by welfare legislation rather than 'floor of rights' type labour legislation is considered to be more at fault.[19] To address this a summit was held in Luxembourg in December 1997 to consider the problems of unemployment throughout Europe. It is clear that despite worries and concerns addressed at the Luxembourg summit most Europeans are committed to a par-

[18] The EU average rate of unemployment is stated to be 8.2% by Eurostat figures provided in September 2000. In the decade 1991–2000, it has varied between 8.2% and 11%. Interestingly however, despite similar legal environments the figures vary considerably from country to country with Luxembourg at around 3.7% and Denmark at 5.8% at the lower end of the spectrum with Italy 12.1%, France 12.6% and Spain 19.9%. In fact countries such as Luxembourg and the Netherlands (5.4%) where the figures are very low provide over the minimum level of employee protection required by EU law.

[19] M Mathiopoulos, *The Closed Society and its Friends* (??? 1997) where the author considers issues surrounding the future of the German economy and faults what she terms the 'welfare dictatorship' for some of the present ills such as the 10% German unemployment figures. In addition the 'welfare dictatorship' is stifling innovation and leading to the 'social and economic petrifaction of Germany'. The author is of the view that Germany should adopt some of the characteristics of the undiluted capitalism of America.

ticular social vision which includes provision of extensive welfare to its citizens[20] and a great deal of corporate participation in public policy making.[21] In contrast in the US, Allen clearly identified a dominant political philosophy underpinning the activities of corporate America which had, as one of its elements, a resistance to statist intervention. In general such resistance is regarded as fundamental to the law and economics analysis of corporate governance. Yet resistance to state intervention has in reality had a chequered career in the US. Thus we see a high level of regulation of corporate activity in certain areas including for example activities concerning securities transactions and activities which have an impact on environmental issues. Despite these examples, resistance to state intervention in relation to issues of employee welfare is trenchant, in certain sectors at least.

FUTURE STRATEGIES

Practical proposals are also important. These proposals involve the tempering of management decisions justified by reference to the shareholder wealth maximisation principle through legislatively mandated employee protection devices such as legislation prohibiting dismissal without cause. Other approaches consider the restructuring of internal corporate structures to facilitate employee representation. One underlying imperative exists and that is the acceptance that the corporation is indeed a public actor in relation to employee welfare issues. As such the corporation is subject to government regulation in pursuit of goals which may have little immediate effect on generating wealth for shareholders, but much to do with striking a desirable balance between this goal and the broader concerns of government and society.

[20] A discussion of welfare or the US Social Security provisions in any detail is outside the scope of this work. It would seem, however, that it is not actually employee protection or participation legislation, which affects employment figures insofar as the legal environment has any impact at all. It seems more probable that extensive welfare legislation has a more direct impact on firstly how unemployment figures are calculated, secondly on the willingness of individuals to become employed in badly paid jobs, and thirdly on the ability of employers to create attractive jobs at the lower end of the wage scale. In this latter regard the provision of extensive social welfare benefits in effect creates a minimum wage which employer groups sometimes claim to be unable to compete with at the lower end of the jobs market. These issues have more resonance when one considers the phenomenon of the 'working poor' in the US which is described in ch 1.

[21] In the December 1997 bulletin from European Information Service it was stated that the European Commission has approved guidelines for member states in relation to employment policies following the European Jobs Summit in Luxembourg in November. The bulletin notes that the guidelines set out a number of specific targets for member states, including targets for re-starting the employment of young and long-term unemployed people and targets regarding access to training for the unemployed. The bulletin also notes that it is clearly stated by the Commission that the employment policies are based on '*the four pillars of employability, entrepreneurship, adaptability and equal opportunities*'. Note that prior to the formal adoption by the Commission of the employment strategies, the Economic and Social Committee of the Commission had issued an opinion: OJ C287 22/09/1997 P.008 where the Committee had again emphasised the importance of the relationship between social policy 'and the social security schemes that spring from it' and economic policy.

It seems that to best protect the interests of employees a combination of some features discussed in chapters four and five might be most likely to yield the best results. Thus providing employees through mandated legislation with what is often referred to as 'a floor of rights' would seem vital. As in Europe, it would seem these would have to take place in the United States at a Federal level to prevent the 'race to the bottom' problems already discussed in the context of corporate law. Protection from dismissal without cause would seem to be an essential and simple device to underline firm-specific investment by employees in a firm and furthermore to encourage such investment. Not only does this kind of legislation achieve this purpose but such a proposal provides an indispensable building block towards the sort of loyalty or trust required to promote employee commitment and productivity in a wider sense. An employee will be less likely to contribute ideas or opinions (especially good ones!) where he or she has no belief that an equal commitment is being made by his company to him. Similarly, an employee may be discouraged from contributing through fear of reprisal through dismissal. Thus it has been argued here that participatory models of any type must be supported by certainly minimum elements of what has been described as the Proprietorial Interest Model.[22]

Participatory models may take a number of different forms. Included are any structures mandating representation of employees on boards and any structures such as works councils involving legislatively mandated representation of workers and management at certain corporate levels. Also included however, would be any form of participation conducted through traditional trade union channels which could arguably be as effective as either of the former type of model if fostered in the right manner. Participatory models seem to contribute to the overall efficiency of the corporation.

There are other reasons why according a 'floor of rights' beyond simply protection from unjust discharge to include mandated leave rights, regulation of working hours and atypical labour contracts seem appropriate. This takes us back to the issue of the function of the corporation. Thus if we have the view, justified by reference to any number of different theories that the corporation has a public function, in contributing to the creation of well-paying, high quality jobs providing sustained employment opportunities with good working conditions we will accept that it is necessary for the corporation and management to take part in public discourse as to the nature of work and the welfare of employees. This goes to our understanding of the ethical function of the corporation.

[22] In combining certain features of co-determination models O'Connor argues that her 'neutral referee model' which she describes as a variation on co-determination would be supplemented by directors' fiduciary duties to employees obliging directors to inform and consult workers about decisions affecting job security and working conditions. However, as stated, the fiduciary model presents an unattractive alternative to reform of contract. O'Connor admits that elements of her co-determination model are based on the European works council so it is even more difficult to understand her opting for a fiduciary model over a contract model, the latter being an integral part of EU strategy.

The final issue then, in relation to legislative proposals is whether we can ensure accountability of management. This issue will be particularly acute in relation to incidents of ownership, which do not relate to proprietorial interest issues, but relate to incidents of control and voice. In other words, how do we ensure that even if we establish consultative and information structures for employees, that management will seriously consider and pay heed to employee input? The fiduciary model purports to provide an answer here. The employee to whom the fiduciary duty is owed can sue to enforce the obligations imposed on management to consider their interests. Unfortunately it is not clear how such a duty would be clearly articulated by the courts or enforced on a case by case basis. Interestingly trade union representation supported by the collective action of groups of employees seems to provide a clear and practical solution here. A parallel can be drawn here with the apparent control exercised over management through the markets, and of course more latterly through activist institutional shareholding—the axiom that the shareholder will vote with their feet on the performance of management may equally apply to a unionised workforce supported by the collective organisation and protected from reprisal by management. It is by no means intended to propose trade unionism as a panacea for all ills but simply in light of its critical demise in the US to highlight some of its advantages.[23]

Finally, it is clear from the European experience that legislation creates a different context over time and eventually reshapes public understanding so that even where obligations are not legally enforced a contextually different approach and understanding are brought to bear.

[23] On this point Rogers makes interesting comparisons between the type of trade unionism prevalent in the US compared with European countries, both displaying substantially different characteristics. Thus in Europe Rogers notes that high density centralised unionism is much more prevalent compared with what he terms a low-density decentralised union movement, which is found in the US. Rogers goes on to note differences between these systems. In high density systems there will usually be sectoral and national level bargaining agreements and 'more generic political regulation of the labor market' Because of the presence of 'society-wide terms' imposed on employers, they do not regard trade unions as a burden but more of the normal costs of doing business. Similarly Rogers is of the view that because the trade unions in HDCU contexts are more 'secure in their social position' they are more 'willing to make sure that business was done.' See further Joel Rogers, 'Reforming US Labor Relations' (1993) 69 *Chicago-Kent Law Review* 97, 103. The modern European approach emphasises the positive benefits of this type of approach and continues to foster the social partnership elements to the relationship. Rogers has observed this phenomenon himself: 'In such systems, labor and management appeared, in stark contrast to the United States, as genuine "social partners"-intent on improving economic performance within certain social bounds . . ."

10

The Global Corporation: Does Governance Matter?

THE IDEA THAT there are two forms of capitalism—the European model and the US model—is now becoming a matter for extensive debate, even to the extent that it is now being considered in popular publications.[1] In considering comparative corporate governance models it is clear that there is some correlation between ownership structures, consequent governance models and in turn outcomes in relation to the position of employees. There is an impact on the facility with which employees can be included as stakeholders, or to put this in an alternative way, the facility with which employees can be accorded certain 'incidents of ownership.' Although many US corporate governance scholars refer to either the Japanese corporate governance model, or to the German model, it is now more appropriate to consider a European governance model.[2] The fact that there are two competing forms of capitalism has a number of consequences.

GLOBAL COMPETITIVENESS

The first issue to be considered is the issue of competitiveness. Writers in the corporate governance area who defend the 'US Megacorp' model of corporate

[1] See Sally Wheeler, *The Third Way* (Hart Publishing, Oxford, 2001). For example *Time* magazine ran an article in December 1997 regarding the European search for what it termed the 'Third Way'. *Time*, 13 Dec 1997. Overstating the idea that the European Jobs Summit represented a departure from established European policies to some other Third Way, (which is not really the case) the article nevertheless adopted the idea that there are two fundamentally different approaches to many social issues represented in the US and EU model: 'The current search for the Third Way shows that . . . though the days of high growth, excessive welfare benefits and jobs for life may be over, the American model—with its economic brutalities and social fractures—is not inevitable. . . . Europeans can chart their own course through the changing landscape of the new global economy—but only if they have the brains, the heart and the nerve.'

[2] Thus for example in a collection of articles prepared for a Conference on Employees and Corporate Governance at Columbia Law School in November 1996 only one out of ten articles referred to the European experience as a distinct experience and this was in a rather dismissive, disparaging manner: 'The persistently high unemployment rates in the welfare-state economies of Western Europe, likely due in part to labor market rigidities resulting from employee-protective legislation, remind us that no law yet devised can protect employees against perhaps the largest risk they face-not being hired in the first place.' Sloan Project on Corporate Governance: Employees and Corporate Governance, (Columbia Law School, 22 November 1996).

governance are fond of the argument that given the productivity figures for the last decade and a half for the American worker as compared with every other worker, the US approach must be the superior approach.[3] Others are not so sure. Michael Jensen, in an article written in 1993,[4] underlines the fact that macroeconomic data from the 1980s show major productivity gains, noting that in the period 1981–1990 '[N]ominal unit labor costs stopped their 17-year rise, and real unit labor costs declined by 25% . . . and that these came . . . from increased productivity.' However Jensen, although a supporter of the market as a control device, notes that this period is now unique in that it was the period of the hostile take-over. He also realises that this period is 'generally portrayed by politicians, the media and others as a decade of greed and excess' despite the 'gains in productivity, efficiency and welfare' which he describes. Jensen refers to Lipton as expressing a common view of the 1980s when he has claimed that the take-over activity of the 1980s 'imposed short-term profit maximisation strategies on American Business at the expense of research and development and capital investment.' Lipton is also of that view that this phenomenon has reduced the ability of US companies 'to compete in world markets and *still maintain a growing standard of living at home*.' (My emphasis).[5] In the same article Jensen expresses the opinion that the problems which the market for control sought to address are still present in the US: 'Throughout corporate America, the problems that motivated much of the control activity of the 1980s are now reflected in lacklustre performance, financial distress, and pressures for restructuring.'[6] Reviewing other economic indicators based on OECD compilation of national accounts there is no reason to assert that the US is fairing *significantly* better than Europe. Figures[7] for 1998, 1999 and 2000 indicate the

[3] See for example Bainbridge, Macey and Miller, referred to in ch 7.

[4] Michael Jensen, 'The Modern Industrial Revolution, Exit and Control Systems' (1993) 48 *Journal of Finance* 831, 837.

[5] Mark Lipton, 'Corporate Governance: Major Issues for the 1990s' (Address to the Third Annual Corporate Finance Forum at the J Ira Harris Center for the Study of Corporate Finance, University of Michigan School of Business (6 April 1989) referred to in Jensen *ibid* n 4 at p 837. Jensen describes Lipton as a 'prominent defender of American CEOs'.

[6] Jensen, *ibid* n 4 at p 852. Jensen describes 4 different types of control, which can be exercised on the corporation including capital markets; legal/political/regulatory controls; product and factor markets and internal control systems operated by the board. Noting that the era of the capital markets has come to an end amid 'intense controversy and opposition from corporate managers', assisted by charges of fraud, insider dealing and the rise in bankruptcies, Jensen is of the opinion that the legal control is 'too blunt an instrument to handle the problems of wasteful managerial behaviour'; that product and factor markets are 'too slow to act as a control force' and posits that 'the internal control systems of publicly held corporations have generally failed to cause managers to maximise efficiency and value.'

[7] OECD Economic Outlook, May 2001. It appears that growth in GDP figures for the period 1990–1996 has been similar in the US and the EU15 except that the actual figures are higher in the EU. OECD National Accounts Vol 1 (1996) 10–12.Comparing import and export figures for 1994 in billions of US dollars EU15 exported 2057.28 compared with 706.40 for the US and EU15 imported 1941.64 compared with US 816.90. Similar figures pertain for 1993. It is interesting to note that US import figures are higher than export figures, which is not the case for the EU15. See further OECD National Accounts Vol 1 (1996) 120–132.

percentage growth of GDP as 3.4 per cent for EU15 and 4.2 per cent for the US. Interestingly there is some variation as between member states of the EU, despite similar labour market structures, with Ireland displaying an average growth of 9 per cent between 1994 and 2000 and other countries figures much closer to the average. In fact in some cases the contrary proposition pertains. Thus we can only assume that the market for corporate control theory, in identifying an effective monitoring device, is not borne out by reality.

Leaving the actual figures aside two important points should be made. Firstly the EU15 is now a much bigger trading block than the US with a greater workforce than that of the US, and it continues to grow.[8] There are no similar possibilities for the growth of the US. Thus it is important to understand the significance of the claims made here in relation to a European governance model. The characteristics of that governance model cannot be dismissed as simply the rather eccentric quasi-socialist inclinations of one country. In fact the EU model represents a committed and extensive implementation of a different strategy amongst many of the most important trading countries and corporations in the world:

> The United States is no longer hegemonic in economic terms. Its share of world output has dropped below a quarter and its share of trade is even less. The EU is larger on both counts and the creation of the euro will end America's monetary dominance.[9]

Secondly comparing US with EU15 figures, there is no basis for concluding that EU15 is faring worse than the US on the basis of any significant indicator with the exception of unemployment figures. This is certainly offset by the US phenomenon of the 'working poor'.[10] In relation to overall corporate performance there does not seem to be any justification for the proposition that current governance structures within the European company have had any negative impact on comparisons with US corporations. Thus it is most probably the case that corporate governance models, *particularly regarding the inclusion of other stakeholders*, are of relatively small importance in relation to overall corporate performance. Arguably this would certainly be the case compared with other factors such as management of new product development, market competitiveness, use of technology and other management techniques such as just-in-time manufacturing, in addition to external environmental factors. In other words it could be the case that different corporate governance models are neither significantly

[8] At the Luxembourg Summit in 1997 the accession of a number of former Eastern European countries was agreed to in principle, including Poland and The Czech Republic. This is now reflected in the terms of the Nice Treaty 2000 awaiting ratification by members states. The current population of EU15 is 375 millon, 1.4 times approximately the population of the US, although interestingly the geographic area is one third the size of the US. www.usatrade.gov

[9] Michael Bergstein, 'American Politics; Global Trade: Clinton Fast-Track to Negotiate Trade Agreement' *The Economist* 27 Sept. 1997.

[10] See further ch 1.

efficient nor inefficient in the real sense of the word.[11] In similar fashion Charny, in answer to the question of whether worker-managerialist institutions contribute to firm value, canvasses the possibility of what he calls 'multiple equilibria' in the relationship of workers to issues of corporate governance in advanced industrialised countries. These 'multiple institutional solutions . . . are both stable in themselves and are not likely to be improved by small changes in the direction of greater or lesser participation.'[12]

Although considering the role of employees as stakeholders is the focus of this work, choice of overall governance system has become an increasingly important issue in relation to the development of emerging economies. The OECD Project on Governance and the Report of the World Bank, previously referred to in chapter eight, highlight important features of any governance system. The latter acknowledges that 'there is no one size fits all blueprint for corporate governance.'

THE GLOBAL ECONOMY AND THE WORKER

At Home

If we hypothesise for the moment that efficiency and performance are not significantly affected by governance structures either in an adverse or negative way we must then question whether there are other reasons for considering changes. Charny, for example considers, an additional question as to the role of law in constituting governance systems and in answering this question he makes a number of important points. Noting, that for the well informed contractor, law is probably largely irrelevant he states that 'law has an important role to play, however, in settings where the parties are poorly informed or face barriers to transactional co-operation.' This will apply to the employment relationship where many employees will not be equal to the employer in terms of information available to them. But Charny highlights a different kind of informational problem which also exists, and that is that over time, in an employment situation unanticipated circumstances will arise, leaving both the employee and the employer at a disadvantage. Against this background Charny argues that

[11] This seems to be borne out by two important studies in this area: Klaus Gugler (ed) *Corporate Governance and Economic Performance* (Oxford University Press, Oxford, 2001) and Fabirizio Barca and Marco Becht (eds), The Control of Corporate Europe (Oxford University Press, Oxford, 2001). See ch 3 on the meaning of efficiency. However, reference has been made in this work to many commentators who hold the contrary view that participation in particular yields significant outcomes in relation to corporate performance.

[12] David Charny, 'Workers and Corporate Governance: The Role of Political Culture' in Sloan Project on Corporate Governance: Employees and Corporate Governance (Columbia Law School, 22 November 1996). However, it should be noted that Charny cites no figures in this article to support these assertions.

> the advantage of legally mandated institutions is that they serve as fixed reference points for exploration of future possibilities, while (if properly structured) remaining open to deliberate revision of institutional role.[13]

There are other reasons for supporting legally mandated worker governance systems proffered by Charny, which resonate with themes explored here. He argues, in apparent contradiction of his earlier assertion regarding 'multiple equilibria', that worker governance 'may while *increasing firm value* (my emphasis) also permit diversion of a larger share of surplus to workers as a group' and that because shareholders or managers may wish to avoid such redistribution such structures should be mandated. It is hoped that this work may have convinced some readers of the value of such a view. Most importantly Charny is of the view that the effectiveness of worker governance structures may depend in many cases on a 'highly reticulated set of supportive background institutions' such as trade unions and financial monitors and 'public institutions for social welfare entitlements.'[14] These statements resonate with many aspects of EU policy, which as described earlier, take a more 'holistic' approach to many of the issues raised, whether these pertain to competitiveness, economic policy or social policy. Thus questions of the proper role of the corporation, corporate responsibility and management accountability are regarded as only parts in the puzzle. Implicitly recognising that there are considerable public choice issues here Charny states that individual firms cannot create the necessary supportive institutions, which he has briefly described. These institutions are 'products of political action.'[15]

Therefore we have at least four additional reasons why governance structures should be reconsidered. Firstly, to reverse informational imbalances within the employment relationship. Secondly, to allow greater ability to adapt to changing circumstances in the corporate environment which would not have been anticipated by either party in the employment relationship. Thirdly, to allow for redistribution of the increase in firm value achieved through worker governance systems. Fourthly, worker governance structures should be altered to allow for a redistribution of corporate wealth on a more equitable basis in any event, ie regardless of whether redesigned governance systems significantly increase firm value.

Professor Freeman[16] also considers the claim that there is a more equitable approach to the redistribution of corporate wealth. He considers issues which

[13] *Ibid* p 26.

[14] See Alan Hyde, 'In Defense of Employee Ownership' (1991) 67 *Chicago-Kent Law Review* 159.

[15] In a recent paper Charny hypothesises that inter-jurisdictional competition may exert substantial pressure 'on rules with distributive impacts' and argues that democratic theory and a 'commitment to global equity' may call for the transnational setting of labour standards. D Charny, 'Regulatory Competition and the Global Coordination of Labor Standards' (2000) 3 *Journal of Interntional Economic Law* 281.

[16] Professor Freeman is the Herbert Ascherman Professor of Economic at Harvard University and programme director for labour studies at the National Bureau of Economic Research, Cambridge MA.

are also highlighted by both practical examples provided in chapter one of this work and by the work of sociologists such as Schor which are also referred to in that section. In a somewhat chilling introduction to his article *Toward an Apartheid Economy*[17] Freeman describes the phenomena outlined in the beginning of this work:

> Rising inequality. Stagnant real wages. A declining middle class. High levels of child poverty. Insecure workers. A waning union movement. Homeless people in every city. Bursting jails and prisons. A fraying social safety net.

Accordingly Freeman argues that while the US economy is still performing in relation to productivity, technology leadership and rates of economic growth there is clearly 'something wrong with the US economy' and that is the failure to address the issue of redistribution of the benefits of economic growth. Freeman states that

> For many the rise in AT&T 's stock after it announced plans to lay off 40,000 employees crystallised the picture of an economy gone haywire with shareholders gaining and employees losing as a result of innovation and advances in productivity.

Most significantly Freeman points out that amidst the apparent economic boom there has been a significant decline in real wages amongst workers in the lowest paid category so that, as he states, this 'fall in the real earnings of the low paid means that a substantial number of working men earn less than their fathers did two or three decades ago.' From figures provided by Freeman we can see that the problems of the lowest paid American worker are acute. In the US the male worker in the bottom 10 per cent of the earnings distribution earns 38 per cent of the median worker's income compared with 61 per cent of the median earned by a Japanese worker who is similarly placed and 68 per cent for the European worker. The knock-on effects have been widely debated amongst politicians 'from US secretary of labour Robert Reich on the left to presidential candidate Patrick Buchanan on the right' according to Freeman as well as in the business press and popular media. This work has put forward the argument that efforts to redistribute more fairly the fruits of economic success involve not only the provision of good wages but also the provision of related benefits such as pensions and insurance benefits, other benefits such as job security, mandated leave rights, and others correlating to the incidents of ownership described in chapter three. In addition, the consideration of different models in chapters four and five has pointed us in particular directions because certain solutions seem to work better in protecting employees than others.[18]

[17] Richard Freeman, Toward an Apartheid Economy' (1996) *Harvard Business Review* 114.

[18] In recent papers Freeman has noted the effects of different forms of capitalism but argues also that different institutional structures will provide 'peak status' in relation to some criteria (for example the US in relation to employment and productivity) but not for others (the US record in distribution). National Bureau of Economic Research Working Paper No. w7757 and NBER Working Paper W7556. http://papers.ssrn.com

And Abroad

In a global context the role of multinational corporations have a number of implications for all workers. In the US and in particular in certain sectors, the question is what sort of opportunities are presented to multinational European companies for lower cost production than their European counterparts. This is borne out by the type of experience related in chapter one regarding the location of a BMW plant in South Carolina where the hourly rate employees were to earn at that plant was about half of that earned in Germany. This concern can be countered by the argument that this simply amounts to an investment in jobs, that such investment will continue to encourage economic growth and that this kind of investment is therefore a good thing. However, the argument is not that simple. The big question in relation to the attraction of investment concerns the type of jobs being created.[19] Whether the jobs provided by BMW in South Carolina are the least skilled, least rewarding of the jobs provided by a company such as BMW with all the high skilled, high tech jobs remaining in Germany is an important, not incidental question here. This is particularly so in relation to the US where in the 1950s and 1960s the same type of workers would have been regarded as the best trained, most well paid in the world. In addition, even if the jobs created are providing employment and this employment contributes to economic growth, it is not clear how long this cycle takes. Questions can be legitimately asked regarding the quality of jobs provided in the short term. In other words this phenomenon is not the product of a deliberate policy choice but an accidental by-product of the actions of corporations in relation to their workers over a sustained period of time. Corporations viewed as private actors in the market place are free to regard themselves as having no ethical or legal responsibility for the creation or resolution of these problems.

A converse point can also be made. Obviously investment goes the other way and many American multinationals invest in Europe for a number of different reasons. One of the main reasons is access to the huge and expanding EU market, both in terms of distance and in terms of tariff-free access. Another reason has been also the lower wages paid in certain sectors in Europe. Nevertheless, employees of American multinationals operating in the EU, whether American or European benefit from the different response to employees mandated in Europe. All will enjoy the incidents of ownership described in this work, even to the extent that the US multinational will be obliged to negotiate at a relatively senior level with representatives of European employees through the Works Council system. The same corporate groups will not, however, have to extend the same benefits to their own workers at home. Yet although of great benefit to individual European workers, the accordance of such rights will never be sufficient to deter investment by those companies. In short, for the individual the

[19] See Reich below.

rights are really important, whereas for the corporation these rights are only a very small part of a much bigger set of issues.[20]

A further argument may be that Europe will not sustain this climate in the face of competition from other low cost locations, such as China, where the daily rate of pay is something similar to an hourly rate of pay in Europe. The answer here is that if there are such losses to suffer, the US worker will similarly lose out, and will suffer more. In terms of wage competition in a global economy the US and EU have more in common than not. The competition will be for the high quality, high skilled jobs and the question for each trading bloc is whether they are positioned to compete in that market. The approach taken in the US may not, over time, create an environment which nurtures firm-investment by workers leading to skills training and development. In contrast it seems that EU policy-makers have deliberately addressed their position in a competitive market and have placed themselves in a situation where there has been a concentrated development of high quality, highly skilled workers, supported in a climate where innovation, research and development are encouraged as part of a competitive strategy.

THE GLOBAL FUTURE

Robert Reich has attempted to address some of the issues raised in the brief discussion above. In *The Work of Nations*[21] Reich argues that national identities in terms of corporations will become less and less important as the multinational corporation extends its activities throughout the globe. What will be important for a particular society identified by nationhood will be the *kinds of jobs* available to its citizens. There are, according to Reich, three types of jobs for the future: what he terms the routine production job, the in-person services job and the symbolic-analyst job.[22] The distinctions between these categories and the ability of individuals to perform these tasks depend, according to Reich, almost exclusively on the level of education received by the individual and on the skills brought to bear on the task.

From this analysis, Reich continues to argue that the disparities in earning power currently prevalent in the US, (and in the EU) and which are continuing to grow, arise from the difference in how these three categories of workers have fared in the global economy. Noting what he terms 'important clues' as to the reasons for continuing inequality, Reich refers to the fact that 'the growth in inequality within the United States (as well as in many other nations) has been dramatic even among people who already hold jobs' and that the 'widening

[20] See Charny, above n 15 who provides a useful distinction between what he terms 'purely efficient' rules and 'distributive impacts' arguing that inter-jurisdictional competition is unlikely to affect the former but likely to 'exert substantial pressure' on the latter.

[21] Reich, Robert, *The Work of Nations* (Simon and Schuster, London, 1991).

[22] *Ibid*. See generally ch 14.

income gap is closely related to the level of education.'[23] Developing this argument Reich is of the opinion that when we consider these three different types of jobs we need to ensure that we are aware where the wealth lies in relation to each job. Furthermore we should ensure that the wealth thus created is distributed.

Therefore Reich notes that in terms of generating wages and wealth the routine production job is in decline, under threat from low cost global competition and technological advances; the in-person service job, although not directly threatened by global competition, is under threat from competition from dislocated routine production workers and from the way this job is typically performed, on a part-time basis by women. In contrast the symbolic—analyst is in the ascendant.

CONCLUSION

From this analysis Reich makes a number of policy proposals, particularly in relation to education and training, not all of which, obviously, are relevant to this work. However the following passage is instructive:

> Herein lies the new logic of economic nationalism: The skills of a nation's workforce and the quality of its infrastructure are what makes it unique, and uniquely attractive, in the world economy. Investments in these relatively immobile factors of world-wide production are what chiefly distinguish one nation from another; money by contrast moves easily around the world.
>
> A workforce that is knowledgeable and skilled at doing complex things, and which can easily transport the fruits of its labors into the global economy, will entice global money to it. The enticement can develop into a virtuous relationship: well-trained workers and modern infrastructure attract global webs of enterprise, which invest and give workers relatively good jobs; these jobs in turn, generate additional on-the-job training and experience, thus creating a powerful lure to other global webs. As skills increase and experience accumulates, *a nation's citizens add greater and greater value to the world economy-commanding ever-higher compensation and improving their standard of living.*[24] (emphasis added)

The really important questions in corporate governance are the basic ones. What are the guiding principles in relation to corporate decision-making? For whose benefit are the decisions made and by whom? In relation to workers, a particular case can be made that they should also be considered, along with shareholders, as an important group to benefit from and participate in corporate decisions.

In addition, the answers provided by the different legal and political structures in the US and the EU, and the manner in which these answers are enforced,

[23] *Ibid*. See ch 16 pp 203–05.
[24] *Ibid*. See ch 22 p 265.

have implications beyond the everyday position of the workers themselves. There are implications for the workforce as a whole, for the development of cultures and society and for future success in the context of global competition. For these reasons it is argued here that these questions are too important to be left solely to the corporation to resolve as a private actor. The role of the corporation as a public actor is a question of immediate and growing importance. As Reich points out, the American corporation and its management has become less and less accountable to any of its stakeholders. But this is not entirely accurate, for in fact the American corporation is already understood to be a public actor, and together with its management is subject to a high degree of regulation in relation to issues such as the environment and securities transactions. That is true of the European corporation also except that there is more recognition of employees as stakeholders. In contrast in the US, viewing the corporation as a public actor in relation to issues of employee welfare, does not seem to be an acceptable position to take, with one exception, and that is in relation to discrimination issues. Thus the reality in regard to corporate and management accountability and in relation to the acceptance or otherwise of 'statist intervention' is fragmented. Inherent in this reality are clear and fundamental contradictions within currently dominant corporate law theories.

Bibliography

BOOKS

Applebaum, E and Butt, R. *High Performance Work Systems.*

Barca, Fabrizio and Becht, Marco. *The Control Of Corporate Europe* (eds, Oxford University Press, Oxford, 2001).

Berle, Adolph A Jr and Means, Gardner C. *The Modern Corporation and Private Property* (Commerce Clearing House Inc, New York, 1932).

Blair, Margaret M. *Ownership and Control* (Brookings Institute, Washington DC, 1995).

Reviewed by Lipton, Martin *et al.* 70 N.Y.U.L. Rev. 1144 (1995).

—— *Wealth Creation and Wealth Sharing* (Brookings Institute, Washington DC, 1996).

Blasi, JR. *Employee Ownership, Revolution or Rip-off?* (Ballinger, Cambridge, MA, 1988).

—— *Employee Ownership and Participation: The Facts and the Trends, The Problems and the Policy Options: Analysis for the Clinton Transition Team.*

Cheffins, Brian. *Company Law: Theory, Structure and Operation* (Clarendon Press, Oxford, 1997).

Craig, Paul and De Búrca, Gráinne. *EC Law Text, Cases and Materials* (Clarendon Press, Oxford, 1995).

Davies, Paul and Freedland, Mark. *Cases and Materials on Labour Law* (Weidenfeld and Nicholson, London, 1986).

Dooley, Michael P. *Fundamentals of Corporation Law* (Foundation Press, New York, 1995).

Dorresteijn, Adriaan, Kuiper, Ina, and Morse, Geoffrey. *European Corporate Law* (Kluwer, Deventer, The Netherlands, 1994).

Easterbrook, Frank H and Fischel, Daniel R. *The Eonomic Structure of Corporate Law* (Harvard University Press, Cambridge, Mass, 1991).

Fennell, Caroline and Lynch, Irene. *Labour Law in Ireland* (Gill and MacMillan, Dublin, 1993).

Galambos, L and Pratt J. *The Rise of The Corporate Commonwealth* (Basic Books, New York, 1989).

Galbraith, JK. *American Capitalism: The Concept of Countervailing Power* (ME Sharpe, White Plains, NY, 1956).

—— *The Affluent Society* (Houghton, Mifflin, Boston, 1976).

—— *The New Industrial State* (3rd edn, Mentor, New York, 1978).

—— and Salinger N. *Almost Everyone's Guide to Economics* (Houghton Mifflin Co, New York, 1978).

Gamble, Andrew, Kelly, Gavin and Parkinson, John (eds). *The Political Economy Of The Company* (Hart Publishing, 2000).

Gower LCB. *Principles of Modern Company Law* (6th edn, Sweet and Maxwell, London, 1997).
Gugler, Klaus. *Corporate Governance and Economic Performance* (ed, Oxford University Press, Oxford, 2001).
Hamel and Prahalad. *Competing for the Future* (Harvard Business School Press Cambridge, MA, 1994).
Hill, Henry P. *Accounting Principles for the Autonomous Corporate Entity* (Quorum Books, New York, 1987).
Hoschschild, Arlie and Machung, Anne. *The Second Shift: Working Parents and the Revolution at Home* (Avon Books, New York, 1989).
See the following reviews Ward, Debbie. 16 Journal of Health Politics, Policy and Law 823–830. Boyd, Susan. 4 Canadian Journal of Women and the Law 325–330 (1990).
Hurst. *Law and Social Order in the United States* (Cornell University Press, Ithaca, New York, 1977).
Hutton, W. *The State We're In* (Vintage, London, 1995).
Jacoby, Neil H. *Corporate Power and Social Responsibility* (Macmillan Publishing, New York, 1973).
Journal of Law and Society. *Special Issue on Enterprise and Community: New Directions and Corporate Governance.* Vol 24, March 1997.
Kerckhofs, P. *20 Years of European Worker Council Dynamics* (European Trade Union Institute, Belgium, 2001).
Lasok D and Bridge JW. *Law and Institutions of the European Communities* (5th edn, Butterworths, London, 1991).
Mathiopoulos, M. *The Closed Society and Its Friends.*
Maw NG. *Corporate Governance* (Dartmouth, Aldershot, England, 1994).
Michaels, M, Marginson, Paul, and Sisson, Keith. *The European Works Councils: Planning for the Directive* (1994).
Mitchell, LE (ed). *Progressive Corporate Law* (Westview Press, Boulder CO, 1996).
Monks, Robert and Minnow, Nell. *Corporate Governance* (Blackwell, Cambridge, MA, 1995).
Parkinson, JE. *Corporate Power and Responsibility* (Clarendon Press, Oxford, 1993).
Porter, Michael E. 1990. *The Competitive Advantage of Nations* (Macmillan, London, 1990).
Prentice, D and Holland, PRJ (eds). *Contemporary Issues in Corporate Governance* (Oxford University Press, 1993).
Reich, R. *The Work of Nations* (Simon and Schuster, London, 1991).
Romano, R. *Foundations of Corporate Law* (Oxford University Press, New York, 1993).
Rose, S. *The Shareholder* (Mercury Books, London, 1989).
Sloan Project On Corporate Governance: Employees And Corporate Governance, Columbia Law School: November 22, 1996.
Schor, Juliet. *The Overworked American: The Unexpected Decline of Leisure* (Basic Books, New York, 1993).
Reviewed in (1993) 46 Industrial and Labor Relations Review 419–420.
—— *The Overspent American:Upscaling, Downshifting, and the New Consumer* (Basic Books, New York, 2001).
Sealy, LS. *Cases and Materials in Company Law* (6th ed, Butterworths, London, 1996).
Smith, (ed). *The Modern Theory of Corporate Finance.*

Steil, Benn *et al. The European Equity Markets: The State of the Union and an Agenda for the Millennium* (Kluwer, London, 1996).

Stetson Law Review Symposium. *Corporate Malaise—Stakeholder Statutes: Cause or Cure?* Vol XXIII (1991).

Szyszczak, Erika. *EC Labour Law* (Longman European Law Series, 2000).

Tomasic, Jackson, Pentony and Woellner. *Corporation Law: Principles, Policy and Process* (Butterworths, Sydney, 1990).

University of Toronto Law Journal. *Special Issue on the Corporate Stakeholder Debate* 43 University of Toronto Law Journal (1993).

Weiler, Paul. *Governing the Workplace: The Future of Labor* (Harvard University Press, Cambridge, Mass, 1990).

Reviewed in Hyde, Alan. 'Endangered Species' 91 *Colum. L. Rev.* (1991) 457.

Wheeler, S. *The Third Way* (Hart Publishing, Oxford, 2001).

Willborn *et al. Employment Law: Cases and Materials* (Michie Company, Charlottesville, VA, 1993).

Wolgast, Elizabeth. *Ethics of an Artificial Person* (Stanford University Press, Stanford, 1992).

ARTICLES

Alchian, Armen A and Demsetz, Harold. 'Production, Information, Costs and Economic Organisation' 62 *Am. Econ. Rev.* 777–783 (1972).

Allen, William T. 'Contracts and Communities' 50 *Wash. & Lee L. Rev.* 1 (1993).

—— *Inherent Tensions in the Governance of US Public Corporations: The Uses of Ambiguity in Fiduciary Law*, NYU School of Law, Working Paper Series, (1998).

—— http://papers.ssrn.com.

Bainbridge, Stephen. 'In Defense Of The Shareholder Wealth Maximization Norm: A reply to Professor Green' 50 *Wash. & Lee L. Rev.* 1423 (1993).

—— 'Community and Statism: a conservative contractarian critique of progressive corporate law scholarship' *Cornell L. Rev.* 856 (1997).

—— 'Corporate Decision Making and the Moral Rights of Employees: Participatory Management and Natural Law'.

Barnard J. *Institutional Investors and the New Corporate Governance.* 69 *N. C. L. Rev.* 1146 (1991).

Baums, Theodore J. 'Takeovers versus Institutions in Corporate Governance' in Germany in *Contemporary Issues in Corporate Governance*: 174 (D Prentice and PRJ Holland, eds, 1993).

Bergstein, Michael. 'American Politics; Global Trade: Clinton Fast-Track to Negotiate Trade Agreement' *The Economist*, Sept. 27, 1997.

Berle, AA. 'For Whom Corporate Managers are Trustees: A Note' 45 *Harv. L. Rev.* (1932) 1365.

Black, Bernard. *Corporate Law and Residual Claimants* Columbia Law School: Sloan Project on Corporate Governance: Employees and Corporate Governance, November 22, 1996.

Blair, Margaret and Stout, Lynn A. 'A Team Production Theory of Corporate Law', 85 *Va. L. Rev.* 247 (1999).

Bolodeoku, Ige Omotayo. 'Economic Theories of the Corporation and Corporate Governance: A Critique' [2002] *Journal of Business Law* 411.

Bratton, William W. 'Confronting the Ethical Case against the Ethical Case for Constituency Rights' 50 *Wash. & Lee L. Rev.* 1464 (1993).

Brown, C, Reich, M and Stern, D. 'Becoming a Higher Performance Worker Organisation: The Role of Security, Employee Involvement and Training' (1993) 4 *International Journal of Human Resource Management* 247.

Brudney, Victor. 'The Independent Director-Heavenly City or Potemkin Village' 95 *Harv. L. Rev.* 597 (1982).

Cadbury, Adrian. *Highlights of the Proposals of the Committee on Financial Aspects of Corporate Governance (the* Cadbury Report) in D Prentice and PRJ Holland (eds), Contemporary Issues in Corporate Governance (Oxford, OUP, 1993).

Carley, Mark and Hall, Mark. 'The Implementation of the European Works Councils Directive' 29 *Industrial Law Journal* 103 (2000).

Carney, William J. 'Comment: Two Modes Of Discourse In The Stakeholder Debate' 43 *Toronto Law Journal* 379 (1993).

Carreau, D and Martin, JY. 'La Reforme du Regime der Offrer Publiques', (1992)

Caver, Paul. 'Employee Owned Airlines: The Cure for an Ailing Industry?' 61 *Journal of Air Law & Commerce* 641 (1996).

Charness, Gary and Levine David I. 'When are Layoffs Acceptable? Evidence from a Quasi—Experiment in Universitat Pompeu Fabra, Working Paper Serioes No. 369 http://papers.ssrn.com.

Charny, David. 'Workers and Corporate Governance: The Role of Political Culture' in *Sloan Project on Corporate Governance: Employees and Corporate Governance*, Columbia Law School: November 22, 1996.

—— 'Regulatory Competition and the Global Coordination of Labor Standards' 3 *Journal of International Law* 281 (2000).

Coase, RH. 'The Nature of the Firm' 4 *Economica (N.S.)* 386 (1937).

—— 'The Problem of Social Cost' 3 *Jounral of Law & Economics* 1 (1960).

Coffee, John C. 'Beyond the Shuteyed Sentry: Toward a Theoretical View of Corporate Misconduct and an Effective Legal Response' 63 *Virginia Law Review* 1099 (1977).

Conard, Alfred. 'Comparative Law: The Supervision of Corporate Management: A Supervision of Developments in European Community and United States Law' *Michigan Law Review* 1459 (1984).

Cosh A, Hughes J, and Singh, A. 'Analytical and Policy Issues in the UK Economy' in *Takeovers and Short Termism in the UK* (Institute for Public Policy Research, Cambridge, 1996).

Craypo, Charles. 'The Impact of Changing Corporate Strategies on Communities, Unions and Workers in the United States of America' 24 *Journal of Law and Society* 10 (1997).

Daniels, Ronald. 'Stakeholders and Takeovers: Can Contractarianism Be Compassionate?' 43 *University of Toronto Law Journal* 315 (1993).

Donaldson,Thomas and Preston, Lee E. 'The Stakeholder theory of the Corporation: Concepts, Evidence and Implications' 20 *Academy of Management Review*, 65 (1995).

Dooley, Michael P. 'Two Models of Corporate Governance' 47 *Business Law* 461(1992).

Easterbrook, Frank H, and Fischel, Daniel R. 'The Proper Role of a Target's Management in Responding to a Tender Offer' 94 *Harvard Law Review* 1161 (1981).

Eisenberg, Melvin A. 'Legal Models of Management Structure in the Modern Corporation: Officers, Directors and Accountants' 63 *California Law Review* 375 (1975).

Epstein, RA. 'In Defence of the Contract at Will' 51 *University of Chicago Law Review* 947 (1984).

Estreicher, Samuel. 'Unjust Dismissal Laws: Some Cautionary Notes' 33 *American Journal of Comparative Law* 310 (1985).

Fama, Eugene F. 'Agency Problems and the Theory of the Firm' 88 *Journal of Political Economy* 288 (1988).

—— 'Efficient Capital Market Markets' 46 *Journal of Finance* 1575 (1991).

Forbath William E. 'History of the American Labor Movement' 102 *Harvard Law Review* 1111 (1989).

Freeman, Richard. 'Towards an Apartheid Economy' *Harvard Business Review* (1996).

—— 'Single Peaked vs. Diversified Capitalism: The Relation Between Economic Institutions and the Outcomes' *National Bureau of Economic Research (NBER)* Working Paper No. W7556. http://papers.ssrn.com.

Geu, Thomas Earl and Davis, Martha S. 'Work: A Legal Analysis in the Context of the Changing Transnational Political Economy' 63 *University of Cincinnatti Law Review* 1679 (1995).

Ghilarducci Teresa, *et al.* 'Labor's Paradoxical Interests and the Evolution of Corporate Governance' 24 *Journal of Law and Society* 26 (1997).

Gilson, Ronald J. 'Essay: The Political Ecology of Takeovers: Thoughts on Harmonizing the European Corporate Governance Environment' 61 *Fordham Law Review* 161 (1992).

Gilson, Ronald J, and Kraakman, Reinier. 'Investment Companies as Guardian Shareholders: The Place of the MSIC in the Corporate Governance Debate', 45 *Stanford Law Review* 985 (1993).

Gilson, Ronald J, and Roe, Mark J. 'Understanding the Japanese Keiretsu: Overlaps between Corporate Governance and Industrial Organization' 102 *Yale Law Journal* 871 (1993).

Goll, Irene. 'Environment, Corporate Ideology and Employee Involvement Programs' 30 *Industrial & Labour Relations Review* 138 (1991).

Gould, William B. 'Job Security in the US: Some Reflections on Unfair Dismissal and Plant Closure legislation from a Comparative perspective' 67 *Nebraska Law Review* 28 (1988).

Grantham, Ross. 'The Doctrinal Basis of the Rights of Company Shareholders' 57 *Cambridge Law Journal* 554 (1998).

Green, Ronald M. 'Shareholders as Stakeholders: Changing Metaphors of Corporate Governance' 50 *Washington & Lee Law Review* 1415 (1993).

Groshen. 'Why Wages Vary Among Employers' *Industrial and Labour Relations Review* 36 (1991).

Hermann Donald HJ, and Sor, Yvonne S. 'Property Rights in One's Job: The Case For Limiting Employment at Will' 24 *Arizona Law Review* 765 (1982).

Hopt, Klaus J. 'New Ways in Corporate Governance: European Experiments with Labor Representation on Corporate Boards' 82 *Michigan Law Review* 1338 (1984).

Howse, Robert and Treibilcock, Michael J. 'Protecting the Employment Bargain' 43 *Univeristy of Toronto Law Journal* 751 (1993).

Hyde, Alan. 'In Defense of Employee Ownership' 67 *Chicago-Kent Law Review* 159 (1991).

—— 'Endangered Species: A Review of Weiler: Governing the Workplace: The Future of Labor Relations'.
—— 'Ownership, Contract and Politics in the Protection of Employees Against Risk' 43 *University of Toronto Law Journal* 721 (1993).
Ireland, P. *et al*. 'The Conceptual Foundations of Modern Company Law' 14 *Journal of Law Society* 149(1987).
—— 'Company Law and the Myth of Shareholder Ownership' 62 *Modern Law Review* 32 (1999).
Iskander, MR and Chamlou, N. 'Corporate Governance: A framework for Implementation' (The World Bank, Washington DC, 2000).
Jeffrey, Mark. 'The Commission Proposals on' Atypical Work': Back to the Drawing Board . . . Again" 24 *Industrial Law Journal* 296 (1995).
Jensen, Michael C. 'The Modern Industrial Revolution, Exit and Control Systems' 48 *Journal of Finance* 831 (1993).
Karmel. 'Is it time for a Federal Corporation Law?' 57 *Brooklyn Law Review* 55 (1991).
Kelman, Mark. 'Consumption Theory, Production Theory and Ideology in the Coase Theorem' 52 *Southern California Law Review* (1979).
Klare, Karl E. 'Workplace Democracy and Market Reconstruction: An Agenda for Legal Reform' 38 *Catholic University Law Review* 1 (1988).
Kohler, Thomas C. 'Lessons from the Social Charter: State, Corporation and the Meaning of Subsidiarity' 43 *University of Toronto Law Journal* 607 (1993).
Langille, Brian and Daniels, Ronald. 'Introduction to the Toronto Symposium on the Corporate Stakeholder Debate' 43 *University of Toronto Law Journal* 297 (1993).
LaPorta, Rafael, Lopez-de-Silanes, Florencio, Shliefer, Andrei and Vishny, Robert W. 'Legal Determinants of External Finance' 52 *Journal of Finance* 1131 (1997).
—— 'Law and Finance' 106 *Journal of Political Economy* 1113 (1998).
—— 'Corporate Ownership Around the World' 54 *Journal of Finance* 471 (1999).
Laudauess, Carl. 'Review of Progressive Corporate Law' (1996) 84 *California Law Review* 1694.
Macey, Jonathan R. 'Externalities, Firm Specific Capital Investments, and the Legal Treatment of Corporate Changes' *Duke Law Journal* 173 (1989).
—— 'An Economic Analysis of the Various Rationales for Making Shareholders the Exclusive Beneficiaries of Corporate Fiduciary Duties' 21 *Stetson Law Review* 37 (1991).
—— and Miller, P. 'Corporate Governance and Commercial Banking: A Comparative Examination of Germany, Japan and the United States' 48 *Stanford Law Review* 73 (1995).
—— 'Good Finance, Bad Economics: An Analysis of the Fraud on the Market Theory' 42 *Stanford Law Review* 4059 (1990).
Manning Bayliss. 'Life in the Boardroom After Van Gorkom' 41 *Business Law* 51 (1985).
Meier-Schatz, Christian J. 'Corporate Governance and Legal Rules: A Transnational Look at Concepts of International Management Control' 13 *Journal of Corporate Law* 431–80 (1980).
Millon, David. 'Communitarianism in Corporate Law: Foundations and Strategies' in Lawrence E Mitchell (ed) *Progressive Corporate Law* 1 (1995).
—— 'Redefining Corporate Law' 24 *Industrial Law Review* 223 (1991).
—— 'New Directions in Corporate Law' 50 *Washington & Lee Law Review* 1373 (1993).
—— 'Default Rules, wealth distribution and corporate law reform: employment at will, versus job security' *University of Pennsylvania Law Review* 975 (1998).

—— 'New Game Plan or Business as Usual? A Critique of the Team Production Model of Corporate Law' 86 *Virginia Law Review* 1001 (2000).

Mitchell, Lawrence, 'Groundwork of the Metaphysics of Corporate Law' 50 *Washington & Lee Law Review* 1477 (1993).

—— 'Trust, Contract, Process' in Lawrence E Mitchell (ed) *Progressive Corporate Law* 185 (1995).

O'Connor, Marleen A. 'Promoting Economic Justice in Plant Closings: Explaining the Fiduciary/Contract Law Distinction to Enforce Implicit Employment Agreements' in Lawrence E Mitchell (ed) *Progressive Corporate Law* 219 (1995).

—— 'A Socio-Economic Approach To The Japanese Corporate Governance Structure' 50 *Washington & Lee Law Review* 1529 (1993).

—— 'The Human Capital Era: Reconceptualizing Corporate Law To Facilitate Labor Management Cooperation' 78 *Cornell Law Review* 899 (1993).

—— 'How Should We Talk About Fiduciary Duty? Directors' Conflict Of Interest Transaction And The ALI's Principles Of Corporate Governance' 61 *George Washington Law Review* 954 (1993).

—— 'Corporate Malaise—Stakeholder Statutes: Cause or Cure?' 21 *Stetson Law Review* 3 (1991).

—— 'Restructuring The Corporations Nexus Of Contracts: Recognizing A Fiduciary Duty To Protect Displaced Workers' 69 *Northern California Law Review* 1189 (1991).

Orts, Eric W. 'The Complexity and Legitimacy of Corporate Law' 50 *Washington & Lee Law Review* 1565 (1993).

—— 'Beyond Shareholders: Interpreting Corporate Constituency Statutes' 61 *George Washington Law Review* 26 (1992).

—— 'The Legitimacy of Multinational Corporations' in Lawrence E Mitchell (ed) *Progressive Corporate Law* 247 (1995).

Parker, J Wilson. 'At Will Employment and the Common Law: A modest proposal to De-Marginalize Employment Law' 81 *Iowa Law Review* 347 (1995).

Pope, James Gray. 'Labor and the Constitution' 65 *Texas Law Review* 1076 (1987).

Pound, J. 'The Rise of the Political Model of Corporate Governance and Corporate Control' 68 *New York University Law Review* 1003 (1993).

Prentice, DD. 'Some aspects of the Corporate Governance Debate' in Prentice and Holland (eds) *Contemporary Issues in Corporate Governance* (1993).

Rajan, Raghuram G. and Zingales, Luigi. 'What do we know about Capital Structure? Some Evidence from International Data' 1 *Journal of Finance* 1421 (1995).

Roe, Mark. 'A Political Theory of American Corporate Finance' 91 *Columbia Law Review* 10 (1991).

—— 'Some Differences in the Corporate Structure in Germany, Japan and the United States' 102 *Yale Law Journal* 1927 (1993).

Rogers, Joel. 'Reforming US Labor Relations' 69 *Chicago-Kent Law Review* 97 (1993).

St Antoine, Theodore J. 'A Seed Germinates: Unjust Discharge Reform Heads Towards Full Flower' 67 *Nebraska Law Review* 56 (1988).

—— 'Dedication to Cornelius J Peck: The Making of the Model Employment Termination Act' 69 *Washington Law Review* 361 (1994).

Schwab, Stuart. 'Coase Defends Coase: Why Lawyers Listen and Economists Do Not' 88 *Michigan Law Review* 1171 (1989).

—— 'Realigning Corporate Governance: Shareholder Activism by Labor Unions' 96 *Michigan Law Review* (1998).

Sen, Amartya. 'Goals Commitments and Identity' *Journal of Law, Economics & Organisation* 341 (1985).
Simon, William H. 'What difference does it make whether corporate managers have public responsibilities?' 50 *Washington & Lee Law Review* 1697 (1993).
Singer, Joseph William. 'Jobs and Justice: Rethinking the Stakeholder Debate' 43 *University of Toronto Law Journal* 475 (1993).
—— 'The Reliance Interest in Property' 40 *Stanford Law Review* 713 (1987–1988).
Solomon, Lewis D. 'Restructuring the Corporate Board of Directors: Fond Hope-Faint Promise?' 76 *Michigan Law Review* 581 (1978).
Stokes, Mary. 'Company Law and Legal Theory' in *Legal Theory and the Common Law* (eds, Twining; Blackwell, Oxford, 1986).
Stone, Katherine Van Wetzel. 'Employees as Stakeholders under State Nonshareholder Constituency Statutes' 21 *Stetson Law Review* 54 (1991).
—— 'Policing Employment Contracts within the Nexus of Contracts Firm—The Adequacy of Stakeholder Contractual Protection' 43 *University of Toronto Law Journal* 353 (1993).
Summers, Clyde. 'Labor Law as the Century Turns: A Changing of the Guard' 67 *Nebraska Law Review* 7 (1988).
Verkerke, J. Hoult. 'An Empirical Perspective on Indefinite term Employment Contracts: Resolving the Just Cause Debate' 4 *Wisconsin Law Review* 838 (1995).
Villiers, Charlotte. 'The Rover Case (1)—The Sale of Rover Cars by BMW—the Role of the Works Council' 29 *Industrial Law Journal* 386 (2000).
Werner, Walter. 'Corporation Law in Search of its Future' 81 *Columbia Law Review* 1611 (1981).
Wolfe, Alan. 'The Modern Corporation: Private Agent or Public Actor' 50 *Washington & Lee Law Review* 1673 (1993).
Williamson, Oliver E. 'Corporate Governance' 93 *Yale Law Journal* 1197.
Wyermeesch, E. 'The Corporate Governance Discussion in some European States' in Prentice and Holland (eds) *Contemporary Issues in Corporate Governance* (1993).

OTHER SOURCES

Policy documents and Economic Reports

OECD

OECD National Accounts Vol 1 (1996), (1999).
OECD Principles of Corporate Governance SG/CG (99)5.
Corporate Governance in OECD Member Countries: Recent Developments and Trends: OECD Steering Group on Corporate Governance (April, 2001).

EU

Commission of the European Communities COM(93) 551 final. [17.11.93].
Commission of the European Communities COM(94) 333 final/1. [27.07.1994].
Commission of the European Communities COM(94) 333 final/2 . [27.07.1994].

Communication from the Commission to the Council, the European Parliament, the Economic and Social Committee and the Committee of the Regions on the Social Policy Agenda COM (2000) 379 28.6.2000.

Communication from the Commission to the Council, the European Parliament, the Economic and Social Committee and the Committee of the Regions on Employment and Social Policies: a framework for investing in quality. Com (2001) 313 20.6.2001.

Communication from the Commission to the Council, the European Parliament, the Economic and Social Committee and the Committee of the Regions on Promoting Core Laboaur Standards and improving social governance in the context of globalisation. Com (2001) 416 18.7.2001.

Green Paper on Promoting a European Framework for Corporate Social Responsibility COM (2001) 366.

European Commission–DGV CE–06–97–343-EN-K: Termination of Employment relationships: Legal situation in the Member States of the European Union.

EuroStat Information Service (European Commission, Brussels, Belgium).

US

The Economic Report of the President 1998 (Government Publications Office, Washington DC, 1998).

The Economic Report of the President 2000 (Government Publications Office, Washington DC, 2000).

American Law Institute Corporate Governance Project. Final Draft (1994).

UK

The Cadbury Report: Report of the Committee on the Financial Aspects of Corporate Governance (London, December, 1992).

MPR Executive Pay Report 1995–1996 also known as the Greenbury report published by Incomes Data Services (UK, 1995).

The Hempel Report (1997).

UK Company Law Reform Project. www.dti.gov.uk.

LEGISLATION

EEC

Council Regulation 2084/93: OJ 1993, L193.

Council Regulation 2332/89.

Council Regulation 2157/2001 2001 OJ (L294).

[European Company Statute 1970 OJ (C 124)].

Directive EEC 78/660 1978 OJ (L 222) 4th Company Law.

Directive EEC 83/349, 1983 OJ (L 193) 7th Company Law.

Directive EEC 84/253, 1984 OJ (L 126) 8th Company Law.

5th Draft Directive on Company Law 1972 OJ (C.7) and amendments thereto in 1983 OJ (C 240) and 1991 OJ (C 7).
Council Directive 75/129/EEC 1975 OJ (L 48).
Council Directive 77/187/EEC 1977 OJ (L 61).
Council Directive 80/987/EEC 1980 OJ (L283) 23.
Council Directive 91/383/EEC 1991 OJ (L 206).
Council Directive 92/85/EC 1992 OJ (L 328).
Council Directive 93/104/EC 1993 OJ (L 307).
Council Directive 94/45/ EC 1994 OJ (L 254).
Council Directive 96/34/EC 1996 OJ (L 145).
Council Directive 98/23 1998 OJ (L 131).
Council Directive 97/81 1998 OJ (L 14).
Council Directive 98/59/EC 1998 OJ (L 225).
Council Directive 98/50/EC 1998 OJ (L 201).
Council Directive 2001/86/EC 2001 OJ (L 294).
Official Journal 1990 C 224.
European Parliament Resolution on the closure of the Renault plant at Vilvoorde.
1997 OJ (C115).

United States

Family and Medical Leave Act, USC (1993).
Workers Adjustment and Retraining Notification Act, 29 U.S.C. 2101–2109 (1988).
National Labor Relations Act (Wagner Act) 29 U.S.C. 151–169 (1982 & Supp. II 1984).

United Kingdom

1985 Companies Consolidation Act (UK).
Employment Protection Act (as amended) of 1971.

Ireland

1990 Companies Act (Irl).
The Transnational Information and Consultation Act 1996.
The Unfair Dismissals Act of 1977 (as amended) www.dti.gov.uk.

CASES

Clark v Workman (1920) 1 IR.
Kinsela v Russell Kinsela Properties Ltd (1986) 10 ACLR 395.
Re Frederick Inns Ltd [1994] ILRM 387.
Smith (Howard) Ltd v Ampol Petroleum Ltd [1974] AC 821.

US States Steelworkers v United States Steel 631 F 2d 12264 (6th Cir, 1980).
Winkworth v Edward Baron Development Co Ltd [1987] 1 All ER 114.
Ypsilanti v General Motors Corp 506 NW 2d 566 (Mich Ct App 1993).

COMMENTARIES

Coopers and Lybrand: EC Commentaries (Coopers and Lybrand, London, 1995)
European Information Service (European Commission, Brussels, Belgium).

Index